STUDY GUIDE on SHAKESPEARE'S

MACBETH

MADE SUPER SUPER EASY

TEXT EXPLAINED IN GREAT DETAIL

ACHIEVE TOP GRADES
A MUST FOR ALL STUDENTS

EVELYN SAMUEL on Shakespeare

Shakespeare's Hamlet
Made Super Super Easy
First Edition Published by Evelyn Samuel

EveMadeSuperEasyBooks
www.EveSuperEasyBooks.com
evesupereasybooks@gmail.com

DEDICATED TO

I dedicate this book to my mother, Narainamal.
You will always be my Idol.

REVIEWS

★★★★★ **A great help**
Reviewed 6 February 2022
This book is an informative guide that will help you study and raise your grades. Not only that but it has small details that will surprise the inspectors. This book is a real gem that everyone studying macbeth should own.

★★★★★ **Fantastic book**
Reviewed 4 November 2020
This book is excellent and is very helpful in explaining the themes and language in Macbeth. It is full of information that can help you achieve top grades and has helped me massively. I highly recommend this book to anybody considering to buy it.

★★★★★ **Brilliant!!!**
Reviewed 15 October 2020
I highly recommend this book. It explains a Macbeth in detail, and it is easy to understand as a student. My grade has also improved a lot

★★★★★ **A must buy for you**
Reviewed 10 October 2020
It is a very good book and has helped me so much in Macbeth work. It is a very great buy and I would recommend to anyone doing Macbeth!

★★★★★ **Fantastic resource!**
Reviewed 25 August 2021
Easy to follow guide. The kids absolutely love it! Definitely recommending this to my friends and family.

★★★★★ **This book is one of a kind helps you with anything you need about Macbeth**
Reviewed 23 October 2021
I love this book great for exam season helps me with everything I need about Macbeth

★★★★★ **it's very helpful**
Reviewed 6 November 2021
It's really good

★★★★★ **This book is exceptional!!**
Reviewed 6 October 2020
I bought for this my son who is in year 11 right now. He has told me that he was so grateful for the book as he used the detailed explanations and judicious quotes and well as notes and explanations on structure and alternative intelligent interpretations of characters. He used the contents of this book in his September exam and had done exceptionally better than last year being bumped up by 3 grades and his teacher giving him high predicted grades. I wanted to thank the author of this book as it has really given my son the confidence to achieve high grades.

PREFACE

To all students reading my study guide **MACBETH made super super easy**. I do hope that my wealth of information will assist you to achieve the highest possible grades. I have formulated a unique structure where detailed explanations are next to the text to make it super super easy for you to connect and understand the book, and to revise without the need to resort to more than one book.

Each ACT is defined by a Summary followed by in-depth explanations which are highlighted with relevant important quotes. Within the explanations, connotated meaning, imagery, symbolism, and linguistic devices are identified.

A detailed explanation of each main character in the book is provided so that the fabric of their relationships can be better understood. To further create understanding, the Structure, Form, Language, and Themes within the play are explored. Typical exam questions are included to give some idea of the scope sought by the Exam Boards. Further details can be found in the Specification published by each Exam Board on their websites.

Finally, sample essays are provided to give you some idea of the standard expected by the Exam Boards.

Good Luck with your studies and your exam results.

FOREWARD

What a **super super easy** way to study and understand Shakespeare's **MACBETH**. No need to match text with explanation when both are next to each other.

I really enjoyed looking left at the text and then right at the explanation. The structure and content of this fantastic study guide is a solid base to get to grip with the revenge, the madness, the supernatural, and the final demise of thane Macbeth who through greed and lust for power, spurred on by his ambitious wife, kills King Duncan and usurps his crown.

Tragically, thane Banquo is murdered by hired killers sent by Macbeth to silence him, but his son Fleance escapes to Wales. Macduff's wife and son are also murdered by the hired killers. But the witches third prophecy as manifested by the third apparition, is realized when in the final battle Malcolm, King 'Duncan's son, and his army advance on Macbeth shielded by trees,

'Great Birnam Wood to high Dunsinane Hill shall come against him'.

Macbeth is slain by Macduff who is of Caesarean birth 'ripped from his mother's womb', thus fulfilling the witches' second prophecy. The first prophecy being Macbeth would be King, but Macduff is a threat.

I can recommend this study guide to all students, and hope they gain as much insight, as I did, into Shakespeare's **MACBETH**.

Teacher of English

BOOKS PUBLISHED IN THE SERIES
MADE SUPER SUPER EASY

Shakespeare's
MACBETH
ROMEO AND JULIET
OTHELLO
HAMLET

Priestley's
AN INSPECTOR CALLS

Dickens'
A CHRISTMAS CAROL

SOON TO FOLLOW IN THE SERIES
MADE SUPER SUPER EASY

Shakespeare's
THE TEMPEST
TWELFTH NIGHT
A MIDSUMMER'S NIGHT DREAM
THE MERCHANT OF VENICE

www.EveSuperEasyBooks.com
EveSuperEasyBooks@gmail.com

CONTENT

TEXT AND EXPLANATIONS 22

CONTEXT

- •• William Shakespeare, one of the greatest playwrights of the era, wrote the play around 1603, during the reign of King James 1 of England.
- •• At the time this play was written, Scotland and England were united under one king.
- •• Shakespeare's plays reflect the social, economic, and historical elements of that period.
- •• King James' concerns and fascination about witchcraft and the supernatural were reflected in the play.

SUPERNATURAL and witchcraft

- •• King James published a book, Demonology, on the subject. God and the church played a vital role in England at that time. People believed in God and the devil, fate and the supernatural.
- •• Because people accused them of associating with the devil and, thereby, being evil, witches were condemned and burned.
- •• The play is filled with dark imagery, and it is one of Shakespeare's most interesting and compelling plays.

TRAGIC Hero

- •• Macbeth is a tragedy where we see the rise and fall of a hero.
- •• Macbeth is a typical tragic hero who fell from grace because of a tragic flaw in his character: greed and ambition. His greed led to serious consequences - several murders, his mental and psychological demise, disruption of the natural order, severed ties with God, the destruction of a country, and, at the end, his own death.

DIVINE Right of Kings

- •• Most importantly, the play explores the issues of kingship and loyalty. It was believed that God had designed a symbiotic balance for nature and humanity. If corruption sets in, then the normal order, instituted by God, is violated. It is then that chaos reigns; this is evidenced in Macbeth's decision to kill King Duncan. It was considered a sin to violate this "divine right of God", no matter the person.
- •• Kings were given the 'divine right' to rule by God; the king had absolute power and was seen as being next to God. If anyone violated this divine appointment and sought to harm the king in any way, it disturbed the natural order of God's will. Macbeth's killing of King Duncan had disturbed the natural order and, hence, invited God's wrath, culminating with death.

CHARACTERS

MACBETH	Thane of Cawdor who kills King Duncan and usurps his throne
Lady MACBETH	Macbeth's wife the driving force behind his ambition
SEYTON	Macbeth's servant
DUNCAN	King of Scotland murdered by Macbeth
MALCOLM	Duncan's eldest son
DONALBAIN	Duncan's youngest son
BANQUO	leader with Macbeth of Duncan's Army murdered by Macbeth's hired killers, but whose children will inherit the throne as prophesied by the witches
FLEANCE	Banquo's son who survives Macbeth's attempt by hired killers
MACDUFF	Thane who kills Macbeth in battle as predicted by the witches' third prophecy
Lady MACDUFF	Macduff's wife murdered by Macbeth's hired killers
Son	murdered by Macbeth's hired killers
SIWARD	Earl of Northumberland, Malcolm's uncle, leader of the English Army against Macbeth
Young SIWARD	Siward's son, killed by Macbeth in the final battle
LENNOX	Thane against Macbeth
ROSS	Thane against Macbeth
MENTEITH	Thane against Macbeth
ANGUS	Thane against Macbeth
CAITHNESS	Thane against Macbeth
Three WITCHES	the instigators of the three prophecies which Macbeth fails to understand
HECATE	the goddess of witchcraft who helps the three witches work their mischief
Others	**A Captain, A Porter, An Old Man, the three hired killers, An English Doctor, A Scottish Doctor, A Gentlewoman attending Lady Macbeth, Apparitions, Lords, Attendants, Soldiers, Servants, Messengers** **The Ghost of Banquo**

SYNOPSIS

In Act I, the audience is introduced to an initial incident, termed **the Exposition**, where in seven scenes the protagonist Macbeth fails to understand the implication of the strange prophecies told to him and Banquo by the three witches on the heath, thinking by killing King Duncan the prophecies would be fulfilled. When King Duncan arrives at Dunsinane, Macbeth's castle, Macbeth suddenly departs the state dinner, worried by what he is planning to do, the murder of Duncan. Lady Macbeth berates him for his cowardice in not carrying out the deed. She alleviates his anxiety by hatching a plan where the two guards outside Duncan's chambers will be drugged and the blood-stained daggers laid in their hands, so they will be blamed not him.

In Act 2, the audience is introduced to a growth in tension, termed **the Rising Action**, where in four scene Macbeth murders Duncan but is tormented by his actions. Lady Macbeth plants the daggers on the guards. Macduff discovers Duncan murdered body and raises the alarm. Macbeth slays Duncan's guards to cover his crime claiming he did it in fury. Duncan's sons, Malcolm and Donalbain, escape fearing for their lives. Macbeth succeeds to the throne, but Macduff is absent at the coronation.

In Act 3, the audience is introduced to a climax, termed **the Climax**, where in six scenes Macbeth seeks to secure the crown by eliminating any threat. He perceives Banquo as a threat, and consequently hirers three murderers to kill Banquo and his son, Fleance. Banquo is killed but Fleance escapes to Wales. At the next banquet, Banquo's ghost sits in Macbeth chair, although no one but Macbeth sees it, causing Macbeth to claim there is no place for him to sit. Ross announces that Macbeth is not well.

Macbeth sees Banquo's ghost disappears, reappear, then disappear again. He tries to convince Lady Macbeth of its presence but to no avail. Meanwhile the three witches and their queen Hecate prepare for their next Macbeth. Somewhere in Scotland, Lennox and an unnamed Lord lament the political upheaval so far with Malcolm and Macduff at the English court to raise an army to defeat the usurper Macbeth.

In Act 4, the audience is introduced to an unravelling of the story, termed **the Falling Action**, where in three scenes Macbeth seeks reassurance from the three witches and their queen Hecate about his prospects; Macbeth's hired killers murder Lady Macduff and her son; and Malcolm with Macduff join with the English to invade Scotland to depose Macbeth. Macduff learns of the deaths of his wife and son.

In Act 5, the audience is introduced to resolution, termed **the Denouement**, where in nine scenes first Lady Macbeth and then Macbeth meet their demise. The third witches' prophecy is realised as Great Birnam Wood comes against high Dunsinane hill: the English army use the branches of trees from Birnam Wood as camouflage to approach Dunsinane castle, vanquishing Macbeth's army. Macbeth kills Young Siward, son of the English commander, but is then killed by Macduff who fulfils the witches' second prophecy that Macbeth will be killed by someone who did not have a natural birth. Macduff was ripped from his mother's womb. Malcolm, son of murdered King Duncan, is proclaimed the next King.

SETTING

The play is set in and around Macbeth's castle at Dunsinane, in Scotland. The action takes place:

- Macbeth's castle at Inverness before he becomes king
- Duncan's castle at Forres
- The heath near Forres where Macbeth meets the three witches
- Macbeth's castle at Dunsinane after he becomes king
- English court in England
- Birnan Wood just outside Dunsinane castle

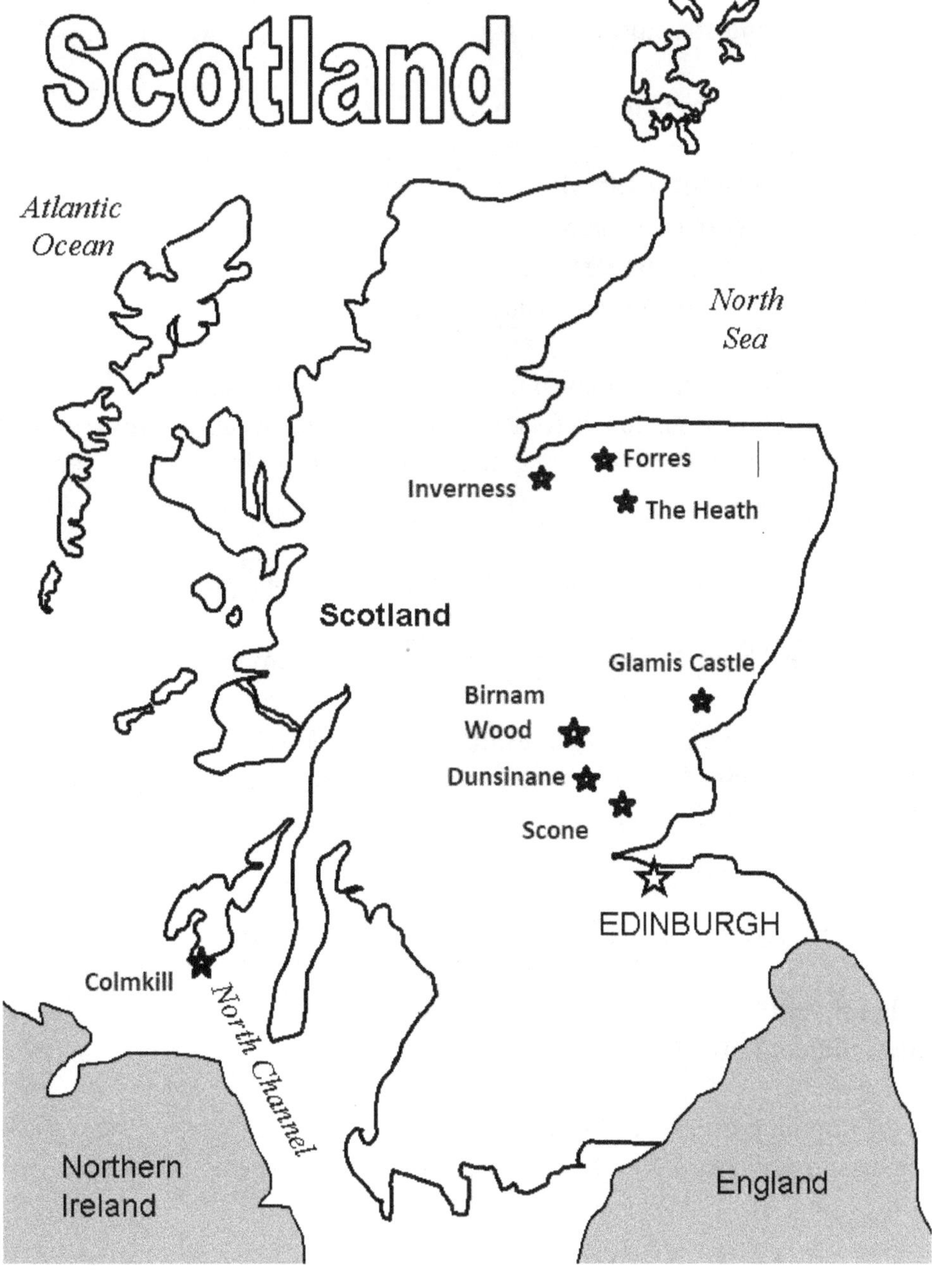

FORM

Shakespeare's Macbeth takes the form of a play made up entirely of dialogue where the audience discover through words delivered by actors, the type of characters, their motives, their relationships together with the storyline.

Shakespeare's aim was to educate and entertain ordinary people in an age when few people could read - to draw out the emotions in people. In this case, to expose the dark side of human desire where jealousy, lust and ambition destroy people through connivance and deceit.

Shakespeare writes in prose and verse. Prose is normal speech without rhyme.
Verse always has a set rhyme and structure.

In Macbeth there are four places where prose is used:

- In **Act 1 scene 5** - Macbeth's letter to his wife
- In **Act 2 scene 3** - the Porter comical soliloquy
- In **Act 4 scene 2** - the conservation between Lady Macduff and her son
- In **Act 5 scene 1** - the conservation between Lady Macbeth and the Doctor

Blank verse is made up of roughly ten syllables of unrhymed iambic pentameter, organised into five groups of two, where an unstressed syllable is followed by a stressed syllable. This creates an air of authority and identifies higher status characters such as Macbeth from lower characters such as servants who speak in ordinary prose.

In Act 5 scene 8 line 5, Macbeth in **Blank Verse** (iambic pentameter unstressed, stressed syllables)

But get thee back-my soul is too-much charged (iambic syllables)

Rhyming verse is used by Shakespeare to end lines in a memorable way so that the audience recall it in later scenes; to make characters complete each other's rhymes to emphasise unity in thought, action, ideas, and moods between them. Hamlet frequently uses them in his monologues and soliloquies.

In Act 4 scene 1 line 20, the Witches speak in **Rhyming Verse** (verse with homonym endings)

Double, double toil and TROUBLE
Fire burn, and cauldron BUBBLE

The Witches speak in **Rhyming Couplets** throughout the play. This separates them from the other characters who mostly speak in **Blank Verse**. Shakespeare switches rhyme and meter to capture the audience's attention.

STRUCTURE

The play '*Macbeth*' is edited into five Acts, each containing several scenes. The storyline is straightforward based on the classical five-part structure:

•an initial incident - termed **Exposition**
•a growth in tension - termed **Rising Action**
•a climax to the drama - termed **Climax**
•an unravelling of the plot - termed **Falling Action**
•a resolution to the drama - termed **Denouement**

There are no subplots and therefore the play conforms to the structure of place, action, and time. The action moves apace from the opening scene where after the success of battle, Macbeth happens upon three witches prophesying events to come predicting he will be king. Driven on by Lady Macbeth, Macbeth kills King Duncan and takes the throne but finds himself opposed by other Thanes. His response is to hire three murderers to eliminate the opposition. Banquo but not his son Fleance, is murdered. Paranoid, Macbeth hallucinates seeing Banquo's ghost appear at a state banquet. Lady Macbeth and guest are startled at his behaviour. With Malcolm and Macduff forming an alliance with the English king, Macbeth seeks out the witches to find out what will happen next. Meanwhile, Macbeth's hired murderers kill Macduff's wife and son.

The fifth part of the structure sees resolution as those who have suffered finally eliminate Macbeth on the battlefield. Just before he is killed, a messenger informs Macbeth that Lady Macbeth is no more. Malcolm, Duncan's son, is crowned king. ALL the prophecies spouted by the three witches are fulfilled!

LANGUAGE

Shakespeare uses different language devices to make the play more tragic, more appealing, and to make themes more understandable. The devices make Macbeth plight and transformation into the tragic hero, resonate with his flawed ambition of greed and power via the instrument of murder.

The **device of Imagery** is used throughout Macbeth in the form

- **Simile** - when one thing is compared with another (using 'like' or 'as')
- **Metaphor** - when something is described as if it actually is something else
- **Personification** - when something that is not human is given human characteristics

The **imagery of light and darkness** is used as metaphors for **good and evil**. Night is personified as something that can blind Day. Nocturnal animals rule the Night.

In **Act 3 scene 2 line 41**, Macbeth exclaims

Ere the bat hath flown
His cloister'd flight, ere to black Hecate's summons

The **imagery of religion** is used to judge Macbeth's actions.

In **Act 1 scene 7 line 18**, Macbeth in his soliloquy, contemplates heaven's view on the demise of Duncan

his virtues
Will plead like angels, trumped-tongu'd against
The deep damnation of his taking-off

In contrast, Malcolm dismisses Lady Macbeth as a 'fiend-like queen', and both Malcolm and Macduff compare Macbeth with the devil

In **Act 4 scene 3 line 56**, Macduff states

Not in the legions
Of horrid hell can come a devil more damn'd
In evils to top Macbeth

The **imagery of blood and milk** is used to identify **Macbeth** with **blood** whereas **kindness** is **milk**.

Lady Macbeth in her soliloquy, yearns for her milk to be turned to gall, so like a man she could stomach killing Duncan herself rather than spurring on the wavering Macbeth.

The **imagery of disease** is personified by the Witches who infect Macbeth with evil.

The **imagery of nature** is personified by animals. Macduff compares Macbeth to a bird of prey as well as to a dog.

The **imagery of time** is manifested by the Witches three predictions. In **Act 1 scene 3 line 56**, Banquo questions the Witches,

If you can look into the seeds of time,
And say which grain will grow and which will not
Speak then to me

The **device of Symbolism** is used to stand for a theme or idea. The symbol of power which drives Macbeth to murder to acquire it. The symbols of strength and freedom portray by traits exhibited by animals. Macbeth is a bird of prey waiting to pounce on the unsuspecting King Duncan to devour his power.

In **Act 1 scene 5 line 64**, Lady Macbeth tells her husband,

Look like th'innocent flower,
But be the serpent under't

The **device of irony** and **of dramatic irony** occurs frequently in the play. In **Act 1 scene 6 line 14**, Duncan praises Lady Macbeth as a hostess, not suspecting that she with her husband Macbeth plan to murder him. Duncan says,

How you shall bid God yield us for your pains
And thank us for your trouble

Dramatic irony puts the audience one step ahead of the characters on stage, so they know what to expect. When Ross brings Macduff the appalling news about his family's demise, the audience is already aware of it.

The **device of Repetition** is used to emphasis an idea or symbol increasing its significance. Repetition of words like 'done', 'lost', 'fair', 'foul'. Repetition of ideas like blood, nature, power, greed.

MONOLOGUE

The monologue is a literary device used by Shakespeare to express the inner thoughts and feelings of the characters in the play, so that the audience gains a better insight into the drama unfolding. The character speaks in the presence of one or more characters. Perhaps, the most famous monologue in Macbeth occurs in **Act 5 scene 5 line 9**. Macbeth does not fear the outcome.

MACBETH

Monologue	ACT	scene	line	length	first line
1	1	7	1	28	If it were done when 'tis done
2	**5**	**5**	**9**	7	I have almost forgot the taste of fears

LADY MACBETH

Monologue	ACT	scene	line	length	first line
1	1	5	1	30	They met me in the day of success
2	1	7	36	11	Was the hope drunk wherein you dress'd yourself

MALCOLM

Monologue	ACT	scene	line	length	first line
1	4	3	114	24	Macduff, this noble passion

LENNOX

Monologue	ACT	scene	line	length	first line
1	3	6	1	24	My former speeches have but hit your thoughts

PORTER

Monologue	ACT	scene	line	length	first line
1	2	3	1	19	Here's a knocking, indeed!

SERGENT

Monologue	ACT	scene	line	length	first line
1	1	2	11	17	Doubtful it stood; As two spent swimmers

SOLILOQUY

The Soliloquy is a literary device used by Shakespeare to express the inner thoughts and feelings of the characters in the play, so that the audience gains a better insight into the drama unfolding. Unlike the monologue, the character speaks to her or himself. Perhaps, the most famous soliloquy in Macbeth occurs in **Act 1 scene 5 line 37**. Lady Macbeth fears her husband is not up to the task of killing Duncan.

MACBETH

Soliloquy	ACT	scene	line	length	first line
1	1	7	1	29	If it were done when 'tis done
2	2	1	33	28	Is this a dagger which I see before me
3	3	1	49	24	To be thus is nothing
4	5	5	18	9	Tomorrow, and tomorrow, and tomorrow

LADY MACBETH

Soliloquy	ACT	scene	line	length	first line
1	1	5	14	16	Glamis thou art, and Cawdor, and shalt be
2	**1**	**5**	**37**	16	The raven himself is hoarse

TEXT AND EXPLANATION

The Shakespearean text is written in the left column, and the explanation and interpretation, in the right column.

Important quotes and phrases in the text are highlighted and reproduced in the explanation column for discussion, on the same page. Consequently, there is no need to turn pages!

A summary of each Scene precedes the text and explanation to give an overall perspective of the events in the play.

MACBETH SUMMARY	**ACT 1 scene 1**	p23

The three evil witches meet in the gothic, eerie setting of the heath in 'thunder and lightning'. There's a sense of foreboding when Shakespeare present the evil witches right at the beginning of the play.

They plan to meet Macbeth to create havoc and misery in his life.

They sing in rhyme and rhythm, "fair is foul, and foul is fair, hover through the fog and filthy air". This rhyming couplet means, 'good is bad and bad is good'.

It's as though they are singing a jubilant song in trapping Macbeth to carry out their foul deeds.

The witches create a reversal of the normal order, and they disrupt and violate God's natural order with their evil deeds.

In the opening scene, Shakespeare also creates an atmosphere of mystery and suspense to set the tone and pace of the gory events to follow.

During King James' rule people believed in witches and if caught meddling in witchcraft, they would be put to death. King James also wrote a book, 'Demonology' describing witchcraft as, 'High Treason against God.'

The witches rightfully prophesied that Macbeth would become the Thane of Cawdor and king of Scotland.

Macbeth is thrilled and this message sets the 'wheels turning' for his desire to become king.

Battlefield: thunder and lightning

Victory for King Duncan

MACBETH
TEXT

The battlefield

Thunder and lightning
ENTER three Witches

FIRST WITCH
When shall we three meet again
In thunder, lightning, or in rain?
SECOND WITCH
When the hurlyburly's done,
When the battle's lost and won.
THIRD WITCH
That will be ere the set of sun.
FIRST WITCH
Where the place?
SECOND WITCH
Upon the heath.
THIRD WITCH
There to meet with Macbeth.

The Witches hear the calls of their spirit friends or 'familiars', which look like animals – cat or toad

FIRST WITCH *(calling to the cat)*
I come, Graymalkin!
SECOND WITCH *(hearing the toad)*
Paddock calls.
THIRD WITCH
Anon.
ALL
Fair is foul, and foul is fair:
Hover through the fog and filthy air.

Exeunt

Three Witches: Fair is Foul, and Foul is Fair

ACT 1 scene 1
EXPLANATION

The bare surroundings of the heath create a scary and ominous atmosphere. Shakespeare uses pathetic fallacy

"In thunder, lightning or rain."

Whenever the witches enter. This can suggest that the plotting of their evil deeds is as destructive and boisterous as the weather.
This has a profound impact on the mood of the opening scene, implying that nature is angry and at odds with itself because the divine right of kings is about to be violated.

During King James rule, kings were seen as chosen by God, and any attack on a king can be seen as a violation of the divine right of kings.

That will be ere the set of sun.

The witches want to meet in the "set of sun". Note the use of dark imagery to highlight the chaos that they are about to cause in Macbeth's life. The ugly-looking, evil witches create an eerie atmosphere in the bare surroundings of the heath, and the miserable weather adds to this eeriness. This setting foreshadows all the gory scenes to follow, like all the horrible murders.
The Elizabethan audience was accustomed to seeing witches being condemned and executed, and King James believed in the power of the witches. They were even blamed for terrible weather like this. Shakespeare ends this scene with a rhyming couplet:

Fair is foul, and foul is fair:
Hover through the fog and filthy air.

This paradox of "good is bad and bad is good" will recur throughout the play. This can be associated with the evil deeds of Macbeth and Lady Macbeth, which the witches see as being good because they are so evil. The witches make evil look good and good look evil. The play has many contrasting images of light and darkness. For example, Macbeth can be seen as the light until after he meets the witches. Once they predict his kingship, he becomes dark just like them. The witches disappear as quickly as they came in the "Fog and Filthy air". This alliterative device highlights the witches, evil, ugly behaviour, and the doom that they are about to cause in Macbeth's life

MACBETH SUMMARY	**ACT 1 scene 2**	

In Act 1, Scene 2, we see Macbeth's bravery and heroism on the battlefield described with such zest and vigour to king Duncan.

He fought ferociously, tackling the enemy and

"like valour's minion carved out his passage".

King Duncan is so pleased and called Macbeth,

"O valiant cousin, worthy gentleman".

Macbeth had come home victorious, and he has now become a celebrated war hero and Duncan was overwhelmed by Macbeth's bravery when he killed the rebel Macdonald and bravely overcame the Norwegian forces.

Duncan, very graciously, awards him the title of Thane of Cawdor immediately hence, sealing his own dreadful fate.

Shakespeare uses dramatic irony and takes us on a spell-binding journey as we sadly witness this celebrated war hero becoming a tragic hero because of a flaw in his character and that is - his untold greed for ambition.

King Duncan

Donaldbain, Malcolm, sons of King Duncan

MACBETH
TEXT

A camp near Forres

Alarum within.
ENTER DUNCAN, MALCOLM, DONALBAIN, LENNOX, with Attendants, meeting a bleeding Sergeant

DUNCAN
What bloody man is that? He can report,
As seemeth by his plight, of the revolt
The newest state.
MALCOLM
This is the sergeant
Who like a good and hardy soldier fought
'Gainst my captivity. Hail, brave friend!
Say to the king the knowledge of the broil
As thou didst leave it.
SERGEANT
Doubtful it stood;
As two spent swimmers, that do cling together
And choke their art. The merciless Macdonwald–
Worthy to be a rebel, for to that
The multiplying villanies of nature
Do swarm upon him–from the western isles
Of kerns and gallowglasses is supplied;
And fortune, on his damned quarrel smiling,
Show'd like a rebel's whore: but all's too weak:
For brave Macbeth–well he deserves that name–
Disdaining fortune, with his brandish'd steel,
Which smoked with bloody execution,
Like valour's minion carved out his passage
Till he faced the slave,
Which ne'er shook hands, nor bade farewell to him,
Till he unseam'd him from the nave to the chaps,
And fix'd his head upon our battlements.
DUNCAN
O valiant cousin! worthy gentleman!

Soldier and blooded Sergeant recounting the battle

ACT 1 scene 2
EXPLANATION

At the beginning of Act 1, Scene 2, we should look at Shakespeare's use of auditory imagery, which is often ignored but plays a very vital role in the play. For example, when Lady Macbeth dies off stage, we hear the screams. The alarum bell sounds by trumpets, signalling victory on the battlefield and excitement. This can be compared to the knelling of the bells later in the play, which signals Duncan's death; "ring the alarum bell! Murder and Treason." This sound can also be juxtaposed with thunder and lightning earlier in the play when the witches arrive, which is frightening, while the bell here is signalling triumph and victory.

What bloody man is that?

At the beginning, Duncan asks,
"What bloody man is that?" The motif of blood runs throughout the play. For example, the brutal killings throughout the play are visceral. Malcolm tells Duncan that Macbeth is a "good and hardy" soldier who saved him from captivity. Shakespeare creates a vivid picture, describing Macbeth's bravery, enabling the reader to visualise the gory scenario. This is seen in the sergeant's report that Macbeth struck a foe so that

Till he unseam'd him from the nave to the chaps,
And fix'd his head upon our battlements.

Here, unbeknown to us we are given a first glimpse of Macbeth's brutality and ferocity.

King Duncan listens to the Sergeant

MACBETH TEXT

SERGEANT
As whence the sun 'gins his reflection
Shipwrecking storms and direful thunders break,
So from that spring whence comfort seem'd to come
Discomfort swells. Mark, king of Scotland, mark:
No sooner justice had with valour arm'd
But the Norweyan lord surveying vantage,
With furbish'd arms and new supplies of men
Began a fresh assault.
DUNCAN
Dismay'd not this
Our captains, Macbeth and Banquo?
SERGEANT
Yes;
As sparrows eagles, or the hare the lion.
If I say sooth, I must report they were
As cannons overcharged with double cracks, so they
Doubly redoubled strokes upon the foe:
Except they meant to bathe in reeking wounds,
Or memorise another Golgotha,
I cannot tell.
But I am faint, my gashes cry for help.
DUNCAN
So well thy words become thee as thy wounds;
They smack of honour both. Go get him surgeons.
Exit SERGEANT, attended

Who comes here?

Enter ROSS and ANGUS
MALCOLM
The worthy thane of Ross.
LENNOX
What a haste looks through his eyes! So should he look
That seems to speak things strange.

ACT 1 scene 2 EXPLANATION

Doubly redoubled strokes upon the foe.

This violent imagery foreshadows Macbeth's violent character. Even Lady Macbeth didn't know about the vicious trait in Macbeth, because she says, "You are too full of the milk of human kindness", suggesting purity and innocence in Macbeth. Duncan was so overwhelmed with Macbeth's bravery that he calls him, "noble Macbeth." He praised Macbeth's bravery.

They smack of honour both.

Even Duncan is unaware of Macbeth's ruthlessness. Ironically, later, when Lady Macbeth asks Macbeth to murder Duncan, he says, "He's here in double trust", as king and cousin.

The sergeant goes on to describe Macbeth and Banquo's bravery, how they charged at the enemy to, perhaps, "memorize another Golgotha". Golgotha is the "place of skulls" where Christ was crucified, and it is compared to the bloody battlefield.

Shakespeare uses Biblical imagery to describe the scenery of bloodshed. This can be associated to Christ's crucifixion and the blood he shed on the cross. Duncan was good and pure like Christ, and he too shed his blood when he died. Furthermore, the repetition of thunders and storms foreshadows King Duncan's fate.
There's a storm looming over Duncan's fate, and the witches' prophecy is about to be fulfilled.

The Sergeant says,
So from that spring whence comfort seem'd to come
Discomfort swells

Duncan listens as Thane Ross recounts the battle

Defeated Thane of Cawdor, Macdonald

MACBETH TEXT

ROSS
God save the king!
DUNCAN
Whence camest thou, worthy thane?
ROSS
From Fife, great king;
Where the Norweyan banners flout the sky
And fan our people cold. Norway himself,
With terrible numbers,
Assisted by that most disloyal traitor
The thane of Cawdor, began a dismal conflict;
Till that Bellona's bridegroom, lapp'd in proof,
Confronted him with self-comparisons,
Point against point rebellious, arm 'gainst arm.
Curbing his lavish spirit: and, to conclude,
The victory fell on us.
DUNCAN
Great happiness!
ROSS
That now
Sweno, the Norways' king, craves composition:
Nor would we deign him burial of his men
Till he disbursed at Saint Colme's inch
Ten thousand dollars to our general use.
DUNCAN
No more that thane of Cawdor shall deceive
Our bosom interest: go pronounce his present death,
And with his former title greet Macbeth.
ROSS
I'll see it done.
DUNCAN
What he hath lost noble Macbeth hath won.

Exeunt

Macbeth: victor and the new Thane of Cawdor

ACT 1 scene 2 EXPLANATION

"Great happiness."

Duncan is clearly very happy with the Macbeth's and Banquo's bravery and exclaims;

No more that thane of Cawdor shall deceive

Ross describes the battlefield to Duncan. He said that the Norwegian banners waved proudly and fanned the Scottish dead soldiers with it.

Norway suffered many causalities even though they were assisted by the traitorous former Thane of Cawdor; he fought a very "dismal" conflict. Macbeth is compared to "Bellona's bridegroom", i.e. Mars, the Roman God of War whose wife was the Roman Goddess of War.

Macbeth bravely confronted the enemy with unmatched courage and skill, thereby winning the war for Scotland.

No more that thane of Cawdor shall deceive

Once again, Duncan shows his appreciation ("Great happiness!").

Our bosom interest: go pronounce his present death,
And with his former title greet Macbeth.

Ironically, the Thane of Cawdor was put to death for being a traitor, and Macbeth, a future traitor, succeeded him.

This foreshadows Macbeth's later act of treachery when he goes against the divine right of kings and kills Duncan. He too ended up a traitor like the previous Thane of Cawdor.

Duncan was happy to give the title of Thane of Cawdor to Macbeth. He said,

What he hath lost, noble Macbeth had won

Once again, King Duncan refers to Macbeth as being 'noble' but is unaware of the treachery lodged deep within him.

MACBETH SUMMARY	**ACT 1 scene 3**	p29

Once again, the witches meet in the dreary heath in thunder.

They meet Macbeth and Banquo who react differently to their prophecies.

They tell Macbeth that he will become Thane of Cawdor and king.

They also tell Banquo that his sons will be in line to become kings. Banquo is very sceptical about them and says that they
"look not like inhabitants of the earth".

Banquo is astonished at Macbeth's reaction towards the witches, and he says that he seems
"rapt withal".

Macbeth is so fascinated with the witches that he urges them
"stay you imperfect creatures, tell me more".

He is surprised that they predicted that he will be Thane of Cawdor, because he says,
"The Thane of Cawdor lives".

Soon after, Ross and Angus bring news that Macbeth has been awarded the title of the Thane of Cawdor because the present Thane of Cawdor has been executed. Macbeth is shocked that the witches' predictions have already materialized, but Banquo warns him that,

"the instruments of darkness tells us truths".

He says that they "win us with honest trifles" to fool and betray us.

Macbeth thinks about becoming king, and he tells Banquo that he wishes to discuss the witches' predictions with him at a later stage.

Witches

Witches' lair somewhere on the heath near Forres

Banquo and Macbeth arrive at the witches' lair

MACBETH
TEXT

ACT 1 scene 3
EXPLANATION

A health near Forres

Thunder
ENTER the three witches

FIRST WITCH
Where hast thou been, sister?
SECOND WITCH
Killing swine.
THIRD WITCH
Sister, where thou?
FIRST WITCH
A sailor's wife had chestnuts in her lap,
And munch'd, and munch'd, and munch'd:–
'Give me,' quoth I:
'Aroint thee, witch!' the rump-fed ronyon cries.
Her husband's to Aleppo gone, master o' the Tiger:
But in a sieve I'll thither sail,
And, like a rat without a tail,
I'll do, I'll do, and I'll do.
SECOND WITCH
I'll give thee a wind.
FIRST WITCH
Thou'rt kind.
THIRD WITCH
And I another.
FIRST WITCH
I myself have all the other,
And the very ports they blow,
All the quarters that they know
I' the shipman's card.
I will drain him dry as hay:
Sleep shall neither night nor day
Hang upon his pent-house lid;
He shall live a man forbid:
Weary se'nnights nine times nine
Shall he dwindle, peak and pine:
Though his bark cannot be lost,
Yet it shall be tempest-toss'd.
Look what I have.

The witches appear on the heath in thunder. This use of this pathetic fallacy is symbolic of the witches' explosive and thunderous intentions for Macbeth.

Notice the bleak, eerie, gothic setting highlighting the witches' sinister, wicked behaviour.

They are discussing how one of them caused havoc in a sailor's life and caused his ship to be wrecked in the stormy seas, because his wife refused to give them her chestnuts.

Sleep shall neither night nor day
Hang upon his pent-house lid;

Note the extent of the witches' evil and the pain and suffering that they had caused the sailor.
This foreshadows their wicked intentions for Macbeth, and they are bent on ruining him.

They are vengeful and caused his ship to be tossed in the stormy seas.

Though his bark cannot be lost,
Yet it shall be tempest-toss'd.

We can once again associate the tempest to the thunder and lightning suggesting that the witches are trifling with nature and God's divine law.

First Witch and Second Witch on the open heath

MACBETH TEXT	ACT 1 scene 3 EXPLANATION

SECOND WITCH
Show me, show me.
FIRST WITCH
Here I have a pilot's thumb,
Wreck'd as homeward he did come.
Drum within

THIRD WITCH
A drum, a drum!
Macbeth doth come.
ALL
The weird sisters, hand in hand,
Posters of the sea and land,
Thus do go about, about:
Thrice to thine and thrice to mine
And thrice again, to make up nine.
Peace! the charm's wound up.

Enter MACBETH and BANQUO
MACBETH
So foul and fair a day I have not seen.

She says,

Here I have a pilot's thumb,
Wreck'd as homeward he did come.

The Third Witch announces;

A drum, a drum!
Macbeth doth come.

Shakespeare maps out their evil character paving the way for their devious actions with Macbeth later on. These weird, mystical, supernatural creatures sing in rhyme and rhythm. "A drum, a drum, Macbeth doth come." Once again, they sing a jubilant song, because they are plotting to cause mischief in Macbeth's life, speaking in half-truths to confuse him. The theme of sleep surfaces here at the beginning of the play.

The first witch says, "Sleep shall neither night or day hang upon his pent-house lid", referring to torturing the sailor with lack of sleep. This is the first mention of sleep, and the motif of sleep runs throughout the play. Macbeth talks about murdering sleep, and Lady Macbeth sleepwalks before she dies. These are but a few examples of the theme of sleep.

So foul and fair a day I have not seen.

Macbeth seems to be echoing the witches' words: "So foul and fair a day I have not seen." Here, he can be associated with the witches' foul deeds, because he goes on to murder later on.

Third Witch

Macbeth [*to the witches*]**: Speak if you can**

MACBETH
TEXT

BANQUO
How far is't call'd to Forres? What are these
So wither'd and so wild in their attire,
That look not like the inhabitants o' the earth,
And yet are on't? Live you? or are you aught
That man may question? You seem to understand me,
By each at once her chappy finger laying
Upon her skinny lips: you should be women,
And yet your beards forbid me to interpret
That you are so.
MACBETH
Speak, if you can: what are you?
FIRST WITCH
All hail, Macbeth! hail to thee, thane of Glamis!
SECOND WITCH
All hail, Macbeth, hail to thee, thane of Cawdor!
THIRD WITCH
All hail, Macbeth, thou shalt be king hereafter!
BANQUO
Good sir, why do you start; and seem to fear
Things that do sound so fair? I' the name of truth,
Are ye fantastical, or that indeed
Which outwardly ye show? My noble partner
You greet with present grace and great prediction
Of noble having and of royal hope,
That he seems rapt withal: to me you speak not.
If you can look into the seeds of time,
And say which grain will grow and which will not,
Speak then to me, who neither beg nor fear
Your favours nor your hate.
FIRST WITCH
Hail!
SECOND WITCH
Hail!
THIRD WITCH
Hail!
FIRST WITCH
Lesser than Macbeth, and greater.
SECOND WITCH
Not so happy, yet much happier.
THIRD WITCH
Thou shalt get kings, though thou be none:
So all hail, Macbeth and Banquo!
FIRST WITCH
Banquo and Macbeth, all hail!

ACT 1 scene 3
EXPLANATION

Macbeth is amazed and wants to connect with them. Banquo asks,

What are these
So wither'd and so wild in their attire

The alliteration "withered and so wild" suggests their evil, mysterious appearance. Banquo says

That look not like the inhabitants o' the earth,
And yet are on't?

He is shocked and confused about the appearance of these supernatural creatures and further questions the witches' appearance.

you should be women,
And yet your beards forbid me to interpret
That you are so.

There is a contrast between Macbeth's and Banquo's reaction to the witches. Banquo is sceptical of the witches' predictions whilst

All hail, Macbeth, hail to thee, thane of Cawdor!

Banquo appears surprised at Macbeth's reaction to the witches.

Good sir, why do you start; and seem to fear
Things that do sound so fair?

He questions Macbeth about his strange behaviour and says that he seems "rapt withal".
The witches give the men their predictions. They tell Macbeth that he will be Thane of Cawdor and king, and they tell Banquo that

Thou shalt get kings, though thou be none:

MACBETH TEXT	ACT 1 scene 3 EXPLANATION

MACBETH
Stay, you imperfect speakers, tell me more:
By Sinel's death I know I am thane of Glamis;
But how of Cawdor? the thane of Cawdor lives,
A prosperous gentleman; and to be king
Stands not within the prospect of belief,
No more than to be Cawdor. Say from whence
You owe this strange intelligence? or why
Upon this blasted heath you stop our way
With such prophetic greeting? Speak, I charge you.
Witches vanish

BANQUO
The earth hath bubbles, as the water has,
And these are of them. Whither are they vanish'd?
MACBETH
Into the air; and what seem'd corporal melted
As breath into the wind. Would they had stay'd!
BANQUO
Were such things here as we do speak about?
Or have we eaten on the insane root
That takes the reason prisoner?
MACBETH
Your children shall be kings.
BANQUO
You shall be king.
MACBETH
And thane of Cawdor too: went it not so?
BANQUO
To the selfsame tune and words. Who's here?

Enter ROSS and ANGUS

ROSS
The king hath happily received, Macbeth,
The news of thy success; and when he reads
Thy personal venture in the rebels' fight,
His wonders and his praises do contend
Which should be thine or his: silenced with that,
In viewing o'er the rest o' the selfsame day,
He finds thee in the stout Norweyian ranks,
Nothing afeard of what thyself didst make,
Strange images of death. As thick as hail
Came post with post; and every one did bear
Thy praises in his kingdom's great defence,
And pour'd them down before him.

Macbeth is keen to hear more and urges the evil witches to stay;

Stay, you imperfect speakers, tell me more:

He is confused and excited, and now the witches have planted a seed of greed in Macbeth that will have serious consequences later in the play.

He also demands that they reveal the source of their information.

Say from whence
You owe this strange intelligence?

Note Macbeth's constant use of question marks suggesting his wonderment at the witches' prophecies, and he demands that they speak to him;

Speak, I charge you.

Macbeth and Banquo discuss their titles predicted by the witches but although they said that Banquo's sons will be kings, he is sceptical about them and warns Macbeth again that they should not trust the witches.

Or have we eaten on the insane root
That takes the reason prisoner?

He warns Macbeth that they should not become the victims of the witches' treachery and lose all sense of reasoning.

Ross with Angus looking on, presents to Macbeth the box containing the chain of Cawdor

MACBETH
TEXT

ANGUS
We are sent
To give thee from our royal master thanks;
Only to herald thee into his sight,
Not pay thee.
ROSS
And, for an earnest of a greater honour,
He bade me, from him, call thee thane of Cawdor:
In which addition, hail, most worthy thane!
For it is thine.
BANQUO
What, can the devil speak true?
MACBETH
The thane of Cawdor lives: why do you dress me
In borrow'd robes?
ANGUS
Who was the thane lives yet;
But under heavy judgment bears that life
Which he deserves to lose. Whether he was combined
With those of Norway, or did line the rebel
With hidden help and vantage, or that with both
He labour'd in his country's wreck, I know not;
But treasons capital, confess'd and proved,
Have overthrown him.
MACBETH
[Aside] Glamis, and thane of Cawdor!
The greatest is behind.
To ROSS and ANGUS
Thanks for your pains.
To BANQUO
Do you not hope your children shall be kings,
When those that gave the thane of Cawdor to me
Promised no less to them?
BANQUO
That trusted home
Might yet enkindle you unto the crown,
Besides the thane of Cawdor. But 'tis strange:
And oftentimes, to win us to our harm,
The instruments of darkness tell us truths,
Win us with honest trifles, to betray's
In deepest consequence.
Cousins, a word, I pray you.

ACT 1 scene 3

EXPLANATION

Angus and Ross enter and give Macbeth the great news that the king wishes to show him his appreciation by awarding him the title of the thane of Cawdor.

He bade me, from him, call thee thane of Cawdor:

Banquo is absolutely startled and utters in shock;

What, can the devil speak true?

Note that he refers to them as the 'Devil' associating them with the utmost evil. We can see that Banquo is level-headed and capable of seeing that the witches have an evil plan, yet Macbeth is excited at this news and asks,

why do you dress me
In borrow'd robes?

Shakespeare's use of the metaphor is poignant because ironically Macbeth will usurp Duncan's crown and will wear his stolen robes.

Macbeth is thrilled and he goes aside and says,

Glamis, and thane of Cawdor!
The greatest is behind.

We can clearly see Macbeth's mounting ambition and greed after this announcement.

He asks Banquo if he doesn't wish for his children to become kings, but he warns Macbeth once more;

The instruments of darkness tell us truths

Macbeth holding the chain of office declaring him to be the Thane of Cawdor

MACBETH TEXT

ACT 1 scene 3 EXPLANATION

MACBETH
[*Aside*] Two truths are told,
As happy prologues to the swelling act
Of the imperial theme.–I thank you, gentlemen.
This supernatural soliciting
Cannot be ill, cannot be good: if ill,
Why hath it given me earnest of success,
Commencing in a truth? I am thane of Cawdor:
If good, why do I yield to that suggestion
Whose horrid image doth unfix my hair
And make my seated heart knock at my ribs,
Against the use of nature? Present fears
Are less than horrible imaginings:
My thought, whose murder yet is but fantastical,
Shakes so my single state of man that function
Is smother'd in surmise, and nothing is
But what is not.
BANQUO
Look, how our partner's rapt.
MACBETH
[*Aside*]
If chance will have me king, why, chance may crown me
Without my stir.
BANQUO
New horrors come upon him,
Like our strange garments, cleave not to their mould
But with the aid of use.
MACBETH
[*Aside*] Come what come may,
Time and the hour runs through the roughest day.
BANQUO
Worthy Macbeth, we stay upon your leisure.
MACBETH
Give me your favour: my dull brain was wrought
With things forgotten. Kind gentlemen, your pains
Are register'd where every day I turn
The leaf to read them. Let us toward the king.
Think upon what hath chanced, and, at more time,
The interim having weigh'd it, let us speak
Our free hearts each to other.
BANQUO
Very gladly.
MACBETH
Till then, enough. Come, friends.

Exeunt

Macbeth is just thrilled with this news that already two of the witches' predictions have come true,

Two truths are told,
As happy prologues to the swelling act

Note the use of the verb, 'swelling' can suggest that Macbeth is swelling up with greed for power. Shakespeare presents us with a very graphic imagery of Macbeth's swelling greed.

Whose horrid image doth unfix my hair
And make my seated heart knock at my ribs

He talks of his murderous intentions to kill Duncan and steal the crown and says that it is just a fantasy,

My thought, whose murder yet is but fantastical,

Macbeth goes on to say,

If chance will have me king, why, chance may crown me

We can assume that Macbeth is willing to allow his ambitious greed to take over his sense of reasoning because he is convinced that fate wants him to become king and that he will be king. We see the beginning of Macbeth's demise because of his greed and evil thoughts Banquo is shocked at Macbeth's reaction, and he uses a clothing imagery and says that Macbeth is uncomfortable in his new title,

Like our strange garments, cleave not to their mould

Macbeth wearing his new title Thane of Cawdor

MACBETH SUMMARY **ACT 1 scene 4**

King Duncan receives Macbeth and Banquo with grace and heartfelt gratitude for their outstanding achievements on the battlefield.

Duncan enquires of Malcolm if the Thane of Cawdor has been executed. Duncan learns that the Thane of Cawdor has confessed to his treasons and had asked for Duncan's pardon, and he repented for what had done.

"Implore your highness' pardon and set forth a deep repentance."

Duncan says, "There's no art to find the mind's construction in the face."

Ironically, Duncan had built an absolute trust in Macbeth. He said,

"You just cannot read what's on a men's mind just by looking at his face."

Here, Macbeth's evil intentions of killing Duncan is lurking within him. He begins to develop

"black and deep desires"

to get the crown for himself; however, Duncan could not see his intentions on his face.

Duncan tells Macbeth that he will be visiting them at the castle.

Macbeth tells Duncan that Lady Macbeth will be delighted, and he leaves to prepare for Duncan's arrival.

The palace at Forres

King Duncan awaiting to welcome Macbeth

MACBETH **TEXT**

ACT 1 scene 4 **EXPLANATION**

The palace at Forres

Flourish of trumpets sound,
ENTER King DUNCAN, his sons MALCOLM and DONALBAIN, Thane LENNOX, and ATTENDANTS

DUNCAN
Is execution done on Cawdor? Are not
Those in commission yet return'd?
MALCOLM
My liege,
They are not yet come back. But I have spoke
With one that saw him die: who did report
That very frankly he confess'd his treasons,
Implored your highness' pardon and set forth
A deep repentance: nothing in his life
Became him like the leaving it; he died
As one that had been studied in his death
To throw away the dearest thing he owed,
As 'twere a careless trifle.
DUNCAN
There's no art
To find the mind's construction in the face:
He was a gentleman on whom I built
An absolute trust.
Enter MACBETH, BANQUO, ROSS, and ANGUS
O worthiest cousin!
The sin of my ingratitude even now
Was heavy on me: thou art so far before
That swiftest wing of recompense is slow
To overtake thee. Would thou hadst less deserved,
That the proportion both of thanks and payment
Might have been mine! only I have left to say,
More is thy due than more than all can pay.
MACBETH
The service and the loyalty I owe,
In doing it, pays itself. Your highness' part
Is to receive our duties; and our duties
Are to your throne and state children and servants,
Which do but what they should, by doing every thing
Safe toward your love and honour.
DUNCAN
Welcome hither:
I have begun to plant thee, and will labour
To make thee full of growing. Noble Banquo,
That hast no less deserved, nor must be known
No less to have done so, let me enfold thee
And hold thee to my heart.

Duncan asks,

Is execution done on Cawdor?

This foreshadows the fact that Duncan gave the title of Thane of Cawdor to Macbeth, who, just like the deceased Thane of Cawdor, proved to be a traitor.

[ENTER MACBETH, BANQUO, ROSS, and ANGUS]

O worthiest cousin!

King Duncan addresses Macbeth as "worthiest cousin", yet Macbeth is secretly plotting to kill him. Macbeth says,

The service and the loyalty I owe,
In doing it, pays itself.

He is far from loyal to Duncan. Shakespeare uses dramatic irony here; the audience already knows that Macbeth intends to kill Duncan.

I have begun to plant thee, and will labour
To make thee full of growing.

Ironically Duncan uses the imagery of a tree because he says that he will grow Macbeth and make him successful. Sadly, the witches have planted a seed and Macbeth is growing into a despot and tyrant and his growing desire to kill Duncan is alarming and shocking to the Elizabethan audience because Kings were seen as next to God and Macbeth is planning on violating the Divine Right of Kings which is ordained by God.

Duncan [*to Macbeth*]**: O worthiest cousin**

MACBETH TEXT

ACT 1 scene 4 EXPLANATION

BANQUO
There if I grow,
The harvest is your own.
DUNCAN
My plenteous joys,
Wanton in fulness, seek to hide themselves
In drops of sorrow. Sons, kinsmen, thanes,
And you whose places are the nearest, know
We will establish our estate upon
Our eldest, Malcolm, whom we name hereafter
The Prince of Cumberland; which honour must
Not unaccompanied invest him only,
But signs of nobleness, like stars, shall shine
On all deservers. From hence to Inverness,
And bind us further to you.
MACBETH
The rest is labour, which is not used for you:
I'll be myself the harbinger and make joyful
The hearing of my wife with your approach;
So humbly take my leave.
DUNCAN
My worthy Cawdor!
MACBETH
[Aside] The Prince of Cumberland! that is a step
On which I must fall down, or else o'erleap,
For in my way it lies. Stars, hide your fires;
Let not light see my black and deep desires:
The eye wink at the hand; yet let that be,
Which the eye fears, when it is done, to see.

Exit

DUNCAN
True, worthy Banquo; he is full so valiant,
And in his commendations I am fed;
It is a banquet to me. Let's after him,
Whose care is gone before to bid us welcome:
It is a peerless kinsman.

Flourish fanfare
Exeunt

Duncan announces that his son, Malcolm, will succeed him as the Prince of Cumberland.

Our eldest, Malcolm, whom we name hereafter
The Prince of Cumberland; which honour must
Not unaccompanied invest him only

Duncan tells Macbeth that he is visiting his palace at Inverness, and Macbeth tells him that he will tell his wife the good news, which will make her very happy.

But signs of nobleness, like stars, shall shine
On all deservers.

Duncan's kindness and Macbeth's evil desires is in complete contrast. Duncan addresses Macbeth as "My worthy Cawdor". We once again see Duncan's complete trust and love for Macbeth displayed.

Macbeth is shocked at the news that Malcolm is the Scottish heir apparent.

that is a step
On which I must fall down, or else o'erleap

He feels that Malcolm is standing in his way of becoming king.

Shakespeare uses light and dark imagery to contrast the character of Duncan and Macbeth, light versus darkness.

Duncan says, "Nobleness like stars shall shine." The simile implies people who are noble can shine like stars. Duncan was the picture of nobleness.

In contrast, Macbeth says, "Stars hide you fires." Here, Macbeth does not want light to see his "black and deep desires." The colour imagery of "black" is associated with his evil intentions of killing Duncan. He wants to hide his evil thoughts. There is a certain eeriness and darkness brooding throughout the play. This motif of darkness surfaces here when Macbeth talks about his "black and deep desires", referring to the killing of Duncan.

MACBETH SUMMARY | **ACT 1 scene 5** |

Macbeth sends a letter to Lady Macbeth telling her about his success on the battlefield and of the witches' prophecies and their prediction that he will become king.

She is fearful that his calm nature will prevent him from achieving his dreams of becoming king. "Yet do I fear thy nature, it is too full of the milk of human kindness".

Here, milk suggests innocence and purity associated with Macbeth's character, but we see how he slides from a celebrated war hero to a ruthless killer.

Lady Macbeth is ruthless in her manipulation of Macbeth to become king. She fears that he will be too weak to kill Duncan. He also told her that he

"burned with desire to question them but they vanished".

While he stood amazed and fascinated, there was a message from the king, awarding him the title of Thane of Cawdor, the exact title that the witches predicted.

This revelation got him very excited. It is ironic that Macbeth addresses Lady Macbeth as
"my dearest partner in greatness".

Unfortunately, she later proves to be his greatest partner in destruction. She says that he does not possess the necessary evil to achieve the crown by foul means. "The illness should attend it".

The use of the alliteration 'highly' and 'holily' suggest that Macbeth will only achieve his ambition by playing fair.

Macbeth's castle at Inverness

Lady Macbeth receives a letter from Macbeth

MACBETH
TEXT

Inverness. Macbeth's castle.

ENTER Lady MACBETH reading a letter

LADY MACBETH
[*Reads*] 'They met me in the day of success: and I have learned by the perfectest report, they have more in them than mortal knowledge. When I burned in desire to question them further, they made themselves air, into which they vanished. Whiles I stood rapt in the wonder of it, came missives from the king, who all-hailed me 'Thane of Cawdor;' by which title, before, these weird sisters saluted me, and referred me to the coming on of time, with 'Hail, king that shalt be!' This have I thought good to deliver thee, my dearest partner of greatness, that thou mightst not lose the dues of rejoicing, by being ignorant of what greatness is promised thee. Lay it to thy heart, and farewell.'
Glamis thou art, and Cawdor; and shalt be
What thou art promised: yet do I fear thy nature;
It is too full o' the milk of human kindness
To catch the nearest way: thou wouldst be great;
Art not without ambition, but without
The illness should attend it: what thou wouldst highly,
That wouldst thou holily; wouldst not play false,
And yet wouldst wrongly win: thou'ldst have, great Glamis,
That which cries 'Thus thou must do, if thou have it;
And that which rather thou dost fear to do
Than wishest should be undone.' Hie thee hither,
That I may pour my spirits in thine ear;
And chastise with the valour of my tongue
All that impedes thee from the golden round,
Which fate and metaphysical aid doth seem
To have thee crown'd withal.

ENTER a Messenger

LADY MACBETH
What is your tidings?
MESSENGER
The king comes here to-night.
LADY MACBETH
Thou'rt mad to say it:
Is not thy master with him? who, were't so,
Would have inform'd for preparation.

ACT 1 scene 5
EXPLANATION

Lady Macbeth berates her husband's lack of purpose to seize the crown and she fears his calm nature.

yet do I fear thy nature;
It is too full o' the milk of human kindness

Art not without ambition

Lady Macbeth can be seen as the fourth witch, because she behaves like the witches.

pour my spirits in thine ear.

She intends to entice him into killing King Duncan and reap the benefits of becoming king by foul means.

"valour of my tongue."

She will use her words to entice him and, with her words, correct the things that are stopping him.

In her mind, his kindness "impedes thee" from achieving the "golden round", i.e. the crown. She is convinced that the hand of fate and the supernatural will help him to achieve the crown by foul means.

Which fate and metaphysical aid doth seem
To have thee crown'd withal.

Lady Macbeth hears news that the king will be visiting the palace, and this can set her evil plans into motion.

Lady Macbeth reads Macbeth's letter

MACBETH TEXT

ACT 1 scene 5 EXPLANATION

MESSENGER
So please you, it is true: our thane is coming:
One of my fellows had the speed of him,
Who, almost dead for breath, had scarcely more
Than would make up his message.
LADY MACBETH
Give him tending;
He brings great news.
EXIT Messenger

The raven himself is hoarse
That croaks the fatal entrance of Duncan
Under my battlements. Come, you spirits
That tend on mortal thoughts, unsex me here,
And fill me from the crown to the toe top-full
Of direst cruelty! Make thick my blood;
Stop up the access and passage to remorse,
That no compunctious visitings of nature

Lady Macbeth continues reading the letter

Lady Macbeth is excited and says that the messenger has delivered great news. This visit from Duncan will give her the opportunity to carry out her evil deeds.

He brings great news.

Shakespeare uses the imagery of a raven.

The raven himself is hoarse.

The raven is said to be a bird of ill omen often heralding death. This can foreshadow the death of Duncan. One can imply that, since the raven's voice is 'hoarse', it is trying to warn Duncan of his terrible fate. The continuous call of the raven, and the wearing out of it's voice is the continuous warning of death.

Shakespeare goes on to say that the raven, 'croaks' the fatal entrance of Duncan. Frogs generally croak, but, here, the raven is 'croaking', which is unnatural. Hence, its voice is hoarse from croaking; one can imply that the raven is trying to warn Duncan of his terrible plight.

Here, we see the reversal of the natural order. This can be associated with the violation of the divine right of kings. Here, Lady Macbeth is planning to kill Duncan. The verb 'fatal' further foreshadows and intensifies Duncan's horrible fate.

Lady Macbeth's ruthless and cold character is shown. "Make thick my blood." She asks to be free of any emotions and feelings.

Come, you spirits
unsex me here,
And fill me from the crown to the toe top-full
Of direst cruelty!

Make thick my blood;
Stop up the access and passage to remorse

Lady Macbeth calls on the supernatural spirits to "unsex me".

MACBETH TEXT	ACT 1 scene 5 EXPLANATION

LADY MACBETH
Shake my fell purpose, nor keep peace between
The effect and it! Come to my woman's breasts,
And take my milk for gall, you murdering ministers,
Wherever in your sightless substances
You wait on nature's mischief! Come, thick night,
And pall thee in the dunnest smoke of hell,
That my keen knife see not the wound it makes,
Nor heaven peep through the blanket of the dark,
To cry 'Hold, hold!'

Enter MACBETH
Great Glamis! worthy Cawdor!
Greater than both, by the all-hail hereafter!
Thy letters have transported me beyond
This ignorant present, and I feel now
The future in the instant.

Enter Macbeth to greet Lady Macbeth inside his castle

To take away all her 'soft, warm, womanly feelings, and to make her more masculine to carry out her evil deeds 'of direst cruelty'. She wants to be cruel and does not want to feel any regret. "Stop up the access and passage to remorse." She calls on the evil spirits to, "take my milk for gall." The noun 'milk' is associated with innocence and purity as we see Macbeth when he was a war hero at the beginning.

Lady Macbeth wants her milk of innocence to turn to bitter gall so that pity cannot flow through her veins, and she doesn't feel any compassion.

Lady Macbeth uses dark imagery. She welcomes the night so that she can carry out her evil plans in the veil of darkness. "Come thick night." The use of the verb 'pall' is associated with death. She asks the night to be shrouded with the smoke of hell so that her evil deeds will be hidden. "My keen knife sees not the wound it makes."

Shakespeare also uses biblical imagery, "Nor heaven peep" and the metaphor "blanket of dark" to create an atmosphere of evil and dread intensifying Lady Macbeth's determination. She commands heaven not to intrude and stop her plans of her achieving her dream

She doesn't want nature to stop her. "To cry, 'Hold, hold!" Note the repetition 'Hold, hold', emphasising that she will stop at nothing to achieve her vile ambition to become Queen.

She addresses Macbeth by the titles that Duncan gave him. "Great Glamis! Worthy Cawdor!" Note the repeated exclamation marks suggesting Lady Macbeth's excitement.

She's imagining how he will be greeted in the future as King. Lady Macbeth echoes the witches' words.

all-hail hereafter!

Once again Lady Macbeth is associated to the witches and their evil. She says that the letters excited her beyond belief. "Transport me beyond." She's imaging being Queen already.
I feel now
The future in the instant.

MACBETH TEXT	ACT 1 scene 5 EXPLANATION

MACBETH
My dearest love,
Duncan comes here to-night.
LADY MACBETH
And when goes hence?
MACBETH
To-morrow, as he purposes.
LADY MACBETH
O, never
Shall sun that morrow see!
Your face, my thane, is as a book where men
May read strange matters. To beguile the time,
Look like the time; bear welcome in your eye,
Your hand, your tongue: look like the innocent flower,
But be the serpent under't. He that's coming
Must be provided for: and you shall put
This night's great business into my dispatch;
Which shall to all our nights and days to come
Give solely sovereign sway and masterdom.
MACBETH
We will speak further.
LADY MACBETH
Only look up clear;
To alter favour ever is to fear:
Leave all the rest to me.

Exeunt

Macbeth says, "my dearest love", this juxtaposes Macbeth's remarks when she dies, "She had to die someday".

Vile Lady Macbeth tells Macbeth to pretend to be the perfect host when Duncan visits the palace. but he must have murderous intentions of killing Duncan.

Your hand, your tongue: look like the innocent flower,
But be the serpent under't. He that's coming

There is a clear lack of emotions here and we can trace how their relationship has dwindled at the end. The use of the simile, "look like the innocent flower but be a serpent under",

This imagery clearly depicts the theme of appearance versus reality. Lady Macbeth wants to take full control for the preparations of killing Duncan

you shall put
This night's great business into my dispatch.

She says that their days will be filled with success

our nights and days to come
Give solely sovereign sway and masterdom.

The scene ends with a very confident and bold Lady Macbeth. She tells Macbeth not to fear, for

To alter favour ever is to fear:
Leave all the rest to me.

Macbeth [*to Lady Macbeth*]**: Duncan comes here tonight**

Lady Macbeth [*to Macbeth*]**: look like th' innocent flower But be the serpent under't**

MACBETH SUMMARY **ACT 1 scene 6**

King Duncan arrives at Inverness castle with his attendants.

Lady Macbeth is very gracious in receiving them.

However, Shakespeare uses dramatic irony when Duncan admires the atmosphere of the castle with delight.

Lady Macbeth pretends to be the perfect host, and she has a very pleasant demeanour. We know that, in reality, she is plotting to kill him.

We see the emerging theme of appearance versus reality here.

The atmosphere in the castle is pleasant and welcoming, yet the audience knows that it is in this very castle that Duncan will be killed. Furthermore, Lady Macbeth appears to be so innocent and gracious, but, in reality, she is a cold and calculating killer

"Look like the innocent flower but be the serpent underneath".

This is exactly what she proved to be.

There is a juxtaposition between the exterior and the interior of the castle. Duncan says that

"the air nimbly and sweetly recommends itself",

and Banquo says that "heaven's breath smells wooingly here".

Trumpets heralding King Duncan's arrival

Donaldbain, Malcolm following their father Duncan, arriving at Macbeth's castle, Inverness

MACBETH TEXT

ACT 1 scene 6 EXPLANATION

Inside Macbeth's castle at Inverness

Hautboys and torches.
ENTER King DUNCAN, his sons MALCOLM, DONALBAIN, his commander BANQUO, Thane MACDUFF, Thane LENNOX, Thane ROSS, Thane ANGUS, and Attendants

DUNCAN
This castle hath a pleasant seat; the air
Nimbly and sweetly recommends itself
Unto our gentle senses.
BANQUO
This guest of summer,
The temple-haunting martlet, does approve,
By his loved mansionry, that the heaven's breath
Smells wooingly here: no jutty, frieze,
Buttress, nor coign of vantage, but this bird
Hath made his pendent bed and procreant cradle:
Where they most breed and haunt, I have observed,
The air is delicate.

ENTER Lady MACBETH
DUNCAN
See, see, our honour'd hostess!
The love that follows us sometime is our trouble,
Which still we thank as love. Herein I teach you
How you shall bid God 'ild us for your pains,
And thank us for your trouble.
LADY MACBETH
All our service
In every point twice done and then done double
Were poor and single business to contend
Against those honours deep and broad wherewith
Your majesty loads our house: for those of old,
And the late dignities heap'd up to them,
We rest your hermits.

King Duncan arrives inside Macbeth's castle

This castle hath a pleasant seat

Duncan comments on the atmosphere of the castle "pleasant seat". Note the use of dramatic irony, because the audience is aware that Duncan is about to die in this castle. Even Banquo misjudges the atmosphere in the castle.

Ironically, he comments on the House Martin, who generally builds its nest under the eaves of churches but has chosen to build its nest in the castle. Just like the bird, Banquo and Duncan showed their approval for the castle and its surroundings. Banquo also said that the wind "heaven's breath" is delightfully wooing, and the bird has made his nest for breeding here, suggesting that the castle is a safe place.

[ENTER LADY MACBETH]

See, see, our honour'd hostess!

Duncan greets her very cordially as his "honoured hostess". He goes on to say that love can cause trouble, because one becomes indebted to the giver, referring to Lady Macbeth and the love that she's showing. She speaks with a silver tongue, very charming, but, in reality, this is just a façade. She is very insincere in her welcome and her display of love and affection towards Duncan. Duncan says that she should pray to God to show him how to be grateful "for your pains". By promising "all our service, Lady Macbeth, once again, pretends to be gracious and lures Duncan into a false sense of security by saying that she is completely dedicated to serving him

Were poor and single business to contend

but, in reality, she is plotting to kill him. She further cajoles him into saying that she still upholds the many honours that they have held for many years

for those of old

She also says that they will continually pray for him.

We rest your hermits.

MACBETH
TEXT

DUNCAN
Where's the thane of Cawdor?
We coursed him at the heels, and had a purpose
To be his purveyor: but he rides well;
And his great love, sharp as his spur, hath holp him
To his home before us. Fair and noble hostess,
We are your guest to-night.
LADY MACBETH
Your servants ever
Have theirs, themselves and what is theirs, in compt,
To make their audit at your highness' pleasure,
Still to return your own.
DUNCAN
Give me your hand;
Conduct me to mine host: we love him highly,
And shall continue our graces towards him.
By your leave, hostess.

Exeunt

ACT 1 scene 6
EXPLANATION

And his great love, sharp as his spur, hath holp him

We know this is a blatant lie from a cold, calculating woman. Duncan enquires about the whereabouts of Macbeth. Once again, Duncan shows his appreciation of Macbeth's "great love", saying that his great love helped him. The simile "sharp as a spur" is ironic, because, later, the sharp knife helps Macbeth to become king.

Duncan again cordially addresses Lady Macbeth as

Fair and noble hostess

She uses flattery to hide her evil and sinister deeds. She says that she is fully committed into serving him.

Conduct me to mine host: we love him highly

She says that everything belongs to the king and must be paid back to him. The use of the accounting jargon like

"in compt" and "audit", "on account", or "borrowed"

suggest that Macbeth and Lady Macbeth are indebted to Duncan, and the only way to be free of this is to get rid of him.

Duncan asks for her hand. This is a traditional mark of respect, and Duncan asks to be led to his host – Macbeth. Duncan further emphasises his love and gratitude for Macbeth "we love him highly". By now, the audience have become emotionally involved, dreading the dreadful events to come.

King Duncan greets Lady Macbeth

Macbeth watches his intended victim Duncan

MACBETH SUMMARY **ACT 1 scene 7**

In this soliloquy, we get an inkling of Macbeth's troubled mind, full of anguish. He is contemplating whether he should kill King Duncan or not.

He is impatient and wants the deed to be done quickly. He is weighing the pros and the cons of his actions. He is suffering from an inner conflict.

Must I do it or not. He finally decides on the latter and tells Lady Macbeth,

"We will no longer proceed in this business".

She is furious and, with manipulating persuasion, encourages him into killing King Duncan. He cites several reasons why he shouldn't kill Duncan. He says that he was a good king and was

"here in double trust",

kinsman and a guest in his castle.

She is contemptuous, because he refused to kill Duncan, but Lady Macbeth ruthlessly targets his manhood and accuses him of being a coward.

"To live a coward in thine own esteem".

When Macbeth expresses his fear of failure, she reassures him that they will never fail so he finally relents.

"I am settled and bend up Each corporal agent to this terrible feat".

Macbeth's castle battered by thunder and lightning

Musicians playing inside the castle

MACBETH TEXT

ACT 1 scene 7 EXPLANATION

Inside Macbeth's castle at Inverness

Hautboys and torches.
ENTER a Sewer, and divers Servants with dishes and service, and pass over the stage.
Enter MACBETH

MACBETH
If it were done when 'tis done, then 'twere well
It were done quickly: if the assassination
Could trammel up the consequence, and catch
With his surcease success; that but this blow
Might be the be-all and the end-all here,
But here, upon this bank and shoal of time,
We'ld jump the life to come. But in these cases
We still have judgment here; that we but teach
Bloody instructions, which, being taught, return
To plague the inventor: this even-handed justice
Commends the ingredients of our poison'd chalice
To our own lips. He's here in double trust;
First, as I am his kinsman and his subject,
Strong both against the deed; then, as his host,
Who should against his murderer shut the door,
Not bear the knife myself. Besides, this Duncan
Hath borne his faculties so meek, hath been
So clear in his great office, that his virtues
Will plead like angels, trumpet-tongued, against
The deep damnation of his taking-off;

Macbeth's soliloquy: If it were done when 'tis done,

If it were done when 'tis done, then 'twere well

Macbeth is impatient, and he wants to get over the deed of killing Duncan quickly

It were done quickly

the audience can sense his nervousness here. Macbeth says that if the assassination were done quickly with no repercussions, then Duncan's death will bring him success, "his surcease success". Note Shakespeare's use of the alliteration. Macbeth thinks that killing Duncan will solve his problems.

that we but teach
Bloody instructions, which, being taught, return
To plague the inventor

The metaphor "shoal of time" can be interpreted as Duncan being a fish caught in Macbeth's net, from which there is no escape. Macbeth's life is like a sandbank that will eventually be washed away.

Commends the ingredients of our poison'd chalice
To our own lips

He said that we will be judged in the afterlife "We'ld jump the life to come". We commit violence, "teach bloody instructions," and it comes back to haunt us; we get revenge and "plague the inventor".

First, as I am his kinsman and his subject
Macbeth presents two strong arguments not to kill Duncan. "He's here in double trust" as his "kinsman and his subject".

Macbeth acknowledges that he should protect Duncan against his murderer, "shut the door", and he shouldn't be the one to kill him, that he should "Not bear the knife myself". He shows his appreciation of Duncan saying that he is so kind and meek, and he has been a great king. Macbeth describes Duncan's virtue as one that would "plead the angels".

his virtues
Will plead like angels, trumpet-tongued.

MACBETH
TEXT

MACBETH (*continues*)
And pity, like a naked new-born babe,
Striding the blast, or heaven's cherubim, horsed
Upon the sightless couriers of the air,
Shall blow the horrid deed in every eye,
That tears shall drown the wind. I have no spur
To prick the sides of my intent, but only
Vaulting ambition, which o'erleaps itself
And falls on the other.

ENTER Lady MACBETH
How now! what news?
LADY MACBETH
He has almost supp'd: why have you left the chamber?
MACBETH
Hath he ask'd for me?
LADY MACBETH
Know you not he has?
MACBETH
We will proceed no further in this business:
He hath honour'd me of late; and I have bought
Golden opinions from all sorts of people,
Which would be worn now in their newest gloss,
Not cast aside so soon.
LADY MACBETH
Was the hope drunk
Wherein you dress'd yourself? hath it slept since?
And wakes it now, to look so green and pale
At what it did so freely? From this time
Such I account thy love. Art thou afeard
To be the same in thine own act and valour
As thou art in desire? Wouldst thou have that
Which thou esteem'st the ornament of life,
And live a coward in thine own esteem,
Letting 'I dare not' wait upon 'I would,'
Like the poor cat i' the adage?

Macbeth [*to Lady Macbeth*]: **We will proceed no further**

ACT 1 scene 7
EXPLANATION

He also uses biblical imagery of "trumpet-tongued", suggesting that Duncan's kindness and virtue can be associated to the angels in heaven. He further personifies pity as "a naked new-born babe", riding on the storm, angry at the plot to kill Duncan.

I have no spur
To prick the sides of my intent

The horror of the murder will draw the wind. The visual imagery of a horse leaping can be associated to Macbeth's vaulting ambition, leaping high into the air like a horse. He concludes by saying that his decision to kill Duncan will be his great urge to fulfil his ambition to be king.

There's a short conversation between Macbeth and Lady Macbeth. Shakespeare uses a series of rhetorical questions and short, snappy sentences. Macbeth asks,

Hath he ask'd for me?

Lady Macbeth replies, "Know you not he has?" This suggests the pace and urgency for them to do the deed quickly increases and the tension of the situation also increases. Lady Macbeth is asserting her power and dominance over Macbeth. Macbeth refused to kill Duncan.

We will proceed no further in this business

However, he is goaded into it by Lady Macbeth

Was the hope drunk
Wherein you dress'd yourself?

She manipulates him and accuses him of being sick "to look so green and pale". The colour imagery green can be associated with sickness. Note she uses a series of rhetorical questions, and this can be attributed to her mounting anger at Macbeth's refusal to kill King Duncan. She uses her love as a bargaining tool "Such I account thy love". She says if he loves her, he will show it by killing Duncan. She asks him if he is so afraid to act bravely "Art thou afeard?" to achieve the crown, "the ornament of life". She further accuses him of being a coward

And live a coward in thine own esteem

MACBETH
Prithee, peace:
I dare do all that may become a man;
Who dares do more is none.
LADY MACBETH
What beast was't, then,
That made you break this enterprise to me?
When you durst do it, then you were a man;
And, to be more than what you were, you would
Be so much more the man. Nor time nor place
Did then adhere, and yet you would make both:
They have made themselves, and that their fitness now
Does unmake you. I have given suck, and know
How tender 'tis to love the babe that milks me:
I would, while it was smiling in my face,
Have pluck'd my nipple from his boneless gums,
And dash'd the brains out, had I so sworn as you
Have done to this.
MACBETH
If we should fail?
LADY MACBETH
We fail!
But screw your courage to the sticking-place,
And we'll not fail. When Duncan is asleep–
Whereto the rather shall his day's hard journey
Soundly invite him–his two chamberlains
Will I with wine and wassail so convince
That memory, the warder of the brain,
Shall be a fume, and the receipt of reason
A limbeck only: when in swinish sleep
Their drenched natures lie as in a death,
What cannot you and I perform upon
The unguarded Duncan? what not put upon
His spongy officers, who shall bear the guilt
Of our great quell?

Macbeth [*to Lady Macbeth*]**: If we should fail?**

She targets his manhood and compares him to a poor cat who wanted a fish but was afraid of the water. Similarly, Macbeth wanted the crown but was afraid to kill Duncan. Macbeth tries to defend himself, reminding her of his heroism and bravery in the war.

I dare so all that may become a man.

Lady Macbeth is furious and merciless in her attack of Macbeth. She demands the reason for him breaking his promise to her "You break this enterprise to me?". She once again targets his manhood; "When you durst do it, then you were a man". She goads him into saying that only if he kills Duncan, then only can he prove to be a man.

She argues that if he were king, he would

Be so much more the man

Lady Macbeth's ruthlessness is clearly visible when she very coldly gives the reader a visual picture of how she would pluck her suckling child from her breast and

dash'd the brains out had I so sworn

The use of the onomatopoeias, 'pluck'd' and 'dash'd' is a clear indication of Lady Macbeth's untold cruelty.

Macbeth is hesitant and asks her, If we should fail?

He is clearly scared of the repercussions of their actions. However, Lady Macbeth snaps at him, "We fail?" This short, snappy sentence oozes confidence from a very dominating Lady Macbeth who tells Macbeth

screw your courage to the sticking-place,

She reassures him that she will ensure that the guards will be drunk, because she will ply them with liquor. They will be so fast asleep that they would appear to be dead, and they are free to go ahead and kill "the unguarded Duncan". Wicked Lady Macbeth also says that she will ensure that the guards take the blame for Duncan's death

bear the guilt
Of our great quell?

MACBETH
TEXT

ACT 1 scene 7
EXPLANATION

MACBETH
Bring forth men-children only;
For thy undaunted mettle should compose
Nothing but males. Will it not be received,
When we have mark'd with blood those sleepy two
Of his own chamber and used their very daggers,
That they have done't?
LADY MACBETH
Who dares receive it other,
As we shall make our griefs and clamour roar
Upon his death?
MACBETH
I am settled, and bend up
Each corporal agent to this terrible feat.
Away, and mock the time with fairest show:
False face must hide what the false heart doth know.

Exeunt

Macbeth realises that she is more of a man than he is. Her display of masculine qualities shocks him, and he declares,

Bring forth men-children only

She tells him that she will use the guard's own daggers, and it will naturally seem as though they have committed the murder. She further reassures Macbeth that they will make loud exclamations of their grief and sadness at Duncan's death. Once again, the theme of appearance versus reality surfaces because they are pretending to be grieving.

Finally, after much persuasion from a devious Lady Macbeth, he relents,

I am settled

He says they should deceive everybody by appearing happy and their faces must not show the evil intent that their hearts are harbouring.

False face must hide what the false heart doth know.

He is now echoing Lady Macbeth's evil intentions. (Act 1 scene 5)

Look like th' innocent flower
But be the serpent under't

Note the theme of appearance versus reality here.

Duncan's two chamberlains
Scottish dancing between daggers

Lady Macbeth pours wassail (spiced ale) into wine to make the two chamberlain sleep

Banquo is very perceptive. He senses that something is wrong. He gives Macbeth a ring from Duncan as a gift to Lady Macbeth. He relays to Macbeth his dreams about the witches, which is worrying him.

Macbeth lies that he doesn't think about the witches and suggests that they discuss the matter another time. We see a contrast here between the character of Macbeth and Duncan, the theme of good versus evil.

Shakespeare presents us with Macbeth's soliloquy where Macbeth has hallucinations about seeing a dagger hovering in the air.

This is a powerful speech by Macbeth. He speaks to the dagger, believing that it is directing him towards his goal of killing Duncan.

His initial fears of killing Duncan have disappeared. Instead, he has a new determination, and we are faced with Macbeth's inner conflict:

"Must I do it or not?"

The bell rings.

Macbeth prepares himself to kill Duncan and hopes that Duncan will not hear the bell.

"For it is a knell that summons thee to heaven or to hell".

Note Shakespeare's use of auditory imagery when the bell signifies death here.

Banquo with his son Fleance on their way to bed

Macbeth encounters Fleance and Banquo

MACBETH
TEXT

Macbeth's castle

ENTER BANQUO and FLEANCE bearing a torch

BANQUO
How goes the night, boy?
FLEANCE
The moon is down; I have not heard the clock.
BANQUO
And she goes down at twelve.
FLEANCE
I take't, 'tis later, sir.
BANQUO
Hold, take my sword. There's husbandry in heaven;
Their candles are all out. Take thee that too.
A heavy summons lies like lead upon me,
And yet I would not sleep: merciful powers,
Restrain in me the cursed thoughts that nature
Gives way to in repose!

Enter MACBETH, and a Servant with a torch

Give me my sword.
Who's there?
MACBETH
A friend.
BANQUO
What, sir, not yet at rest? The king's a-bed:
He hath been in unusual pleasure, and
Sent forth great largess to your offices.
This diamond he greets your wife withal,

Gives MACBETH the diamond ring

By the name of most kind hostess; and shut up
In measureless content.
MACBETH
Being unprepared,
Our will became the servant to defect;
Which else should free have wrought.
BANQUO
All's well.
I dreamt last night of the three weird sisters:
To you they have show'd some truth.

ACT 2 scene 1
EXPLANATION

Banquo can be seen as a symbol of light; he's trying to bring that light into Macbeth's dark, evil life.
husbandry in heaven
Their candles are all out

Unfortunately, this light will be snuffed out by Banquo's death later on. Banquo enquires about the night, and the mention of the moon gives an atmosphere of darkness and evil.

The Elizabethans associated the moon to witchcraft and the supernatural whereas we now associate the moon to love and light.

Banquo has a premonition that something strange is going to happen.
The moon is down; I have not heard the clock.

Shakespeare uses the symbols of the moon and the clock, which Banquo personifies, going down; ironically, he goes down – killed later in the play.

Banquo gives Macbeth his sword. He says that it is dark. "Their candles are all out" referring to the stars that are not shining. He uses biblical imagery, saying that "heaven" is being economical with it's light. Ironically, it's not long before Banquo will see the light in heaven. Banquo has an uncomfortable feeling that is weighing heavily on his mind, and he compares it to lead.
A heavy summons lies like lead upon me.

The theme of sleep is prevalent here.
And yet I will not sleep.

He cannot sleep because he is thinking about the witches' prophecies, which have unnerved him. When Macbeth enters, Banquo asks for his sword. This highlights his nervousness and suspicions of his premonitions.

Banquo tells Macbeth that the king is very happy, and he is asleep. He *gives Macbeth the diamond ring* that Duncan gave as a gift to Lady Macbeth to show his love.

Banquo tells Macbeth that

I dreamt last night of the three weird sisters:
To you they have show'd some truth.

MACBETH
TEXT

ACT 2 scene 1
EXPLANATION

MACBETH
I think not of them:
Yet, when we can entreat an hour to serve,
We would spend it in some words upon that business,
If you would grant the time.
BANQUO
At your kind'st leisure.
MACBETH
If you shall cleave to my consent, when 'tis,
It shall make honour for you.
BANQUO
So I lose none
In seeking to augment it, but still keep
My bosom franchised and allegiance clear,
I shall be counsell'd.
MACBETH
Good repose the while!
BANQUO
Thanks, sir: the like to you!

Exeunt BANQUO and FLEANCE

MACBETH
Go bid thy mistress, when my drink is ready,
She strike upon the bell. Get thee to bed.
Exit Servant

Is this a dagger which I see before me,
The handle toward my hand? Come, let me clutch thee.
I have thee not, and yet I see thee still.
Art thou not, fatal vision, sensible
To feeling as to sight? or art thou but
A dagger of the mind, a false creation,
Proceeding from the heat-oppressed brain?

Macbeth [*soliloquy*]: Is this a dagger which I see

Macbeth said that he does not think of them, which is obviously a blatant lie; Macbeth is obsessed.

I think not of them.

Macbeth tells Duncan that they will discuss the witches on another occasion.

Shakespeare uses a pun here. Macbeth is referring to the plot to kill Duncan, or, when Duncan dies, he will become king, implying that, if Banquo assists him, he will do favours for him.

If you shall cleave to my consent, when 'tis,
It shall make honour for you

Banquo's reply makes it quite clear that he will not do anything devious and dishonourable. He owes his allegiance to the divine right of kings.

My bosom franchised and allegiance clear,
I shall be counsell'd.

From now on, we see that Macbeth views Banquo as a threat and obstacle to his kingship, and he has to be eliminated.

Shakespeare presents us with Macbeth's soliloquy where he is hallucinating, and he sees a dagger hovering in the air, pointing towards Duncan's room. He speaks to the dagger, "Come let me clutch thee".

Shakespeare uses a series of rhetorical questions to highlight Macbeth's confusion. He imagines the dagger guiding him calling it a "fatal vision", which is ironic, because it is just about to cause Duncan's death.

Macbeth is wondering whether the dagger can be touched. "To feelings as to sight?"

Shakespeare uses sensory imagery here: sight, feeling, touch, which further intensifies Macbeth's confused state of mind. Macbeth questions whether the dagger is a figment of his imagination of a "heat-oppressed brain?" – "A dagger of the mind".
He says that the dagger is real and touchable just like his own dagger.

MACBETH
TEXT

ACT 2 scene 1
EXPLANATION

MACBETH (*continues*)
I see thee yet, in form as palpable
As this which now I draw.
Thou marshall'st me the way that I was going;
And such an instrument I was to use.
Mine eyes are made the fools o' the other senses,
Or else worth all the rest; I see thee still,
And on thy blade and dudgeon gouts of blood,
Which was not so before. There's no such thing:
It is the bloody business which informs
Thus to mine eyes. Now o'er the one halfworld
Nature seems dead, and wicked dreams abuse
The curtain'd sleep; witchcraft celebrates
Pale Hecate's offerings, and wither'd murder,
Alarum'd by his sentinel, the wolf,
Whose howl's his watch, thus with his stealthy pace.
With Tarquin's ravishing strides, towards his design
Moves like a ghost. Thou sure and firm-set earth,
Hear not my steps, which way they walk, for fear
Thy very stones prate of my whereabout,
And take the present horror from the time,
Which now suits with it. Whiles I threat, he lives:
Words to the heat of deeds too cold breath gives.

A bell rings
I go, and it is done; the bell invites me.
Hear it not, Duncan; for it is a knell
That summons thee to heaven or to hell.
Exit

Macbeth [soliloquy] **: A dagger of the mind**

He says that the dagger is guiding him in the direction in which he is going because the dagger is pointing towards Duncan's room,

Thou marshall'st me in the way that I was going.

Macbeth acknowledges that it was the very same "instrument" that he was going to use. His confusion is further intensified when he says that his eyes are deceiving him and playing tricks on him, or it is the only organ that is functioning normally.

Once again, the motif of blood surfaces here, he sees thick "gouts of blood" on the dagger. He acknowledges that killing Duncan is going to be a bloody business. He mentioned "wicked dreams" of "Hecate", the queen of the witches, reminding us, once more, of his strong bond with the witches. The mention of the wolf, its howl, and its stealthy movement can be associated with Macbeth's stealthy actions and movements when killing Duncan.

He creeps stealthily towards his victim

With Tarquin's ravishing strides towards his design

Tarquin was a rapist in ancient Rome, and he "moves like a ghost" towards his victim. The simile can be associated to Macbeth's killing of Duncan. He does not want his footsteps to be heard, because his footsteps can be traced

Thy very stones prate of my whereabouts

Macbeth is now prepared to kill Duncan and says that talking about the murder can only make it difficult to complete.

He hears the bell and hopes that Duncan won't hear it. The bell is symbolic here because the ringing of the bell summons Duncan "to heaven or to hell"

Lady Macbeth waits anxiously for Macbeth to return after he murdered Duncan. He tells her that he has "done the deed".

There is an atmosphere of eeriness, because there is mention of 'owls' and 'crickets', night creatures of ill omens which are associated with death.

Macbeth is a deeply distraught man, and he hallucinates about having heard voices. He is tormented with guilt, and he tells her that one of Duncan's guards cried, "Murder!", the other laughed in his sleep. Then they woke each other and said their prayers. One cried, "Amen!" and the other "God bless us!" but Macbeth said that he could not say, "Amen!" because the word got stuck in his throat.

He was distraught because he was in "most need of blessing". He was alarmed when he heard a voice say, "Sleep no more Macbeth does murder sleep".

Note the theme of sleep surfacing once again. We see a very disorientated and confused Macbeth here.

Lady Macbeth is horrified at seeing Macbeth's hands covered in blood and that he was still holding the daggers.

While Macbeth is a total wreck, Lady Macbeth insists that he must return the daggers to the guards who she had planned to frame for the murders.

She very boldly goes and returns the daggers to the guards.

There is a knocking at the gate, and she orders Macbeth to prepare for bed and to pull himself together. "Be not lost so poorly in your thoughts".

Macbeth is wishing that the knocking will wake Duncan.

Macbeth checks the two chamberlains are asleep

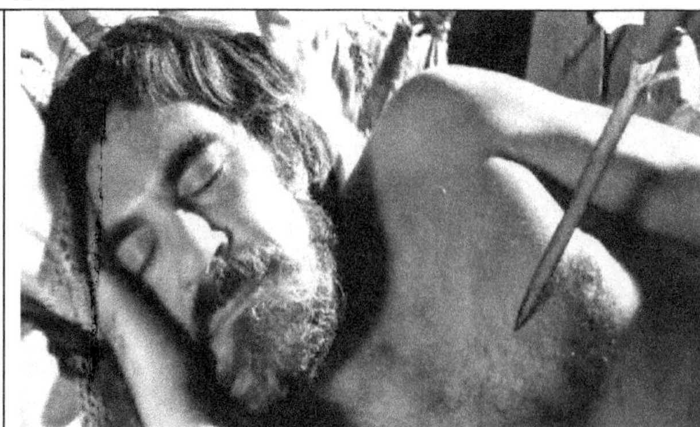

King Duncan stabbed by Macbeth

MACBETH
TEXT

Macbeth's castle

ENTER Lady MACBETH

LADY MACBETH
That which hath made them drunk hath made me bold;
What hath quench'd them hath given me fire.

An OWL shrieks

Hark! Peace!
It was the owl that shriek'd, the fatal bellman,
Which gives the stern'st good-night. He is about it:
The doors are open; and the surfeited grooms
Do mock their charge with snores: I have drugg'd their possets,
That death and nature do contend about them,
Whether they live or die.

Enter MACBETH with two bloody daggers

MACBETH
[Within] Who's there? what, ho!

LADY MACBETH
Alack, I am afraid they have awaked,
And 'tis not done. The attempt and not the deed
Confounds us. Hark! I laid their daggers ready;
He could not miss 'em. Had he not resembled
My father as he slept, I had done't. My husband!

MACBETH
I have done the deed. Didst thou not hear a noise?

Macbeth [*to Lady Macbeth*]**: I have done the deed**

ACT 2 scene 2
EXPLANATION

The drink that has put the guards to sleep had made Lady Macbeth bold and brave.

That which hath made them drunk hath made me bold

It had set her alight with determination to have Duncan killed. She mentions that

An OWL shrieks

Owls were considered to be birds of ill-omen; these night creatures are thought to have heralded Duncan to his death and gave

the stern'st good-night

Lady Macbeth is satisfied that her plot has worked, that the grooms are snoring and sleeping heavily as though in death

That death and nature do contend about them

Shakespeare creates a very tense atmosphere in this scene. It is the pivotal point in the play, and the audience begins to empathise with Duncan's plight.

Lady Macbeth exclaims that if Duncan didn't look like her father, she would have killed him herself. The height of her ruthlessness is once again visible here.

Had he not resembled
My father as he slept, I had done't

Note Lady Macbeth's exclamation,

My husband!

shows her cruel, conniving character, because it's the first time she calls him 'husband', showing her appreciation of him here for killing Duncan.

Shakespeare uses short, snappy sentences that leaves Macbeth breathless, after having committed the murder

I have done the deed. Didst thou not hear a noise?

MACBETH
TEXT

LADY MACBETH
I heard the owl scream and the crickets cry.
Did not you speak?
MACBETH
When?
LADY MACBETH
Now.
MACBETH
As I descended?
LADY MACBETH
Ay.
MACBETH
Hark! Who lies i' the second chamber?
LADY MACBETH
Donalbain.
MACBETH
This is a sorry sight.
Looking on his bloody hands

LADY MACBETH
A foolish thought, to say a sorry sight.
MACBETH
There's one did laugh in's sleep, and one cried 'Murder!'
That they did wake each other: I stood and heard them:
But they did say their prayers, and address'd them
Again to sleep.
LADY MACBETH
There are two lodged together.
MACBETH
One cried 'God bless us!' and 'Amen' the other;
As they had seen me with these hangman's hands.
Listening their fear, I could not say 'Amen,'
When they did say 'God bless us!'
LADY MACBETH
Consider it not so deeply.
MACBETH
But wherefore could not I pronounce 'Amen'?
I had most need of blessing, and 'Amen'
Stuck in my throat.
LADY MACBETH
These deeds must not be thought
After these ways; so, it will make us mad.

ACT 2 scene 2
EXPLANATION

This highlights his nervousness and serves to show his heightened fear.

Lady Macbeth said,

I heard the owl scream and the crickets cry.

These night creatures symbolise death and are considered to herald ominous news. The verbs "scream" and "cry" suggest that nature is weeping for Duncan's terrible fate. This is because Macbeth, in this act of rebellion against God and nature, has violated the divine right of kings.

Shakespeare's effective use of auditory imagery gives us a sense of silence and fear that pervades the air, thereby creating a sense of suspense and tension. Macbeth retorts,

This is a sorry sight

The alliteration suggests his shock and remorse. He couldn't believe or prepare himself for the amount of blood that Duncan shed when he died. This can be associated to Christ's crucifixion on the cross. Duncan was innocent, he was killed, and his blood was shed just like Christ because Christ died to save the world and both were pierced, Duncan by a dagger and Christ by nails.

Lady Macbeth reprimands him for saying this. She tries to allay his fears by rationalising with him. She tells him not to think too deeply about what he had done. He tells her about the guards who got up and said their prayers and that when he said "Amen!" it got stuck in his throat. Macbeth is now aware that he has lost favour with God, and he is overwhelmed with grief.

Lady Macbeth reassures her husband that it is not so, otherwise it will make them descend into madness,

These deeds must not be thought
After these ways; so, it will make us mad

MACBETH
TEXT

MACBETH
Methought I heard a voice cry 'Sleep no more!
Macbeth does murder sleep', the innocent sleep,
Sleep that knits up the ravell'd sleeve of care,
The death of each day's life, sore labour's bath,
Balm of hurt minds, great nature's second course,
Chief nourisher in life's feast,–

LADY MACBETH
What do you mean?

MACBETH
Still it cried 'Sleep no more!' to all the house:
'Glamis hath murder'd sleep, and therefore Cawdor
Shall sleep no more; Macbeth shall sleep no more.'

LADY MACBETH
Who was it that thus cried? Why, worthy thane,
You do unbend your noble strength, to think
So brainsickly of things. Go get some water,
And wash this filthy witness from your hand.
Why did you bring these daggers from the place?
They must lie there: go carry them; and smear
The sleepy grooms with blood.

MACBETH
I'll go no more:
I am afraid to think what I have done;
Look on't again I dare not.

LADY MACBETH
Infirm of purpose!
Give me the daggers: the sleeping and the dead
Are but as pictures: 'tis the eye of childhood
That fears a painted devil. If he do bleed,
I'll gild the faces of the grooms withal;
For it must seem their guilt.
EXIT Lady MACBETH

Knocking within

MACBETH
Whence is that knocking?
How is't with me, when every noise appals me?
What hands are here? ha! they pluck out mine eyes.
Will all great Neptune's ocean wash this blood
Clean from my hand? No, this my hand will rather
The multitudinous seas in incarnadine,
Making the green one red.

ACT 2 scene 2
EXPLANATION

Macbeth thinks he hears an inner voice cry,
Sleep no more!
Macbeth does murder sleep

And when asked by Lady Macbeth about the incident, he replies,

Glamis hath murder'd sleep, and therefore Cawdor
Shall sleep no more; Macbeth shall sleep no more

The imagery of water plays a vital role in the play. Lady Macbeth tells Macbeth to

get some water,
And wash this filthy witness from your hand.

She honestly believed that water will wash away the guilt of the terrible deed that they have committed. When Lady Macbeth asks him to take the daggers back and smear the sleepy grooms with blood, he is horrified at this suggestion and exclaimed,

I am afraid to think what I have done;
look on it again I dare not.

Lady Macbeth is furious that he dares to refuse her request and she retorts, "Infirm of purpose!" Note the use of the exclamation marks highlighting her anger. She says that

the sleeping and the dead
Are but as pictures

By this she means that you can't make out the difference between them, and that Macbeth is scared like a child;

It's the eye of childhood
That fears a painted devil

Macbeth is, once again, gripped with fear, and he is hallucinating sounds.
Whence is that knocking?

Macbeth is so ridden with guilt after killing Duncan that he says,

Will all great Neptune's ocean, wash this blood
Clean from my hand?

MACBETH
TEXT

ACT 2 scene 2
EXPLANATION

RE-ENTER Lady MACBETH

LADY MACBETH
My hands are of your colour; but I shame
To wear a heart so white.

Knocking within
I hear a knocking
At the south entry: retire we to our chamber;
A little water clears us of this deed:
How easy is it, then! Your constancy
Hath left you unattended.

Knocking within
Hark! more knocking.
Get on your nightgown, lest occasion call us,
And show us to be watchers. Be not lost
So poorly in your thoughts.
MACBETH
To know my deed, 'twere best not know myself.

Knocking within
Wake Duncan with thy knocking! I would thou couldst!

Exeunt

Macbeth [*Aside*]: **Will all great Neptune's ocean wash this blood Clean from my hand?**

The motif of blood once again runs through the play. Duncan's blood serves as a symbol of guilt. Macbeth is tortured at the thought of his terrible deed. Neptune is the Roman God of the sea, and he says that all the oceans' water wouldn't be able to rid him of this guilt.

We see a very broken Macbeth here, and we can juxtapose his emotions and behaviour to later in the play where his ruthless killing spree shocks the audience.

Lady Macbeth re-enters to stiffen her husband's resolve

My hands are of your colour; but I shame
To wear a heart so white.

And to relieve his anxiety of being found out as the murderer.

A little water clears us of this deed

The water imagery can be compared to Lady Macbeth's famous sleepwalking in Act 5 scene 1, "Out damned spot! out, I say!" The gentlewoman says that "she seems to be washing her hands". Once again, Lady Macbeth is trying to wash away her guilt. "What will these hands never be clean?" The clothing imagery is also important in the play and appears several times. After Duncan's murder, Lady Macbeth tells Macbeth to

Get on your nightgown, lest occasion call us.

After the witches' prediction that Macbeth will become king, he says, "Why do you dress me in borrowed robes?" and when Lady Macbeth was about to die she says, "Wash your hands, put on your nightgown, look not so pale". Nightgowns can be associated with death because one is in a deathlike state when one is asleep.

As Lady Macbeth said earlier,

The sleeping and the dead are but as pictures.

Hence, we can connote that the clothing imagery of nightgowns are associated with the dead because Duncan, Macbeth, and Lady Macbeth died.

MACBETH SUMMARY

ACT 2 scene 3

Act 2, Scene1 is a very gloomy and tense scene filled with suspense and tension. However, we see that in Act 2 scene 3 Shakespeare very cleverly introduces the Porter and presents him as a very comical character.

This technique was used to cut the tension that was so palpable after the killing of Duncan. We could at least get some relief from these tense nail-biting scenes.

The porter ironically makes many references to the 'devil', 'hell' and 'Beelzebub', suggesting that the castle reeks of evil. He lets MacDuff and Lennox in, and Macbeth goes to greet them while MacDuff goes in to wake the king.

In the meanwhile, Lennox ironically discusses the night with Macbeth. He describes the boisterous, angry weather with 'lamentings' and 'strange screams of deaths'. Shakespeare uses dramatic irony here and the unruly weather can be associated with nature being angry because the 'Divine Right of Kings' has been violated when Macbeth killed the king.

By now we are met with a shocked and horrified MacDuff because he has just discovered that Duncan is dead. He rings the bell to tell everyone that Duncan has been murdered.

Lady Macbeth pretends to be distraught and exclaims, "What in our house?" feigning innocence. Here once again the theme of appearance versus reality rears its head.

Macbeth tells Malcolm and Donalbain that Duncan is murdered. He also tells them that he killed the guards because they were guilty of the murder. At this point Lady Macbeth faints.

Malcolm and Donalbain smell a rat and they came to realise that their lives are in danger, so they flee to England, and they leave the way open for Macbeth to take the crown and become king.

Courtyard inside Macbeth's castle

Porter with key to open castle gate

MACBETH TEXT

ACT 2 scene 3 EXPLANATION

Macbeth's castle

ENTER a drunk PORTER
Knocking within

PORTER
Here's a knocking indeed!
If a man were porter of hell-gate,
He should have old turning the key.
Knocking within

Knock, knock, knock!
Who's there, i' the name of Beelzebub?
Here's a farmer, that hanged himself
On the expectation of plenty:
Come in time; have napkins enow about you;
Here you'll sweat for't.
Knocking within

Knock, knock!
Who's there, in the other devil's name?
Faith, here's an equivocator, that could
Swear in both the scales against either scale;
Who committed treason enough for God's sake,
Yet could not equivocate to heaven:
O, come in, equivocator.
Knocking within

Knock, knock, knock!
Who's there? Faith,
Here's an English tailor come hither,
For stealing out of a French hose:
Come in, tailor; here you may roast your goose.
Knocking within

Knock, knock;
Never at quiet! What are you?
But this place is too cold for hell.
I'll devil-porter it no further:
I had thought to have let in some of all professions
That go the primrose way to the everlasting bonfire.
Knocking within
Anon, anon! I pray you, remember the porter.
PORTER opens the gate

This is a very tense scene; you can cut the tension with a knife. However, the porter helps to ease the tension, and the audience's nervousness is somewhat abated. He calls himself

porter of hell-gate

his reference to 'Beelzebub' and the devil gives us an indication that there is something sinister and evil lurking in the palace.

Shakespeare uses dramatic irony in the porter's speech:

Who committed treason enough for God's sake

The porter is unaware that his foreshadowed utterances had come true because Macbeth did commit treason by killing Duncan.

The porter also speaks of heaven highlighting Duncan's purity and innocence.

"Yet could not equivocate to heaven."
He also speaks of hell where people like Macbeth who commit treason go to.

But this place is too cold for hell.

He further mentions

the everlasting bonfire

referring to hell where Macbeth and Lady Macbeth are heading to, for their unspeakable crimes.

Porter unlocks main castle gate to let in Macduff

MACBETH
TEXT

Enter MACDUFF and LENNOX

MACDUFF
Was it so late, friend, ere you went to bed,
That you do lie so late?
PORTER
'Faith sir, we were carousing till the second cock:
And drink, sir, is a great provoker of three things.
MACDUFF
What three things does drink especially provoke?
PORTER
Marry, sir, nose-painting, sleep, and urine.
Lechery, sir, it provokes, and unprovokes;
It provokes the desire,
But it takes away the performance: therefore,
Much drink may be said to be an equivocator
With lechery: it makes him,
And it mars him; it sets him on,
And it takes him off; it persuades him,
And disheartens him; makes him stand to,
And not stand to; in conclusion,
Equivocates him in a sleep,
And, giving him the lie, leaves him.
MACDUFF
I believe drink gave thee the lie last night.
PORTER
That it did, sir, i' the very throat on me:
But I requited him for his lie;
And, I think, being too strong for him,
Though he took up my legs sometime,
Yet I made a shift to cast him.
MACDUFF
Is thy master stirring?

Enter MACBETH
Our knocking has awaked him; here he comes.

ACT 2 scene 3

EXPLANATION

Once again, the theme of sleep surfaces and the porter personifies sleep using the pronoun 'he.'
"But I requited him for his lie."

Macduff and the porter are discussing the things that drink provokes.

The porter says that it

Equivocates him in a sleep

This is ironic, because Lady Macbeth plied the guards with drink, got them very drunk so they fell into a deep sleep, and blamed them for Duncan's death.

Ironically the porter goes on to list all the things that sleep provokes. He says that it 'mars' man, it 'persuades' him, it 'disheartens' him and lastly it gives him the 'lie' and 'leaves' him.

We can draw a juxtaposition between the porter and Macbeth. The porter says that he can't sleep because of excess drink yet Macbeth couldn't sleep because of his guilty conscience for killing Duncan.

"Macbeth doth murder sleep."

The porter says that he was strong to overcome it's power and;

"He made a shift to cast him."

Yet Macbeth was too weak to overcome Lady's Macbeth's power to entice him to kill Duncan.

Porter, Lennox, and Macduff to wake King Duncan

Macbeth waits with Lennox for Macduff to return

MACBETH
TEXT

LENNOX
Good morrow, noble sir.
MACBETH
Good morrow, both.
MACDUFF
Is the king stirring, worthy thane?
MACBETH
Not yet.
MACDUFF
He did command me to call timely on him:
I have almost slipp'd the hour.
MACBETH
I'll bring you to him.
MACDUFF
I know this is a joyful trouble to you;
But yet 'tis one.
MACBETH
The labour we delight in physics pain.
This is the door.
MACDUFF
I'll make so bold to call,
For 'tis my limited service.
Exit

LENNOX
Goes the king hence to-day?
MACBETH
He does: he did appoint so.
LENNOX
The night has been unruly: where we lay,
Our chimneys were blown down; and, as they say,
Lamentings heard i' the air; strange screams of death,
And prophesying with accents terrible
Of dire combustion and confused events
New hatch'd to the woeful time: the obscure bird
Clamour'd the livelong night: some say, the earth
Was feverous and did shake.
MACBETH
'Twas a rough night.
LENNOX
My young remembrance cannot parallel
A fellow to it.

Re-enter MACDUFF
MACDUFF
O horror, horror, horror!
Tongue nor heart cannot conceive nor name thee!

ACT 2 scene 3
EXPLANATION

[ENTER MACBETH]

MacDuff enquires about the king, and he goes to wake Duncan up.

Is the king stirring, worthy thane?

Lennox tells Macbeth that the

The night has been unruly: where we lay

Shakespeare uses pathetic fallacy, suggesting that nature was at odds with itself and is angry because Macbeth violated the divine right of kings by killing Duncan

Lamentings heard i' the air; strange screams of death

People are saying they heard cries of grief in the air. Macbeth remarks

'Twas a rough night.

Lennox actually foreshadows events that have already happened and are about to happen (the killing of Duncan and the lamenting that are about to happen).

And prophesying with accents terrible

Lennox unwittingly says that the winds were howling and crying with a terrible voice as though they are trying to warn us of something terrible. He also mentions that

the earth
Was feverous and did shake.

Suggesting the earth's anger about Macbeth's violation of nature.

[RE-ENTER MACDUFF]

Macduff is obviously very distraught, having discovered that Duncan is dead. Shakespeare uses a repetition:

O horror, horror, horror!

The use of the repeated exclamation marks in MacDuff's speech can fully sum up the horror of the situation.

MACBETH TEXT

ACT 2 scene 3 EXPLANATION

MACBETH and LENNOX
What's the matter.
MACDUFF
Confusion now hath made his masterpiece!
Most sacrilegious murder hath broke ope
The Lord's anointed temple, and stole thence
The life o' the building!
MACBETH
What is 't you say, the life?
LENNOX
Mean you his majesty?
MACDUFF
Approach the chamber, and destroy your sight
With a new Gorgon: do not bid me speak;
See, and then speak yourselves.
Exeunt MACBETH and LENNOX

Awake, awake!
Ring the alarum-bell. Murder and treason!
Banquo and Donalbain! Malcolm! awake!
Shake off this downy sleep, death's counterfeit,
And look on death itself! up, up, and see
The great doom's image! Malcolm! Banquo!
As from your graves rise up, and walk like sprites,
To countenance this horror! Ring the bell.

Macbeth listens as Macduff alerts him and Lennox to Duncan's murder

MacDuff refers to Duncan as

The Lord's anointed temple

The use of the biblical imagery here shows us how the religious Elizabethan audience viewed the divine right of kings.

They believed that the kings were anointed by God, hence, they were seen as being next to God. That is why Macbeth's actions were abhorred by the Elizabethan audience who wanted to please King James who ruled at that time.

MacDuff tells Macbeth and Lennox that Duncan has been killed.

Macbeth pretends not to know anything

What is 't you say, the life?

Once again, we see the theme of appearance versus reality. He tells them to go to Duncan's room and

Approach the chamber, and destroy your sight

The sight is so horrendous that it might blind you. In line 54, Lennox mentions 'the obscure bird', the owl, the bird of the night.

The horrible scene of Duncan's death is compared to a Gorgon. In Greek mythology, gorgons were two ugly sisters who looked so hideous and frightening that anyone who looked at them turned into stone.

MacDuff rings the bell, and he shouts,

Murder and treason!

There is chaos. He demands Banquo, Malcolm and Donalbain

To countenance this horror!

This scene reflects Armageddon-the judgement day.

MACBETH TEXT

Bell rings
Enter LADY MACBETH
LADY MACBETH
What's the business,
That such a hideous trumpet calls to parley
The sleepers of the house? speak, speak!
MACDUFF
O gentle lady,
'Tis not for you to hear what I can speak:
The repetition, in a woman's ear,
Would murder as it fell.

Enter BANQUO
MACDUFF
O Banquo, Banquo,
Our royal master 's murder'd!
LADY MACBETH
Woe, alas!
What, in our house?
BANQUO
Too cruel any where.
Dear Duff, I prithee, contradict thyself
And say it is not so.

Re-enter MACBETH and LENNOX, with ROSS
MACBETH
Had I but died an hour before this chance,
I had lived a blessed time; for, from this instant,
There 's nothing serious in mortality:
All is but toys: renown and grace is dead;
The wine of life is drawn, and the mere lees
Is left this vault to brag of.

Enter MALCOLM and DONALBAIN
DONALBAIN
What is amiss?
MACBETH
You are, and do not know't:
The spring, the head, the fountain of your blood
Is stopp'd; the very source of it is stopp'd.
MACDUFF
Your royal father 's murder'd.
MALCOLM
O, by whom?

ACT 2 scene 3 EXPLANATION

Lady Macbeth enquires what all the noise was about

What's the business,

She does not show any empathy; instead, she concentrates on the location. She appears startled that it happened in her castle.

[ENTER MACBETH AND LENNOX]

Macbeth shows his hypocrisy when he gives a false speech about life being futile and akin to toys which are trivial. He gives us an imagery of Duncan:

All is but toys: renown and grace is dead;
The wine of life is drawn, and the mere lees
Is left this vault to brag of.

He says that the vault can only now boast of the dregs "lees". The vault can also be referred to as a death chamber in which King Duncan will be buried.

The wine of life is a reference to blood and Christ's crucifixion, because Duncan was innocent like Christ, and his blood was shed like Christ's. Macbeth tells Donalbain,
The spring, the head, the fountain of your blood
Is stopp'd

Let us draw a comparison here; MacDuff's utterance was
Your royal father 's murder'd.

Macbeth embarks on a long-drawn laborious explanation suggesting that he is trying to hide his guilt, whereas MacDuff's response was short and snappy. We can once again trace the motif of blood
the fountain of your blood

Malcolm and Donaldbain shocked by murder

MACBETH TEXT

LENNOX
Those of his chamber, as it seem'd, had done 't:
Their hands and faces were an badged with blood;
So were their daggers, which unwiped we found
Upon their pillows:
They stared, and were distracted; no man's life
Was to be trusted with them.

MACBETH
O, yet I do repent me of my fury,
That I did kill them.

MACDUFF
Wherefore did you so?

MACBETH
Who can be wise, amazed, temperate and furious,
Loyal and neutral, in a moment? No man:
The expedition my violent love
Outrun the pauser, reason. Here lay Duncan,
His silver skin laced with his golden blood;
And his gash'd stabs look'd like a breach in nature
For ruin's wasteful entrance: there, the murderers,
Steep'd in the colours of their trade, their daggers
Unmannerly breech'd with gore: who could refrain,
That had a heart to love, and in that heart
Courage to make 's love known?

LADY MACBETH
Help me hence, ho!

MACDUFF
Look to the lady.

MALCOLM
[Aside to DONALBAIN] Why do we hold our tongues,
That most may claim this argument for ours?

Lady Macbeth and Banquo learn of Duncan's murder as told by Macduff

ACT 2 scene 3 EXPLANATION

Lennox tells Malcolm that the guards killed Duncan, and that there is a lot of evidence to support that. For example, they were "badged with blood", and their daggers were upon their pillows.

Macbeth said that he was furious and killed them. We are exposed to Macbeth's cunning side here. Note the theme of appearance versus reality surfacing constantly in this scene. Macbeth uses a series of verbs, 'wise', 'temperate', 'amazed', and 'loyal' to describe his feelings about Duncan's death. Now he is acting like a 'flower' and being a serpent inside because we know about his pretence to cover up his vile behaviour. He said he acted on impulse, very quickly without a 'pauser.'

Shakespeare gives us a vivid description of Duncan's wounds so that we can visualise it and empathise with Duncan's plight "his silver skin...golden blood".

Note Macbeth's use of colour imagery; he is trying to convince MacDuff of his actions. He goes on to detail his descriptions of the guards as well

Unmannerly breached with gore

They were dressed in blood, and he was so full of love for Duncan, that he "That had a heart to love" would also have the "Courage to make 's love known" by killing the suspected murderers.

At this opportune moment, Lady Macbeth decided to feign a faint.

Help me hence, ho!

Obviously, this scheming action of hers was to try to deflect the attention from Macbeth's explanations in case MacDuff got suspicious.

MACBETH TEXT

DONALBAIN
[Aside to MALCOLM] What should be spoken here, where our fate,
Hid in an auger-hole, may rush, and seize us?
Let 's away;
Our tears are not yet brew'd.
MALCOLM
[Aside to DONALBAIN] Nor our strong sorrow
Upon the foot of motion.
BANQUO
Look to the lady:
LADY MACBETH is carried out

And when we have our naked frailties hid,
That suffer in exposure, let us meet,
And question this most bloody piece of work,
To know it further. Fears and scruples shake us:
In the great hand of God I stand; and thence
Against the undivulged pretence I fight
I fight of treasonous malice.
MACDUFF
And so do I.
ALL
So all.
MACBETH
Let's briefly put on manly readiness,
And meet i' the hall together.
ALL
Well contented.
Exeunt all but Malcolm and Donalbain.

Chamberlain guards murdered by Macbeth to stop them from proclaiming their innocents

ACT 2 scene 3 EXPLANATION

Malcolm and Donalbain become unnerved with the situation and fear a fate similar to Duncan's. They can sense an evil foreboding in the air. They believe that danger is lurking here, and they decide to leave "let's away". Donaldbain said that they did not grieve properly for their father
Our tears are not yet brew'd

Banquo said that when people hide their evil intentions like Macbeth has, they will be exposed.

naked frailties hid, that suffer in exposure

And question this most bloody piece of work,
To know it further

And that they should meet and find the culprit who caused this treacherous deed. He is prepared to fight for this, "In the great hand of God I stand."

The audience becomes nervous now, because Banquo has sealed his fate. He has obviously become a threat to Macbeth, and he is taking the lead into the investigation into King Duncan's brutal murder.

I fight of treasonous malice.

He suspects Macbeth of foul play. Remember, he said that he will be loyal to the king, and that promise is shown here. Macbeth pretends to be brave and says,

Let's briefly put on manly readiness,

Once again, we see the theme of appearance versus reality surfacing here. Macbeth is even bold enough to ask the others to pretend like him.

MACBETH TEXT	ACT 2 scene 3 EXPLANATION

MALCOLM
What will you do? Let's not consort with them:
To show an unfelt sorrow is an office
Which the false man does easy. I'll to England.
DONALBAIN
To Ireland, I; our separated fortune
Shall keep us both the safer: where we are,
There's daggers in men's smiles: the near in blood,
The nearer bloody.
MALCOLM
This murderous shaft that's shot
Hath not yet lighted, and our safest way
Is to avoid the aim. Therefore, to horse;
And let us not be dainty of leave-taking,
But shift away: there's warrant in that theft
Which steals itself when there's no mercy left.

Exeunt

Donaldbain and Malcolm decide it is not safe to stay in Scotland. Donaldbain bolts to Ireland, Malcolm to England to raise an army

Malcolm decides not to associate with them. It's obvious that Malcolm and Donalbain suspect Macbeth of evil, because Malcolm says that showing grief is something

Which the false man does easy.

Malcolm decides to go to England, and Donalbain goes to Ireland

where we are,
There's daggers in men's smiles

They clearly suspect that they will be Macbeth's next victims. He is pretending to be all smiles but he will plot to kill them next so they decide to flee.

Malcolm uses the imagery of a shaft aiming towards them. He says that the killing of Duncan is only the beginning and that it is not over, "Hath not yet lighted."

Malcolm says that

This murderous shaft that's shot

is not over yet. They are its next target and wish

to avoid the aim

They decided not to waste time

not be dainty of leave-taking,
But shift away

Shakespeare uses an imagery of theft to describe their leaving

Which steals itself when there's no mercy left

There is a pun on the verb 'steals.' It can mean the crown that Macbeth is about to steal and Malcolm and Donalbain's hasty departure to avoid being killed

MACBETH SUMMARY	**ACT 2 scene 4**	

This scene highlights the disruption that nature has caused.

Shakespeare uses a traditional old man to voice his concerns about the unnatural occurrences in nature.

This coincides with the Murder of Duncan suggesting that nature is angry because the Divine Right of Kings was violated when Macbeth killed Duncan. Nature is showing its disapproval by behaving in a strange and opposite manner to its normal occurrences.

The old man represents good as opposed to the witches' evil, he can also symbolise, grace, wisdom, and knowledge.

He discusses the reversal of the normal order in Nature for example, the falcon being killed by a mouse which can be interpreted as the powerful king being killed by his mere subject.

The day turned into night. Night is dark imagery associated with death and evil which Macbeth possesses.

"dark night strangles the travelling lamp"

The old man has wisdom and says that heaven is displeased about man's behaviour

"the heaven's, as troubled with man's act"

We learn that Malcolm and Donalbain have fled the country, and now Macbeth will be crowned King at Scone.

Macduff, Ross and Old Man leaving Macbeth's castle

King Duncan's funeral wagon to Colmkill

MACBETH ACT 2 scene 4

TEXT

Somewhere in Scotland. Outside Macbeth,s castle.

Enter ROSS with an OLD MAN

OLD MAN
Threescore and ten I can remember well:
Within the volume of which time I have seen
Hours dreadful and things strange; but this sore night
Hath trifled former knowings.
ROSS
Ah, good father,
Thou seest, the heavens, as troubled with man's act,
Threaten his bloody stage: by the clock, 'tis day,
And yet dark night strangles the travelling lamp:
Is't night's predominance, or the day's shame,
That darkness does the face of earth entomb,
When living light should kiss it?

Ross is told by Old Man he has seen hours dreadful

EXPLANATION

Shakespeare choosing an old man can serve many purposes; for example, he can represent the emotional reactions of the common people to Duncan's murder. He can also represent wisdom, the sense of reasoning and traditions. He acts like a narrator and expresses his horror at Duncan's murder.

He says that, in all his years, he has never seen anything as dreadful and ugly as this

this sore night
Hath trifled former knowings

The old man has knowledge. and he hints that God is angry about man's wicked deeds on earth,

Threaten his bloody stage

This means that the earth is a stage where man commits murder.

Shakespeare uses dark imagery in focusing on "darkness" to show how evil has taken control of the day

And yet dark night strangles the travelling lamp

The use of the onomatopoeia 'strangles' connotes that the night is preventing the sun, or 'lamp', to shine; the day is ashamed to expose or unravel man's dirty deeds and wants the earth to be plunged into darkness to hide its 'shame'

That darkness does the face of earth entomb

The use of the verb 'entomb' is ironic because Duncan will be entombed soon.

We can associate this to the crucifixion of Christ because the earth became dark after his crucifixion. Duncan was pure and good, like Christ. The personification

When living light should kiss?

can be interpreted as questioning why the sun wasn't shining or that Duncan, who should be alive, would be brightening the day with his kindness and love had he not been murdered.

MACBETH
TEXT

OLD MAN
'Tis unnatural,
Even like the deed that's done. On Tuesday last,
A falcon, towering in her pride of place,
Was by a mousing owl hawk'd at and kill'd.
ROSS
And Duncan's horses–a thing most strange and certain
Beauteous and swift, the minions of their race,
Turn'd wild in nature, broke their stalls, flung out,
Contending 'gainst obedience, as they would make
War with mankind.
OLD MAN
'Tis said they eat each other.
ROSS
They did so, to the amazement of mine eyes
That look'd upon't. Here comes the good Macduff.

Enter MACDUFF
How goes the world, sir, now?
MACDUFF
Why, see you not?
ROSS
Is't known who did this more than bloody deed?
MACDUFF
Those that Macbeth hath slain.
ROSS
Alas, the day!
What good could they pretend?
MACDUFF
They were suborn'd:
Malcolm and Donalbain, the king's two sons,
Are stol'n away and fled; which puts upon them
Suspicion of the deed.
ROSS
'Gainst nature still!
Thriftless ambition, that wilt ravin up
Thine own life's means! Then 'tis most like
The sovereignty will fall upon Macbeth.

ACT 2 scene 4
EXPLANATION

In all his wisdom, the old man talks about the natural order being reversed
'Tis unnatural

First, the murder of a king is against the divine right of kings, hence, the reversal of the natural order.

Daylight has been replaced by night, and the falcon, a strong bird of prey, is hunted and killed by an owl.

A falcon, towering in her pride of place,
Was by a mousing owl hawk'd at and kill'd.

Once again, Shakespeare tells us how nature plays a role in man's behaviour, because man has to follow the laws of nature, which Macbeth did not do by killing the king.

Even the horses turned against nature; they

broke their stalls, flung out,
Contending 'gainst obedience

They too broke the laws of nature by eating each other. Ross is shocked at their disobedience and says;

to the amazement of mine eyes

The horses reflected Macbeth's behaviour, because he also did not have any respect for nature's laws when he killed Duncan.

[ENTER MACDUFF]

Macduff thinks that Malcolm and Donalbain were encouraged to kill Duncan, and then they

Are stol'n away and fled

which makes them very suspicious.

Ross, once again, mentions the law of nature that Malcolm and Donalbain disobeyed in killing their father
'Gainst nature still

Now they acknowledge that Macbeth will be king and that he is gone to Scone to be crowned king of Scotland.

MACBETH ACT 2 scene 4

TEXT	EXPLANATION
MACDUFF He is already named, and gone to Scone To be invested. **ROSS** Where is Duncan's body? **MACDUFF** Carried to Colmekill, The sacred storehouse of his predecessors, And guardian of their bones. **ROSS** Will you to Scone? **MACDUFF** No, cousin, I'll to Fife. **ROSS** Well, I will thither. **MACDUFF** Well, may you see things well done there: adieu! Lest our old robes sit easier than our new! **ROSS** Farewell, father. **OLD MAN** God's benison go with you; and with those That would make good of bad, and friends of foes! *Exeunt*	They say that Duncan is to be buried in Colmekill - the holy island where Scottish kings are buried. Carried to Colmekill, The sacred storehouse of his predecessors, And guardian of their bones Ross asks MacDuff whether he is going to Scone for Macbeth's coronation, but he says that he is not going. MacDuff, once again, uses a clothing imagery when he says; Lest our old robes sit easier than our new! We sense that MacDuff is uneasy. He suggests that Macbeth's rule will not be as good as Duncan's. He is referring to Duncan's fair rule and hopes that the 'new robes' which is Macbeth's reign will be just as good. And with those That would make good of bad, and friends of foes! There's a sense of foreboding and a certain premonition in the old man's speech. He foreshadows the animosity that will arise between Macbeth and Macduff which will ultimately lead to the death of Macduff's family and Macbeth's death by Macduff.

Macduff and Ross discuss Duncan's murder

Macduff escorts Duncan's body to Colmkill

MACBETH SUMMARY	**ACT 3 scene 1**	p74

Banquo is distancing himself from Macbeth because he is suspicious of how he achieved the crown. He voices his suspicion about Macbeth gaining the crown. He says,

"Thou playest most foully for't",

implying that Macbeth killed King Duncan for it.
He is also reflecting on the predictions that the witches gave him, that he would be

"the root and father of many kings"

but he is sceptical about the witches' prophesies whereas Macbeth is excited and acts on it.
He says that Macbeth's prophecies from the witches have been fulfilled.

Macbeth and Lady Macbeth enter attired as king and queen and Macbeth invites Banquo to the banquet. Macbeth tells him that they should discuss the threat that Malcolm and Donalbain is posing. They have fled from Scotland and suspicion falls on them for killing Duncan. Macbeth is afraid that they may be plotting against him for the crown.

Banquo plays into Macbeth's hands by telling him that he will go riding with his son Fleance.
This gives Macbeth the perfect plan to kill him.

In his soliloquy Macbeth shows his true feelings towards Banquo. He fears that he is an obstacle to his crown, and he must be eliminated. He acknowledges that his will be,

"A fruitless crown"

Because he has no heir and the witches have predicted that Banquo's sons will be in line to be kings. He manipulates two hired assassins by telling them that since Banquo is their mutual enemy and that they need to kill him and his son Fleance to which agree.

Banquo [aside]**: Thous hast it now, King, Cawdor,all**

Macbeth as King with sword and spectre

MACBETH
TEXT

Macbeth's castle

Enter BANQUO dressed for riding

BANQUO

Thou hast it now: king, Cawdor, Glamis, all,
As the weird women promised, and, I fear,
Thou play'dst most foully for't: yet it was said
It should not stand in thy posterity,
But that myself should be the root and father
Of many kings. If there come truth from them–
As upon thee, Macbeth, their speeches shine–
Why, by the verities on thee made good,
May they not be my oracles as well,
And set me up in hope? But hush! no more.

Sennet sounded.
Enter MACBETH, as king, LADY MACBETH, as queen, LENNOX, ROSS, Lords, Ladies, and Attendants

MACBETH

Here's our chief guest.

LADY MACBETH

If he had been forgotten,
It had been as a gap in our great feast,
And all-thing unbecoming.

MACBETH

To-night we hold a solemn supper sir,
And I'll request your presence.

BANQUO

Let your highness
Command upon me; to the which my duties
Are with a most indissoluble tie
For ever knit.

MACBETH

Ride you this afternoon?

BANQUO

Ay, my good lord.

MACBETH

We should have else desired your good advice,
Which still hath been both grave and prosperous,
In this day's council; but we'll take to-morrow.
Is't far you ride?

BANQUO

As far, my lord, as will fill up the time
'Twixt this and supper: go not my horse the better,
I must become a borrower of the night
For a dark hour or twain.

ACT 3 scene 1
EXPLANATION

Act 3, Scene 1 starts with Banquo's soliloquy.
He is reflecting on the promises of the witches and says that Macbeth has everything that the witches predicted. He is highly suspicious that Macbeth got the crown by foul means.

Thou play'dst most foully for't.

He says if the predictions came true for Macbeth then it will come true for him as well but he did not want to delve further into it. "But hush! No more."
Enter Macbeth declaring Banquo as

our chief guest.

The theme of appearance versus reality comes into play once again, because Macbeth acts all friendly and invites Banquo to a great feast. Macbeth declares Banquo his "chief guest"

Shakespeare uses dramatic irony here, because the audience knows that Macbeth is plotting to kill Banquo. Just like Duncan, Banquo expresses his love and loyalty towards Macbeth as

indissoluble tie For ever knit.

The knitting imagery suggest the love tie that existed between Macbeth and Banquo, which is about to be broken. Macbeth is very sneaky here. He is getting all the information of Banquo's whereabouts

Ride you this afternoon?

so he can deviously plan his murder.

Before Banquo leaves, he tells Macbeth,

I must become a borrower of the night
For a dark hour or twain

This dark imagery foreshadows Banquo's death, because he dies the next night.

MACBETH TEXT

MACBETH
Fail not our feast.
BANQUO
My lord, I will not.
MACBETH
We hear, our bloody cousins are bestow'd
In England and in Ireland, not confessing
Their cruel parricide, filling their hearers
With strange invention: but of that to-morrow,
When therewithal we shall have cause of state
Craving us jointly. Hie you to horse: adieu,
Till you return at night. Goes Fleance with you?
BANQUO
Ay, my good lord: our time does call upon 's.
MACBETH
I wish your horses swift and sure of foot;
And so I do commend you to their backs. Farewell.
Exit BANQUO

Let every man be master of his time
Till seven at night: to make society
The sweeter welcome, we will keep ourself
Till supper-time alone: while then, God be with you!
Exeunt all but MACBETH, and an attendant

Sirrah, a word with you: attend those men
Our pleasure?
ATTENDANT
They are, my lord, without the palace gate.

ACT 3 scene 1 EXPLANATION

He tells Banquo not to forget his feast,

Fail not our feast

and Banquo promises that he will not.

Macbeth tells Banquo that he needs his advice on Malcolm's and Donalbain's actions. Macbeth accuses them of "cruel patricide". He tells Banquo that they are spreading lies and rumours, and both of them need to sort the problem out "craving us jointly". It is obvious here that Macbeth is devious because he wants Banquo's help to fight against Malcolm and Donalbain because they pose a threat to his crown.

Macbeth is acting like a flower – as Lady Macbeth suggested but he has evil intentions like the serpent. Shakespeare's use of dramatic irony can clearly suggest this because we are aware that Macbeth is planning to kill Banquo and his son Fleance.

We see the theme of appearance versus reality here because Macbeth wishes Banquo well and he pretends to to be loving and cordial towards Banquo.

I wish your horses swift and sure of foot.

Macbeth enquires of the servant if the men are waiting for him, and he says that the assassins have arrived and are outside the palace gate. We see Macbeth plunging into the depths of depravity because of his greed by hiring assassins to kill Banquo and Fleance.

Banquo [*to Macbeth*]**: My Lord I will not** [fail you]

Banquo his son Fleance, Macbeth, Lady Macbeth

MACBETH TEXT

MACBETH
Bring them before us.
Exit Attendant

To be thus is nothing;
But to be safely thus.– Our fears in Banquo
Stick deep; and in his royalty of nature
Reigns that which would be fear'd: 'tis much he dares;
And, to that dauntless temper of his mind,
He hath a wisdom that doth guide his valour
To act in safety. There is none but he
Whose being I do fear: and, under him,
My Genius is rebuked; as, it is said,
Mark Antony's was by Caesar. He chid the sisters
When first they put the name of king upon me,
And bade them speak to him: then prophet-like
They hail'd him father to a line of kings:
Upon my head they placed a fruitless crown,
And put a barren sceptre in my gripe,
Thence to be wrench'd with an unlineal hand,
No son of mine succeeding. If 't be so,
For Banquo's issue have I filed my mind;
For them the gracious Duncan have I murder'd;
Put rancours in the vessel of my peace
Only for them; and mine eternal jewel
Given to the common enemy of man,
To make them kings, the seed of Banquo kings!
Rather than so, come fate into the list.
And champion me to the utterance! Who's there!

Re-enter Attendant, with two Murderers
Now go to the door and stay there till we call.
Exit Attendant

Was it not yesterday we spoke together?

Macbeth [soliloquy]**: To be thus is nothing**

ACT 3 scene 1 EXPLANATION

Macbeth then asks the Attendant to bring the murderers in. He tells them,

Our fears in Banquo
Stick deep

He is afraid of Banquo's nobility and honest character.

Shakespeare uses the verb 'reigns', foreshadowing that he will be father of future kings.

There is none but he
Whose being I do fear

He says that he is threatened by Banquo's presence. He draws a comparison between his situation to that of Mark Anthony and Caesar. Mark Anthony was a great statesman and orator, yet he felt intimidated by Caesar.

Macbeth told the murderers that when the witches predicted that he would be king, Banquo challenged them.

Here, we see a very unnerved Macbeth, because the witches prophesied that Banquo will be hailed as "father to a line of kings".

He is distraught that his position as king will be threatened as long as Banquo and his son are alive.

And put a barren sceptre in my gripe

The witches put an empty crown in his grip, because they said that Banquo's descendants and not Macbeth will be father to a line of kings "No son of mine succeeding".

He said that he murdered Duncan and had sinned and it "filed my mind". He uses the imagery of a drinking vessel, where he put bitter drink into it, hence destroying his piece of mind.

Put rancours in the vessel of my peace

Macbeth also said that he had given "mine eternal jewel" (soul) to the devil, "the common enemy of man".

MACBETH
TEXT

FIRST MURDERER
It was, so please your highness.
MACBETH
Well then, now
Have you consider'd of my speeches? Know
That it was he in the times past which held you
So under fortune, which you thought had been
Our innocent self: this I made good to you
In our last conference, pass'd in probation with you,
How you were borne in hand,
How cross'd, the instruments,
Who wrought with them, and all things else that might
To half a soul and to a notion crazed
Say 'Thus did Banquo.'
FIRST MURDERER
You made it known to us.
MACBETH
I did so, and went further, which is now
Our point of second meeting. Do you find
Your patience so predominant in your nature
That you can let this go? Are you so gospell'd
To pray for this good man and for his issue,
Whose heavy hand hath bow'd you to the grave
And beggar'd yours for ever?
FIRST MURDERER
We are men, my liege.
MACBETH
Ay, in the catalogue ye go for men;
As hounds and greyhounds, mongrels, spaniels, curs,
Shoughs, water-rugs and demi-wolves, are clept
All by the name of dogs: the valued file
Distinguishes the swift, the slow, the subtle,
The housekeeper, the hunter, every one
According to the gift which bounteous nature
Hath in him closed; whereby he does receive
Particular addition. from the bill
That writes them all alike: and so of men.
Now, if you have a station in the file,
Not i' the worst rank of manhood, say 't;
And I will put that business in your bosoms,
Whose execution takes your enemy off,
Grapples you to the heart and love of us,
Who wear our health but sickly in his life,
Which in his death were perfect.

ACT 3 scene 1
EXPLANATION

Macbeth asks the murderers if they thought about his proposal to kill Banquo and Fleance;

Have you considere'd of my speeches?

He convinces them that Banquo had deceived them in the past and they thought that it was him. Yet he was innocent of such atrocities and he explained to them that all the evil levelled against them was done by Banquo alone;

That it was he in the times past which held you
So under fortune

We are shocked at Macbeth's art of manipulation and deception. He lies to the men that Banquo has pushed them to an early grave and had made beggars of them and their families.

Whose heavy hand hath bow'd you to the grave
And beggar'd yours for ever?

He asks them if they are so patient and forgiving and if they will pray for someone who hurt them.

Your patience so predominant in your nature
That you can let this go?

Macbeth plays on their conscience, and he also uses mental and psychological blackmail. He uses the comparison of man to dogs and says that man is like dogs and that they fall into different categories – high and low and if they are at the bottom he will bring them up, by getting rid of the enemy. That will bring them closer to him suggesting that their status will be enhanced like his.

He says that he is sick as long as Banquo is alive, but he will be healthy if Banquo is dead.

Which in his death were perfect

MACBETH TEXT

SECOND MURDERER
I am one, my liege,
Whom the vile blows and buffets of the world
Have so incensed that I am reckless what I do
To spite the world.
FIRST MURDERER
And I another
So weary with disasters, tugg'd with fortune,
That I would set my lie on any chance,
To mend it, or be rid on't.
MACBETH
Both of you
Know Banquo was your enemy.
BOTH MURDERERS
True, my lord.
MACBETH
So is he mine; and in such bloody distance,
That every minute of his being thrusts
Against my near'st of life: and though I could
With barefaced power sweep him from my sight
And bid my will avouch it, yet I must not,
For certain friends that are both his and mine,
Whose loves I may not drop, but wail his fall
Who I myself struck down; and thence it is,
That I to your assistance do make love,
Masking the business from the common eye
For sundry weighty reasons.
SECOND MURDERER
We shall, my lord,
Perform what you command us.
FIRST MURDERER
Though our lives...

ACT 3 scene 1 EXPLANATION

The second murderer says that he had been treated so badly by the world that he doesn't care what he does. He is prepared to take revenge for his vile treatment,

Whom the vile blows and buffets of the world
Have so incensed that I am reckless

The first murderer shares the same sentiment about his wrecked life and he says that he will take any chance to fix his life or end it.

So weary with disasters, tugg'd with fortune

Macbeth once again stresses the fact that Banquo is his enemy as well. He says that he can use his power to kill him but they have common friends that he needs.

"With barefaced power sweep him from my sight."

He is very audacious in saying that when Banquo dies, he will be able to cry in public although he has done the killing. Here again we see the theme of appearance vs reality surfacing. Macbeth's shocking pretences.

"But wail his fall who I myself struck down."

He therefore urges them to help him to kill Duncan and Fleance to which they agree.

Murderers listening to Macbeth's instructions

Murderers agree to perform Macbeth commands

MACBETH
TEXT

EXPLANATION

MACBETH

Your spirits shine through you. Within this hour at most
I will advise you where to plant yourselves;
Acquaint you with the perfect spy o' the time,
The moment on't; for't must be done to-night,
An something from the palace; always thought
That I require a clearness: and with him–
To leave no rubs nor botches in the work–
Fleance his son, that keeps him company,
Whose absence is no less material to me
Than is his father's, must embrace the fate
Of that dark hour. Resolve yourselves apart:
I'll come to you anon.

BOTH MURDERERS

We are resolved, my lord.

MACBETH

I'll call upon you straight: abide within.

Exeunt Murderers

It is concluded. Banquo, thy soul's flight,
If it find heaven, must find it out to-night

Exit

He makes plans and gives the murderers instructions

I will advise you where to plant yourselves

We see that Macbeth is working alone, independent of Lady Macbeth. He has acquired a certain confidence and boldness to plan and commit murder on his own.

He tells the murderers that they must not make any mistakes or bungle things up

To leave no rubs nor botches in the work–

He said that Fleance must also

embrace the fate
Of that dark hour

Meaning that Fleance must also meet the same fate as his father and die.

The rhyming couplet at the end of this scene-'flight' coupled with 'tonight'-is rather chilling. It gives a sense of finality when Macbeth seals Banquo's fate.

Banquo, thy soul's flight,
If it finds heaven, must find it tonight.

The use of the biblical imagery 'heaven', suggesting Banquo's innocence, just like Duncan's, will enter heaven.

Macbeth bids Murderers to exit

Macbeth [*Aside*]**: Banquo, thy soul's flight**

MACBETH SUMMARY	**ACT 3 scene 2**	p81

Lady Macbeth enquires about Banquo's whereabouts and says that she wants to speak to Macbeth.

There is a big shift from Act 1 and Act 2.

In Act 3, scene 2, Macbeth is acting independently of Lady Macbeth. In the previous scenes, she held the reigns

"leave this night's business in my hands".

Macbeth follows obediently, but now he is acting alone and is brave enough to actually liaise with murderers.

Shakespeare mirrors Act 1, Scene 5 here, where the order is reversed. Lady Macbeth was planning and plotting Duncan's murder, but now Macbeth is plotting to kill Banquo. He does not communicate his plans to Lady Macbeth.

In Act 1, Scene 5, Lady Macbeth says, "Come, thick night". Macbeth echoes this sentiment in Act 3 scene 2, "Come seeling night".

Shakespeare uses dark imagery when Macbeth and Lady Macbeth call on the darkness to hide their evil intentions. They are both feeling troubled and uncertain, but she boldly asks Macbeth to stop worrying about things "What's done is done".

She also tells him that he should not harbour those terrible memories of the murder in his mind,

"Those thoughts which should indeed have died with them they think on".

Macbeth [*to Lady Macbeth*]**: We have scorch'd the snake , not kill'd it.**

Macbeth [*to Lady Macbeth*]**: O, full of scorpions is my mind, dear wife!**

MACBETH **TEXT**	**ACT 3 scene 2** **EXPLANATION**

Macbeth's castle

Enter LADY MACBETH and a Servant

LADY MACBETH
Is Banquo gone from court?
SERVANT
Ay, madam, but returns again to-night.
LADY MACBETH
Say to the king, I would attend his leisure
For a few words.
SERVANT
Madam, I will.
Exit

LADY MACBETH
Nought's had, all's spent,
Where our desire is got without content:
'Tis safer to be that which we destroy
Than by destruction dwell in doubtful joy.

Enter MACBETH
How now, my lord! why do you keep alone,
Of sorriest fancies your companions making,
Using those thoughts which should indeed have died
With them they think on? Things without all remedy
Should be without regard: what's done is done.
MACBETH
We have scotch'd the snake, not kill'd it:
She'll close and be herself, whilst our poor malice
Remains in danger of her former tooth.
But let the frame of things disjoint, both the
worlds suffer,
Ere we will eat our meal in fear and sleep
In the affliction of these terrible dreams
That shake us nightly: better be with the dead,
Whom we, to gain our peace, have sent to peace,
Than on the torture of the mind to lie
In restless ecstasy. Duncan is in his grave;
After life's fitful fever he sleeps well;
Treason has done his worst: nor steel, nor poison,
Malice domestic, foreign levy, nothing,
Can touch him further.
LADY MACBETH
Come on;
Gentle my lord, sleek o'er your rugged looks;
Be bright and jovial among your guests to-night.

Lady Macbeth is concerned about her husband's depressed state

How now, my lord! why do you keep alone,
Of sorriest fancies your companions making,

She remarks

Things without all remedy
Should be without regard: what's done is done.

But to no avail.

Macbeth is worried and pours out his fears to her.

We have scotch'd the snake, not kill'd it:

implying that they didn't get rid of the problem by killing Duncan, because Banquo and Fleance are still alive and pose a problem to their kingship.

Macbeth talks of things disjointed, and the retribution from others

Ere we will eat our meal in fear and sleep

The affliction of

terrible dreams
That shake us nightly

He said that he is envious that Duncan is so peaceful in death

After life's fitful fever he sleeps well
Treason has done his worst

The theme of sleep surfaces once again here.
Lady Macbeth tells him to be cheerful and be welcoming to their guests for the feast

Be bright and jovial among your guests to-night.

MACBETH TEXT	ACT 3 scene 2 EXPLANATION

MACBETH
So shall I, love; and so, I pray, be you:
Let your remembrance apply to Banquo;
Present him eminence, both with eye and tongue:
Unsafe the while, that we
Must lave our honours in these flattering streams,
And make our faces vizards to our hearts,
Disguising what they are.
LADY MACBETH
You must leave this.
MACBETH
O, full of scorpions is my mind, dear wife!
Thou know'st that Banquo, and his Fleance, lives.
LADY MACBETH
But in them nature's copy's not eterne.
MACBETH
There's comfort yet; they are assailable;
Then be thou jocund: ere the bat hath flown
His cloister'd flight, ere to black Hecate's summons
The shard-borne beetle with his drowsy hums
Hath rung night's yawning peal, there shall be done
A deed of dreadful note.
LADY MACBETH
What's to be done?
MACBETH
Be innocent of the knowledge, dearest chuck,
Till thou applaud the deed. Come, seeling night,
Scarf up the tender eye of pitiful day;
And with thy bloody and invisible hand
Cancel and tear to pieces that great bond
Which keeps me pale! Light thickens; and the crow
Makes wing to the rooky wood:
Good things of day begin to droop and drowse;
While night's black agents to their preys do rouse.
Thou marvell'st at my words: but hold thee still;
Things bad begun make strong themselves by ill.
So, prithee, go with me.

Exeunt

They plan to use the same tactics that they used when Duncan came to the castle.

We once again see the theme of appearance verse reality. Macbeth agrees to carry out the pretence and says,

And make our faces vizards to our hearts,
Disguising what they are.

Here we see a very changed Macbeth from earlier on in the play when he refused to kill Duncan in Act 1 scene 7 "We shall proceed no further in this business"

Macbeth talks about 'dark deeds' referring to Banquo and Fleance's murder. "There shall be done a deed of dreadful note," he tells Lady Macbeth, but he refuses to fully confide in her.

We see a change in Macbeth from the previous scenes, because he has now acquired a boldness to carry out murder without Lady Macbeth's help. We see the theme of evil and darkness in Act 3, Scene 2, because Macbeth and Lady Macbeth want the dark night to hide their evil deeds.

The scene ends when Macbeth tells Lady Macbeth,

O, full of scorpions is my mind, dear wife!

Scorpions are deadly creatures, just like Macbeth. He remains a murderer because of his plan to kill Banquo and Fleance. Macbeth's speech is eerie here, reeking of imageries of darkness and death

the bat hath flown
His cloister'd flight, ere to black Hecate's summons

This dark imagery foreshadows Banquo's death; bats are night creatures found in graveyards and are associated with death, and Macbeth's reference to Hecate, the queen of the witches, also signifies evil and death

there shall be done
A deed of dreadful note.
Determined, Macbeth is now on a mission.

MACBETH SUMMARY | **ACT 3 scene 3** |

This scene takes place in the dark because of its evil nature. This scene is riddled with dark and light imageries.

We can associate the darkness to Macbeth's evil and murderous nature and juxtapose this to Banquo's loyal and kind nature. Macbeth has sunk to the depths of darkness because of his evil deeds.

The murderers, appointed by Macbeth, are ready in waiting to ambush and kill Banquo and his son Fleance.

The two murderers are met by a third, and the second murderer says that Macbeth should trust them since he gave them specific instructions what to do.

It's interesting to note that despite the loyalty of the two murderers, Macbeth was taking no chances. He doesn't trust anybody, and he employs a third murderer to ensure that the deed is done.

"What we have to do to the direction just".

They wait for Fleance and Banquo to approach. They pounce on them and assassinate Banquo but, in the confusion, the light is extinguished, and Fleance escapes hence fulfilling the witches' prediction.

The extinguished light can be symbolic for Banquo's death. Banquo told Fleance that he must get 'revenge'.

The murderers go to tell Macbeth what had happened.

Ambush some distance from Macbeth's castle

Murderers preparing ambush for Banquo and son

MACBETH TEXT	ACT 3 scene 3 EXPLANATION

Some distance from Macbeth's castle

ENTER three MURDERERS

FIRST MURDERER
But who did bid thee join with us?
SECOND MURDERER
He needs not our mistrust, since he delivers
Our offices and what we have to do
To the direction just.
FIRST MURDERER
[*to Third Murderer*] Then stand with us.
The west yet glimmers with some streaks of day:
Now spurs the lated traveller apace
To gain the timely inn; and near approaches
The subject of our watch.
THIRD MURDERER
Hark! I hear horses.
BANQUO
[*Within*] Give us a light there, ho!
SECOND MURDERER
Then 'tis he: the rest
That are within the note of expectation
Already are i' the court.
FIRST MURDERER
His horses go about.
THIRD MURDERER
Almost a mile: but he does usually,
So all men do, from hence to the palace gate
Make it their walk.
SECOND MURDERER
A light, a light!

Macbeth sends the third murderer to join the other two because he doesn't trust anyone.

The murderer says that Macbeth should not mistrust them because he gave them explicit instructions on how to carry out the murder.

Note Shakespeare's constant use of light imagery associated with Banquo.

Ironically as Banquo approaches, the second murderer makes a comment about the west being still alight. One can suggest that Banquo is approaching with glimmers of light. Maybe there is a glimmer of hope left for Macbeth to redeem himself but he rode from the light into darkness and death, hence extinguishing that glimmer of hope.

"The west yet glimmers with some streaks of day."

Just before Banquo dies, he asks for a light

Give us a light there, ho!

It's ironic, because his light (his life) is about to be extinguished. The second murderer also asks for a light;

"A light, a light!

Suggesting that he too needs to see the light because of the dark deed he is about to commit.

Banquo and Fleance passing through wooded area

Banquo attached by Macbeth's two Murderers

MACBETH TEXT

Enter BANQUO, and FLEANCE with a torch

THIRD MURDERER
'Tis he.
FIST MURDERER
Stand to't.
BANQUO
It will be rain to-night.
FIRST MURDERER
Let it come down.

They set upon BANQUO
BANQUO
O, treachery! Fly, good Fleance, fly, fly, fly!
Thou mayst revenge. O slave!

BANQUO dies. FLEANCE escapes

THIRD MURDERER
Who did strike out the light?
FIRST MURDERER
Wast not the way?
THIRD MURDERER
There's but one down; the son is fled.
SECOND MURDERER
We have lost
Best half of our affair.
FIRST MURDERER
Well, let's away, and say how much is done.

Exeunt

ACT 3 scene 3 EXPLANATION

Banquo and Fleance enter with a torch. Note the repetition of the light imagery suggesting that they are bringing the light with them perhaps for Macbeth to see but that light is extinguished.

Note Banquo's dying words

O, treachery! Fly, good Fleance, fly, fly, fly!

He was concerned about his son's safety, and he asks Fleance to seek revenge

Thou mayst revenge

The murderers light got extinguished, and, in the confusion, Fleance escapes

We have lost
Best half of our affair.

Macbeth is going to be furious that Fleance escapes, because now the witches' prophecy will be fulfilled. Banquo dies as the murderers discuss this.

Fleance's escape signals a turning point in the play. The murderers go to tell Macbeth what had happened and how Fleance escaped

Well, let's away, and say how much is done.

Fleance attached by Murderer

Banquo is killed whilst watching Fleance escape

MACBETH SUMMARY	**ACT 3 scene 4**	p87

Shakespeare creates a nail-biting, suspense-filled, tense scene.

Macbeth welcomes his guests. He learns of Banquo's death and Fleance's escape.

This news disturbs him enormously.

Macbeth addresses his guests. He tells them to be seated according to their rank degrees. He tells them that Lady Macbeth will welcome them soon.

When he returns to the table and proposes a toast, he is horrified to see Banquo's ghost, and he accuses the Lords of creating this mischief.

Macbeth is visibly shaken, and Lady Macbeth tries to quell the situation.

Shakespeare toys with our emotions because he makes Macbeth do strange things like hallucinate when he sees the ghost of Banquo, having him fly into fits of rage before he calms his senses and repeats these actions three times, each time seeing the ghost of Banquo.

Lady Macbeth makes an excuse for him by telling everyone that his crazy behaviour can be attributed to a fit that he has suffered since a young boy.

She eventually dismisses the guests and accuses him of being unmanly.

Bear baiting inside Macbeth's castle

Servant tells King Macbeth that his Murderers await

MACBETH TEXT

ACT 3 scene 4 EXPLANATION

The Banqueting Hall with king and queen thrones

Enter MACBETH as King, Lady MACBETH as Queen, Thane ROSS, Thane LENNOX, Lords, and Attendants

Lady MACBETH sits

MACBETH
You know your own degrees; sit down:
At first and last the hearty welcome.
LORDS
Thanks to your majesty.
MACBETH
Ourself will mingle with society,
And play the humble host.
Our hostess keeps her state, but in best time
We will require her welcome.
LADY MACBETH
Pronounce it for me, sir, to all our friends;
For my heart speaks they are welcome.

First Murderer appears at the door
MACBETH
See, they encounter thee with their hearts' thanks.
Both sides are even: here I'll sit i' the midst:
Be large in mirth; anon we'll drink a measure
The table round.

Approaching the door
There's blood on thy face.
FIRST MURDERER
'Tis Banquo's then.
MACBETH
'Tis better thee without than he within.
Is he dispatch'd?
FIRST MURDERER
My lord, his throat is cut; that I did for him.
MACBETH
Thou art the best o' the cut-throats: yet he's good
That did the like for Fleance: if thou didst it,
Thou art the nonpareil.

ENTER MACBETH AS KING AND LADY MACBETH AS QUEEN.

Lady Macbeth plays the perfect host. She tells them to sit according to their ranks from the highest to the lowest.

Previously we witnessed Macbeth's conversation with the two murderers when he tells them that he would raise their ranks if they killed Banquo.

It becomes clear to us how status-conscious both Macbeth and Lady Macbeth are and that they will do anything for status and power even if it means killing.

He says that he will be happy and drink a toast around the table referring to his rejoicing after Banquo's murder.

We see the motif of blood surface once again when Macbeth tells the first murderer that

There's blood on thy face.

The first murderer tells him that it is Banquo's blood and that he had cut Banquo's throat.

Shakespeare uses a verb 'cut-throats' because the murderer cut Banquo's throat and Macbeth calls him a cutthroat and we the audience can call Macbeth a cut-throat because he deceived, robbed, and killed Duncan.

Murderer interrogated by King Macbeth with servant holding torch

MACBETH
TEXT

ACT 3 scene 4
EXPLANATION

FIRST MURDERER
Most royal sir,
Fleance is 'scaped.
MACBETH
Then comes my fit again: I had else been perfect,
Whole as the marble, founded as the rock,
As broad and general as the casing air:
But now I am cabin'd, cribb'd, confined, bound in
To saucy doubts and fears. But Banquo's safe?

FIRST MURDERER
Ay, my good lord: safe in a ditch he bides,
With twenty trenched gashes on his head;
The least a death to nature.
MACBETH
Thanks for that:
There the grown serpent lies; the worm that's fled
Hath nature that in time will venom breed,
No teeth for the present. Get thee gone:
To-morrow we'll hear, ourselves, again.
Exit Murderer

LADY MACBETH
My royal lord,
You do not give the cheer: the feast is sold
That is not often vouch'd, while 'tis a-making,
'Tis given with welcome: to feed were best at home;
From thence the sauce to meat is ceremony;
Meeting were bare without it.

Murderers led away not to be rewarded BUT killed to maintain their silence

When Macbeth hears that Fleance has escaped, he was angry because he said that he had planned the murders so well.

"I had else been perfect."

Macbeth uses the alliteration

cabin'd, cribb'd, confined
to show his feelings of despair and entrapment. He feels that he is now shut up and confined to a small space.

He asks if Banquo is dead

But Banquo's safe?

The murderer gives Macbeth a visual description of Banquo's murder

With twenty trenched gashes on his head;

Macbeth is elated, and he thanks the murderer

There the grown serpent lies

Macbeth said that Banquo is a dead snake, and this gives Macbeth some assurance.

However, he is worried that Fleance had escaped

the worm that's fled

and that he can still cause problems for Macbeth's kingship

that in time will venom breed

Fleance can strike like a snake at Macbeth and claim the crown according to the witches' prophecy, of which Macbeth is afraid.
Lady Macbeth reprimands Macbeth for neglecting the guests. She said that he needs to welcome the guests because courtesy adds spice to the meal.

From thence the sauce to meat is ceremony;
Meeting were bare without it.

MACBETH TEXT

ACT 3 scene 4 EXPLANATION

p90

The GHOST OF BANQUO enters, and sits in MACBETH's place

MACBETH
Sweet remembrancer!
Now, good digestion wait on appetite,
And health on both!
LENNOX
May't please your highness sit.

MACBETH
Here had we now our country's honour roof'd,
Were the graced person of our Banquo present;
Who may I rather challenge for unkindness
Than pity for mischance!
ROSS
His absence, sir,
Lays blame upon his promise. Please't your highness
To grace us with your royal company.
MACBETH
The table's full.
LENNOX
Here is a place reserved, sir.
MACBETH
Where?
LENNOX
Here, my good lord. What is't that moves your highness?
MACBETH
Which of you have done this?
LORDS
What, my good lord?
MACBETH
Thou canst not say I did it: never shake
Thy gory locks at me.

Macbeth welcomes his guests, and he says that all the country's nobility is under

our country's honour roof'd

We see Macbeth's hypocritical character when he praises Banquo in his speech, knowing that he is dead. Macbeth's changing character creates a sense of revulsion in the reader. He has descended from a celebrated war hero into a tragic anarchist.

His cold calculated behaviour is now mirroring Lady Macbeth's. He said that he cannot accuse Banquo of having manners for not being present at the banquet

I rather challenge for unkindness

He goes on to bravely say that he is worried that something bad has happened to Banquo

Than pity for mischance!

Macbeth is shaken to see the ghost of Banquo occupying his seat.

He is so unnerved that he accuses the Lords

Which of you have done this?

The Lords are quite puzzled at Macbeth's behaviour. Macbeth then addresses the ghost of Banquo, denying that he was responsible for his killing.

Shakespeare creates a lot of suspense and tension in this scene. The audience didn't expect a calm atmosphere in the banquet, to turn to one of awe and

The GHOST of Banquo sits in Macbeth's seat at Table

Macbeth [*to ALL*]: Which of you have done this?

MACBETH
TEXT

ACT 3 scene 4
EXPLANATION

ROSS
Gentlemen, rise: his highness is not well.
LADY MACBETH
Sit, worthy friends: my lord is often thus,
And hath been from his youth: pray you, keep seat;
The fit is momentary; upon a thought
He will again be well: if much you note him,
You shall offend him and extend his passion:
Feed, and regard him not. Are you a man?
MACBETH
Ay, and a bold one, that dare look on that
Which might appal the devil.
LADY MACBETH
O proper stuff!
This is the very painting of your fear:
This is the air-drawn dagger which, you said,
Led you to Duncan. O, these flaws and starts,
Impostors to true fear, would well become
A woman's story at a winter's fire,
Authorized by her grandam. Shame itself!
Why do you make such faces? When all's done,
You look but on a stool.
MACBETH
Prithee, see there! behold! look! lo!
How say you?
[*Ghost*]Why, what care I? If thou canst nod, speak too.
If charnel-houses and our graves must send
Those that we bury back, our monuments
Shall be the maws of kites.
GHOST OF BANQUO vanishes

Macbeth [*to Lady Macbeth*]**: see there! behold! look! lo!**

The audience becomes tense when they see Macbeth's expression, and the suspense is heightened when the audience becomes curious about what's going to happen next.

Lady Macbeth was very calm and collected, and she acts very quickly to assure the guests that

The fit is momentary

She tells them that Macbeth will take offence if they place too much emphasis on his behaviour

You shall offend him and extend his passion

She then targets his manhood and belittles him saying,

Are you a man?
She tries to convince him that it is not real, saying,

O proper stuff!
This is the very painting of your fear:

She consoles him further into saying that it's the same when he visualised the dagger that led him to Duncan

the air-drawn dagger which
Led you to Duncan

Lady Macbeth is scared that he is showing guilt
You look but on a stool

The tension is palpable, and Shakespeare is toying with the audiences' emotions, because he makes the ghost of Banquo's appear and disappear.
The ghost reappears and Shakespeare's use of the repeated exclamation marks [!] gives us an indication of Macbeth's absolute terror at seeing the ghost again:

Prithee, see there! behold! look! lo!

He even uses rhetorical questions:
How say you?
Why, what care I?

These depict Macbeth's altered state of mind. He is overcome with fear at seeing Banquo's ghost again.

MACBETH TEXT

ACT 3 scene 4 EXPLANATION

LADY MACBETH
What, quite unmann'd in folly?
MACBETH
If I stand here, I saw him.
LADY MACBETH
Fie, for shame!
MACBETH
Blood hath been shed ere now, i' the olden time,
Ere human statute purged the gentle weal;
Ay, and since too, murders have been perform'd
Too terrible for the ear: the times have been,
That, when the brains were out, the man would die,
And there an end; but now they rise again,
With twenty mortal murders on their crowns,
And push us from our stools: this is more strange
Than such a murder is.
LADY MACBETH
My worthy lord,
Your noble friends do lack you.
MACBETH
I do forget.
Do not muse at me, my most worthy friends,
I have a strange infirmity, which is nothing
To those that know me. Come, love and health to all;
Then I'll sit down. Give me some wine; fill full.

The GHOST OF BANQUO reappears in MACBETH's seat
I drink to the general joy o' the whole table,
And to our dear friend Banquo, whom we miss;
Would he were here! to all, and him, we thirst,
And all to all.
LORDS
Our duties, and the pledge.

The GHOST OF BANQUO reappears in MACBETH's seat

Lady Macbeth is furious at Macbeth's shocking behaviour,

What, quite unmann'd in folly?

But Macbeth insists that he saw the ghost

If I stand here, I saw him

Macbeth is alarmed, and he says that two murders were performed which were

Too terrible for the ear

he thought

That, when the brains were out, the man would die,

But although Banquo endured twenty fatal wounds to his head, he still managed to rise again

And push us from our stools

It is ironic that Banquo sits on Macbeth's stool, because the witches said that his descendants will inherit the title of king.

One can infer that Banquo is claiming the kingship back for his descendants, which Macbeth wrongfully stole.

Macbeth tells the guests not to poke fun at him, because he has "a strange infirmity". This is ironic, because his sickness "is nothing To those that know me", meaning that it is a mental and psychological defect rather than a physical one.

We can compare this to what the doctor said about Lady Macbeth's infirmity in the sleepwalking scene in Act 5, Scene 1 "Infected minds to their deaf pillows will discharge their secrets"

MACBETH TEXT

ACT 3 scene 4 EXPLANATION

MACBETH
Avaunt! and quit my sight! let the earth hide thee!
Thy bones are marrowless, thy blood is cold;
Thou hast no speculation in those eyes
Which thou dost glare with!
LADY MACBETH
Think of this, good peers,
But as a thing of custom: 'tis no other;
Only it spoils the pleasure of the time.
MACBETH
What man dare, I dare:
Approach thou like the rugged Russian bear,
The arm'd rhinoceros, or the Hyrcan tiger;
Take any shape but that, and my firm nerves
Shall never tremble: or be alive again,
And dare me to the desert with thy sword;
If trembling I inhabit then, protest me
The baby of a girl. Hence, horrible shadow!
Unreal mockery, hence!
GHOST OF BANQUO vanishes

Why, so: being gone,
I am a man again. Pray you, sit still.
LADY MACBETH
You have displaced the mirth, broke the good meeting,
With most admired disorder.
MACBETH
Can such things be,
And overcome us like a summer's cloud,
Without our special wonder? You make me strange
Even to the disposition that I owe,
When now I think you can behold such sights,
And keep the natural ruby of your cheeks,
When mine is blanch'd with fear.

MACBETH: When mine is blanch'd with fear.

Macbeth has gained his composure, and he very boldly drinks a toast to Banquo. Macbeth yet again shows his devious character – knowing full well that Banquo is dead.

Once again, Macbeth sees the ghost and he cannot control his fear. He yells at the ghost to leave him alone, to "quit my sight".

Macbeth is visibly shaken and petrified at seeing the ghost again.

At this point, the tension is mounting, and we want to see how Macbeth handles this situation. We are curious to see whether he buckles and shows his guilt. Macbeth is so unnerved

my firm nerves
Shall never tremble

He prefers the ghost to take any shape, even "the rugged Russian bear" but not Banquo's, because he is terrified to see Banquo's ghost.

Macbeth is relieved that the ghost is gone, and he says,

I am a man again

implying that the ghost's appearance created a fear in him that made him feel like a lesser man.

Lady Macbeth accuses Macbeth of spoiling the meeting with his disorderly behaviour and taking away the laughter and joy

You have displaced the mirth, broke the good meeting
With most admired disorder

Macbeth tells Lady Macbeth that he thinks she is so bold and brave and that she will "behold such sights" and won't be affected.

She won't be afraid and will be able to

keep the natural ruby of your cheeks,
When mine is blanched with fear

MACBETH
TEXT

ACT 3 scene 4
EXPLANATION

ROSS
What sights, my lord?
LADY MACBETH
I pray you, speak not; he grows worse and worse;
Question enrages him. At once, good night:
Stand not upon the order of your going,
But go at once.
LENNOX
Good night; and better health
Attend his majesty!
LADY MACBETH
A kind good night to all!
Exeunt Lords and Attendants
except MACBETH and LADY MACBETH

MACBETH
It will have blood; they say, blood will have blood:
Stones have been known to move and trees to speak;
Augurs and understood relations have
By magot-pies and choughs and rooks brought forth
The secret'st man of blood. What is the night?

LADY MACBETH
Almost at odds with morning, which is which.
MACBETH
How say'st thou, that Macduff denies his person
At our great bidding?
LADY MACBETH
Did you send to him, sir?

Ross is confused what Macbeth is talking about

What sights, my Lord?

Lady Macbeth tells Ross not to speak to Macbeth because questions enrage him. She is just making excuses for Macbeth, and she tells everyone to leave and not to bother to leave in order of rank

Stand not upon the order of your going

Macbeth is shocked about the turn of events. He says,

blood will have blood"

meaning that the dead is out to seek revenge on him. Note the motif of 'blood' here. He said that such supernatural things are happening, and he is afraid that the murders that he had committed may be revealed

The secret'st man of blood

Macbeth is unhappy that MacDuff had been so brazen as to deny him the honour of his presence at the banquet. Macbeth views this as arrogance, and it's obvious that Macbeth sees MacDuff as an instant threat who needs to be eliminated.

How say'st thou, that Macduff denies his person
At our great bidding?

Exeunt Lords and Attendants

Macbeth [*to Lady Macbeth*]**: blood will have blood**

MACBETH TEXT

MACBETH
I hear it by the way; but I will send:
There's not a one of them but in his house
I keep a servant fee'd. I will to-morrow,
And betimes I will, to the weird sisters:
More shall they speak; for now I am bent to know,
By the worst means, the worst. For mine own good,
All causes shall give way: I am in blood
Stepp'd in so far that, should I wade no more,
Returning were as tedious as go o'er:
Strange things I have in head, that will to hand;
Which must be acted ere they may be scann'd.

LADY MACBETH
You lack the season of all natures, sleep.

MACBETH
Come, we'll to sleep. My strange and self-abuse
Is the initiate fear that wants hard use:
We are yet but young in deed.

Exeunt

Lady Macbeth and Macbeth retire to bed

ACT 3 scene 4 EXPLANATION

We see Macbeth plunging deeper into the depths of corruption because, now, he is even resorting to bribery. He paid a servant to spy on MacDuff's movements

I keep a servant fee'd

Macbeth is becoming desperate and decides to go to the witches for help. Once again, we see his unnatural association with the witches

I will, to the weird sisters

He wants to know what the future holds for him, is even

bent to know

even if hears the worst of what's going to happen from the 'worst' meaning the witches.

Macbeth says that he is so steeped in blood because of all the murders he has committed, and he wants to know if he has to go further away from the witches and stop his killing.

should I wade no more?

He said that his unnatural delusions are the reason for his fears, and he doesn't have the skills and experience to be hard and cold

Is the initiate fear that wants hard use

He says,

We are yet but young in deed.

This means he is an inexperienced killer and is the reason why he reacts in such an unnatural manner after killing his victims?

MACBETH SUMMARY **ACT 3 scene 5**

Act 3, Scene 5 can be juxtaposed with Act 1, Scene 1.

The witches meet on the gloomy, eerie heath on both occasions when meeting with Macbeth.

They also meet when the weather is wild and angry in thunder on both occasions.

We can infer that nature is once again angry that Macbeth had violated the divine right of kings.

Shakespeare sets the tone and pace for the gory events that follow because he makes the opening mysterious and scary, like the beginning of the play by using pathetic fallacy 'thunder'.

Hecate, the Queen of the witches, is very angry, and she reprimands the other witches for leaving her out of their affairs when dealing with Macbeth. She tells them that Macbeth will be coming the next day to see what the future holds and that their predictions will help to seal his fate.

She says that he has sealed his own fate because he "loves for his own end".

We know that the witches' predictions encouraged Macbeth to commit these devious deeds of murder, but it was also a flaw in his personality hence his descent from a brave hero to a tragic one.

His greed contributed to him falling from grace, from celebrated hero to tragic hero.

A deserted place on the Heath where witches dwell

Witches at the cauldron listening to queen Hecate

MACBETH TEXT

ACT 3 scene 5 EXPLANATION

A deserted place. Thunder

ENTER the three WITCHES, meeting HECATE

FIRST WITCH
Why, how now, Hecate! You look angerly.
HECATE
Have I not reason, beldams as you are,
Saucy and overbold? How did you dare
To trade and traffic with Macbeth
In riddles and affairs of death;
And I, the mistress of your charms,
The close contriver of all harms,
Was never call'd to bear my part,
Or show the glory of our art?
And, which is worse, all you have done
Hath been but for a wayward son,
Spiteful and wrathful, who, as others do,
Loves for his own ends, not for you.
But make amends now: get you gone,
And at the pit of Acheron
Meet me i' the morning: thither he
Will come to know his destiny:
Your vessels and your spells provide,
Your charms and every thing beside.
I am for the air; this night I'll spend
Unto a dismal and a fatal end:
Great business must be wrought ere noon:
Upon the corner of the moon
There hangs a vaporous drop profound;
I'll catch it ere it come to ground:
And that distill'd by magic sleights
Shall raise such artificial sprites
As by the strength of their illusion
Shall draw him on to his confusion:
He shall spurn fate, scorn death, and bear
He hopes 'bove wisdom, grace and fear:
And you all know, security
Is mortals' chiefest enemy.
Music and a song within: 'Come away, come away,' & c

Hark! I am call'd; my little spirit, see,
Sits in a foggy cloud, and stays for me.
Exit
FIRST WITCH
Come, let's make haste; she'll soon be back again.
Exeunt

The three witches enter in the heath. One asks Hecate why she "look angerly".

Hecate says that she is angry because they dare to trade and traffic with Macbeth without her involvement.

Note the alliteration 'trade' and 'traffic'. This gives us a feeling that Macbeth was a mere object to the witches, something to be bought and sold, an object to be traded and trafficked.

Hecate calls him "a wayward son".

This is ironic, because Macbeth has now become one of them through his constant liaison with them.
He has also become a wayward son to God because he cannot say 'amen' anymore.
She says that tomorrow he will know his destiny. She tells the witches to prepare a great spell because

Great business must be wrought ere noon

They plan to wreak havoc in Macbeth's life. He will be fooled into thinking he is greater than fate and he will mock death. They must use magic to raise the "artificial sprites".

Hecate says that the witches must create illusions to confuse Macbeth

the strength of their illusion
Shall draw him on to his confusion

Of course, the main aim of the witches is to make mischief in Macbeth's life and destroy him with false hopes. Hecate says that they must give him a false sense of security, which will build his confidence so that,

He shall spurn fate, scorn death, and bear
He hopes 'bove wisdom, grace and fear

Hecate delivers her speech in rhymes and rhythm, i.e. 'noon – moon'.

It's as though she is singing a triumphant song, because she will be able to destroy Macbeth the mortal and win his soul.

MACBETH SUMMARY | **ACT 3 scene 6** |

Lennox is quite perplexed at the events taking place in Scotland, and he suspects that Macbeth is responsible for all the terrible murders.

He also tells the rebel Lords that he knows the reason why Macbeth killed the guards.

Lennox learns that MacDuff has left Scotland and has joined forces with Malcolm in England. Malcolm is gathering military support to fight Macbeth for his crown.

After the banquet scene Macbeth is isolated because his lords have lost faith in him, and Macduff did not attend the banquet and Macbeth views this as insolence.

Just as Macbeth feared Banquo as a threat, he now views Macduff as a threat which has serious consequences later when he kills his wife and child.

Lennox refers to Macbeth as a 'tyrant', and he is happy that Macduff did not heed Macbeth's call because he was afraid that Macduff would have been his next victim. He hopes that this tyranny will end, and that Scotland will return to its former glory just like the way it was under King Duncan's rule.

"A swift blessing may soon return to this our suffering land"

Somewhere in Scotland inside a Lord's castle

Thane Lennox arrives to meet with other Lords

MACBETH
TEXT

Somewhere in Scotland

Enter LENNOX and another LORD

LENNOX
My former speeches have but hit your thoughts,
Which can interpret further: only, I say,
Things have been strangely borne.
The gracious Duncan
Was pitied of Macbeth: marry, he was dead:
And the right-valiant Banquo walk'd too late;
Whom, you may say, if't please you, Fleance kill'd,
For Fleance fled: men must not walk too late.
Who cannot want the thought how monstrous
It was for Malcolm and for Donalbain
To kill their gracious father? damned fact!
How it did grieve Macbeth! did he not straight
In pious rage the two delinquents tear,
That were the slaves of drink and thralls of sleep?
Was not that nobly done? Ay, and wisely too;
For 'twould have anger'd any heart alive
To hear the men deny't. So that, I say,
He has borne all things well: and I do think
That had he Duncan's sons under his key–
As, an't please heaven, he shall not–they should find
What 'twere to kill a father; so should Fleance.
But, peace! for from broad words and 'cause he fail'd
His presence at the tyrant's feast, I hear
Macduff lives in disgrace: sir, can you tell
Where he bestows himself?

LORD
The son of Duncan,
From whom this tyrant holds the due of birth
Lives in the English court, and is received
Of the most pious Edward with such grace
That the malevolence of fortune nothing
Takes from his high respect: thither Macduff
Is gone to pray the holy king, upon his aid
To wake Northumberland and warlike Siward:
That, by the help of these–with Him above
To ratify the work–we may again
Give to our tables meat, sleep to our nights,
Free from our feasts and banquets bloody knives,
Do faithful homage and receive free honours:
All which we pine for now: and this report
Hath so exasperate the king that he
Prepares for some attempt of war.

ACT 3 scene 6

EXPLANATION

Lennox expresses his fear about the deaths of Duncan and Banquo. He raises his suspicions by saying,

Things have been strangely borne.

He said that it is strange that Duncan was loved by Macbeth, yet he is dead.
Lennox says that it is assumed that Fleance killed Banquo and fled, that Malcolm and Donalbain killed Duncan and also fled. Lennox points the finger at Macbeth

did he not straightIn pious rage the two delinquents tear,
Lennox says that the guards had to die, because, if they were alive, they would deny it, and Macbeth would have been caught for Duncan's murder and he would have been angry.

For 'twould have anger'd any heart alive

He goes on to say that Macbeth would have killed Duncan's sons and Fleance as well to teach them a lesson on what it is to kill a father

they should find
What 'twere to kill a father

MacDuff refused to go to the banquet and, therefore, incurred Macbeth's wrath.
The Lord calls Macbeth a 'tyrant' as well and says that he has usurped the throne from Duncan's son

holds the due of birth

Malcolm is in England and is seeking help from the king. With MacDuff, he seeks to retrieve his stolen crown from Macbeth. MacDuff urges the king to release Northumberland and Siward to help them to fight. Together, with the help of God, they will be able to restore normality in Scotland
Give to our tables, meat, sleep to our nights

They will be "free from our feasts and banquets bloody knives", referring to Macbeth's killing sprees. The Lord said that they are pining for a normal, beautiful life as it was under Duncan's rule, that it was
All which we pine for now

MACBETH
TEXT

LENNOX
Sent he to Macduff?
LORD
He did: and with an absolute 'Sir, not I,'
The cloudy messenger turns me his back,
And hums, as who should say 'You'll rue the time
That clogs me with this answer.'
LENNOX
And that well might
Advise him to a caution, to hold what distance
His wisdom can provide. Some holy angel
Fly to the court of England and unfold
His message ere he come, that a swift blessing
May soon return to this our suffering country
Under a hand accursed!
LORD
I'll send my prayers with him.

Exeunt

ACT 3 scene 6
EXPLANATION

The king is angry at this report, and he is now preparing for war. Lennox is happy that MacDuff didn't go when Macbeth summoned him

Advise him to a caution, to hold what distance
His wisdom can provide

He wants MacDuff to keep his distance from Macbeth, afraid that Macbeth will kill him.

Shakespeare uses biblical imagery

Some holy angel
Fly to the court

to show Lennox's desperation to stop MacDuff from being killed.

Lennox is very passionate when he ends this scene saying that he wishes that things would return to normal

a swift blessing
May soon return

He further emphasises that the country is painfully suffering

our suffering country

under Macbeth's tyrannical, bloody rule.

Thane Lords: Angus, Menteith, Caithness listen to Lennox's doubts about Macbeth's innocence

Lennox *[to ALL]*: **that a swift blessing May soon return to this our suffering country**

MACBETH SUMMARY | **ACT 4 scene 1** |

Once again, the witches meet in an eerie, mysterious setting accompanied by thunder. The thunder is symbolic here.

It can represent Macbeth's tumultuous life after the witches' prophecies. The Witches predict Macbeth's fate and he received three prophecies from them.

The witches first throw ingredients into a cauldron and begin chanting a spell. They are preparing to meet Macbeth, and we see the tone of the play changing. There is a real sense of evil lurking in the air.

When Macbeth approaches, the witches refer to him as "something wicked". They refer to him as "something", an inanimate object having no importance.

They give him his three prophecies:

- he should "beware MacDuff",
- he "cannot be killed by any man of woman born" and, finally,
- he will not lose in battle until "Birnam wood comes to Dunsinane".

The witches speak in riddles and tell Macbeth half-truths; they are very misleading, because it will give Macbeth a false sense of belief that he will be ok. Macbeth then demands to know if Banquo's offspring will be kings.

The witches very mischievously present him with a ghostly apparition of eight kings who have descended from Banquo, leaving Macbeth shocked and confused. Then the witches suddenly disappear.

Lennox tells Macbeth that MacDuff has fled to England. Macbeth is furious and decides to slaughter MacDuff's family as revenge.

We see Macbeth descending even further into corruption and murder. He wants to keep the crown at any cost. We see a similarity with Lady Macbeth's speech in Act 1, Scene 7. She says that she would take her child,

"While it was smiling in my face,
 Have pluck'd my nipple from his boneless gums
 And dash the brains out".

This quote is a clear depiction of Lady Macbeth's cruelty and ruthlessness.

Macbeth has become ruthless and destructive, like his wife, because now he too plans to kill Banquo's son.

MACBETH
TEXT

A dark cavern. Thunder.

ENTER Three WITCHES with a cauldron

FIRST WITCH
Thrice the brinded cat hath mew'd.
SECOND WITCH
Thrice and once the hedge-pig whined.
THIRD WITCH
Harpier cries 'Tis time, 'tis time.
FIRST WITCH
Round about the cauldron go;
In the poison'd entrails throw.
Toad, that under cold stone
Days and nights has thirty-one
Swelter'd venom sleeping got,
Boil thou first i' the charmed pot.
ALL
Double, double toil and trouble;
Fire burn, and cauldron bubble.
SECOND WITCH
Fillet of a fenny snake,
In the cauldron boil and bake;
Eye of newt and toe of frog,
Wool of bat and tongue of dog,
Adder's fork and blind-worm's sting,
Lizard's leg and owlet's wing,
For a charm of powerful trouble,
Like a hell-broth boil and bubble.
ALL
Double, double toil and trouble;
Fire burn and cauldron bubble.
THIRD WITCH
Scale of dragon, tooth of wolf,
Witches' mummy, maw and gulf
Of the ravin'd salt-sea shark,
Root of hemlock digg'd i' the dark,
Liver of blaspheming Jew,
Gall of goat, and slips of yew
Silver'd in the moon's eclipse,
Nose of Turk and Tartar's lips,
Finger of birth-strangled babe
Ditch-deliver'd by a drab,
Make the gruel thick and slab:
Add thereto a tiger's chaudron,
For the ingredients of our cauldron.

ACT 4 scene 1

EXPLANATION

Once again, Shakespeare uses pathetic fallacy to describe the setting, 'thunder'. Note that every time the witches appear, they do so in thunder, the atmosphere is eerie and mysterious; now it's set in a dark cavern.

The witch's speech has a rhythmic beat about it. It also has a somewhat complete rhyme scheme that runs throughout the speech. For example, 'got-pot', 'frog-dog'. We can actually feel their exuberance and joy at their task of destroying Macbeth's life. One can connote that the witches are singing a jubilant song of success. Note the use of the constant plant imagery.

Animal names for plants used in the foulest sense to create their broth. For example, 'toe of frog', 'Adder's fork'. 'Scale of dragon,' 'tooth of wolf.'

They used Macbeth in the same way that they so recklessly make use of the animal names.

Like a hell-broth boil and bubble

We can infer that the witches are concocting their evil broth and preparing Macbeth for his hell, as seen by the use of Shakespeare's biblical imagery, 'Fire' and 'Hell'.

The nouns 'fire' and 'hell' is a foreshadowing of the witches' intent for Macbeth and that was to send him to hell by casting a spell on him using this terrible hell broth.

**Witches: Double, double toil and trouble;
Fire burn, and cauldron bubble.**

MACBETH TEXT

ALL
Double, double toil and trouble;
Fire burn and cauldron bubble.
SECOND WITCH
Cool it with a baboon's blood,
Then the charm is firm and good.
Enter HECATE to the other three WITCHES

HECATE
O well done! I commend your pains;
And every one shall share i' the gains;
And now about the cauldron sing,
Live elves and fairies in a ring,
Enchanting all that you put in.
Music and a song: 'Black spirits,' & c
HECATE retires

SECOND WITCH
By the pricking of my thumbs,
Something wicked this way comes.
Open, locks,
Whoever knocks!

Enter MACBETH
MACBETH
How now, you secret, black, and midnight hags!
What is't you do?
ALL
A deed without a name.
MACBETH
I conjure you, by that which you profess,
Howe'er you come to know it, answer me:
Though you untie the winds and let them fight
Against the churches; though the yesty waves
Confound and swallow navigation up;
Though bladed corn be lodged and trees blown down;
Though castles topple on their warders' heads;
Though palaces and pyramids do slope
Their heads to their foundations; though the treasure
Of nature's germens tumble all together,
Even till destruction sicken; answer me
To what I ask you.

ACT 4 scene 1 EXPLANATION

Hecate compliments the witches for their hard work

O well done! I commend your pains

They dance and sing around the cauldron, because they know that they have won over Macbeth and are sending him to his doom,

And every one shall share i' the gains

Macbeth addresses them as,

How now, you secret, black, and midnight hags!

Note the dark imagery he uses, knowing full well that he is dabbling with these dark, unsavoury characters. He enquires what they are doing, and they say,

A deed without a name

This is ironic because he is about to lose his title as king. He demands to know where they obtain their skills at prediction.

Howe'er you come to know it, answer me:

He goes on to say that they have mighty powers over the winds:

Though you untie the winds and let them fight
Against the churches

Ironically, Macbeth is fighting a mighty battle with the church and against God for all his killings.

Macbeth [*to witches*]**: How now, you secret, black, and midnight hag!**

MACBETH
TEXT

FIRST WITCH
Speak.
SECOND WITCH
Demand.
THIRD WITCH
We'll answer.
First Witch
Say, if thou'dst rather hear it from our mouths,
Or from our masters?
MACBETH
Call 'em; let me see 'em.
FIRST WITCH
Pour in sow's blood, that hath eaten
Her nine farrow; grease that's sweaten
From the murderer's gibbet throw
Into the flame.
ALL
Come, high or low;
Thyself and office deftly show!

Thunder. ENTER First Apparition: an armed Head

MACBETH
Tell me, thou unknown power,–
FIRST WITCH
He knows thy thought:
Hear his speech, but say thou nought.
FIRST APPARITION
Macbeth! Macbeth! Macbeth! Beware Macduff;
Beware the thane of Fife. Dismiss me. Enough.
Descends

MACBETH
Whate'er thou art, for thy good caution, thanks;
Thou hast harp'd my fear aright: but one
word more,–
FIRST WITCH
He will not be commanded: here's another,
More potent than the first.

ACT 4 scene 1
EXPLANATION

The First Apparition sounds out Macbeth's name three times: "

Macbeth! Macbeth! Macbeth! Beware Macduff;

The use of the repetition and the repeated exclamation marks can suggest a finality perhaps death and the repetition of a clear warning of the doom that awaits Macbeth. She tells him to beware Macduff.

Once again, we see the power of the evil witches predicting Macbeth's future. Macbeth becomes Macduff's victim in the end when Macduff kills him.

Macbeth is elated at the witches' revelation, and he feels relieved that everything is fine,

Thou hast harp'd my fear aright.

He says that they have reassured him that their predictions are true and he has nothing to fear. Hence putting all his faith on the witches, who will deliberately lead him on a dangerous path of destruction.

He still badgers them for more information. Then the First Witch shows him a Second Apparition which she says is;

More potent than the first.

First Apparition: an armed head

MACBETH
TEXT

Thunder. ENTER Second Apparition: A bloody Child

SECOND APPARITION
Macbeth! Macbeth! Macbeth!
MACBETH
Had I three ears, I'ld hear thee.
SECOND APPARITION
Be bloody, bold, and resolute; laugh to scorn
The power of man, for none of woman born
Shall harm Macbeth.
Descends

MACBETH
Then live, Macduff: what need I fear of thee?
But yet I'll make assurance double sure,
And take a bond of fate: thou shalt not live;
That I may tell pale-hearted fear it lies,
And sleep in spite of thunder.

Thunder. ENTER Third Apparition: a Child crowned, with a tree in his hand

What is this
That rises like the issue of a king,
And wears upon his baby-brow the round
And top of sovereignty?
ALL
Listen, but speak not to't.

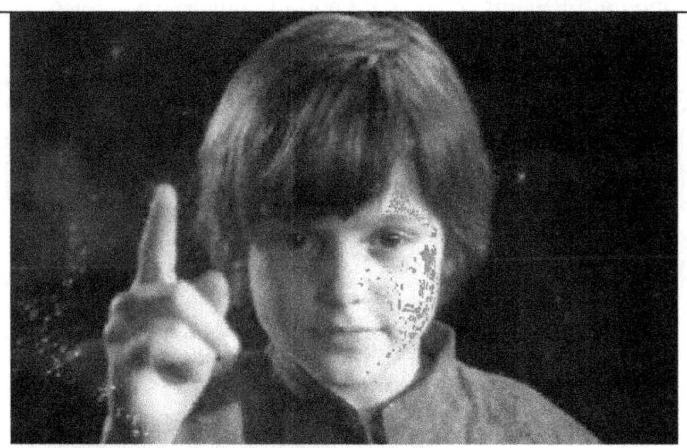

Second Apparition: A bloody Child

ACT 4 scene 1
EXPLANATION

The First Witch tells Macbeth to be

Be bloody, bold, and resolute

This must have peaked Macbeth's interest, because she says that

for none of woman born
Shall harm Macbeth

We are confronted with a very confident and brutal Macbeth here because his speech is very forceful and direct. He is pouring out his venom on MacDuff.

He addresses MacDuff directly saying that he is not scared of him. Macbeth says

But yet I'll make assurance double sure,
And take a bond of fate

that MacDuff will die.

The Third Apparition appears. It is a child crowned with a tree in his hand.

This can symbolically be interpreted as being Malcolm. It also foreshadows

Malcolm coming with a tree in hand to attack Macbeth at the end of the play.

Macbeth is perplexed, and he questions the spirit

That rises like the issue of a king

Macbeth sees that the child is wearing a crown. It is, of course, Malcolm wearing the usurped crown that Macbeth is now wearing, which Malcolm is about to claim back.

The Jacobean audience believed that witches were not to be trusted and view them as a destructive force just like the terrible weather that they always appear in.

THIRD APPARITION
Be lion-mettled, proud; and take no care
Who chafes, who frets, or where conspirers are:
Macbeth shall never vanquish'd be until
Great Birnam wood to high Dunsinane hill
Shall come against him.
Descends

MACBETH
That will never be
Who can impress the forest, bid the tree
Unfix his earth-bound root? Sweet bodements! good!
Rebellion's head, rise never till the wood
Of Birnam rise, and our high-placed Macbeth
Shall live the lease of nature, pay his breath
To time and mortal custom. Yet my heart
Throbs to know one thing: tell me, if your art
Can tell so much: shall Banquo's issue ever
Reign in this kingdom?
ALL
Seek to know no more.
MACBETH
I will be satisfied: deny me this,
And an eternal curse fall on you! Let me know.
Why sinks that cauldron? and what noise is this?
Cauldron descends. Hautboys
FIRST WITCH
Show!
SECOND WITCH
Show!
THIRD WITCH
Show!
ALL
Show his eyes, and grieve his heart;
Come like shadows, so depart!

Third Apparition: a Child crowned with a tree in hand

The Third Apparition gives Macbeth confidence and tells him to

Be lion-mettled, proud; and take no care

It tells him to be brave and proud and not to worry about anything. As we know, there are many half-truths in what these witches are saying, but Macbeth is falling for it completely.

The Third Apparition thrills Macbeth by saying

Macbeth shall never vanquish'd be until
Great Birnam wood to high Dunsinane hill
Shall come against him.

Macbeth is bewildered at the predictions, but he says,

That will never be

because, according to him, a tree cannot unfix itself from its roots and move.
Once again, he cannot grasp the witches' half-truths and lies. Funnily enough, Macbeth's speech here is very dramatic. He has taken on the style of the witches' speech because he speaks in rhyming couplets. For example, 'good-wood' and heart-art.

our high-placed Macbeth
Shall live the lease of nature

Surely, Macbeth appears over-confident and deluded here because he says that he will die a natural death and that he will have a natural lifespan. He is persistent, and he still wants to know if Banquo's children will reign as kings.

shall Banquo's issue ever
Reign in this kingdom?

The witches tell him to

Seek to know no more

He is both adamant and desperate and he threatened them that if he is not informed then

an eternal curse fall on you!

MACBETH
TEXT

A show of Eight Kings, the last with a glass in his hand; GHOST OF BANQUO following

MACBETH
Thou art too like the spirit of Banquo: down!
Thy crown does sear mine eye-balls. And thy hair,
Thou other gold-bound brow, is like the first.
A third is like the former. Filthy hags!
Why do you show me this? A fourth! Start, eyes!
What, will the line stretch out to the crack of doom?
Another yet! A seventh! I'll see no more:
And yet the eighth appears, who bears a glass
Which shows me many more; and some I see
That two-fold balls and treble scepters carry:
Horrible sight! Now, I see, 'tis true;
For the blood-bolter'd Banquo smiles upon me,
And points at them for his.
Exit show of Kings. Exit Apparitions vanish

What, is this so?

FIRST WITCH
Ay, sir, all this is so: but why
Stands Macbeth thus amazedly?
Come, sisters, cheer we up his sprites,
And show the best of our delights:
I'll charm the air to give a sound,
While you perform your antic round:
That this great king may kindly say,
Our duties did his welcome pay.
Music. The witches dance and then vanish, with HECATE

MACBETH
Where are they? Gone? Let this pernicious hour
Stand aye accursed in the calendar!
Come in, without there!

Banquo last of Eight kings with Macbeth in mirror

ACT 4 scene 1
EXPLANATION

The witches show Macbeth eight kings with Banquo's ghost following. Macbeth is furious because one looks like the spirit of Banquo:

Thou art too like the spirit of Banquo: down!

Note that the verb, 'down!' with an exclamation mark suggest Macbeth's anger. He says that Banquo's crown is burning his eyeballs

Thy crown does sear mine eye-balls

Macbeth seems deranged here. We can feel his voice of desperation as he yells at the witches,

Filthy hags!
Why do you show me this?

This, we can say, is the start of Macbeth's decline and downfall. The use of excessive punctuations like rhetorical questions and exclamation marks suggest that he is now becoming a psychological wreck. For example, 'A fourth! Start, eyes!'.

He is also shocked at seeing how long the line of kings are and he questions it:

What, will the line stretch out to the crack of doom?

Puzzled, he questions whether this line will stretch until Judgement-day, and he cannot bear it: "I'll see no more."

Standing before Macbeth is a whole scene from a coronation of kings from England and Scotland until they were united by King James I in 1603. Macbeth is horrified and has finally grasped the truth that the witches had tricked him when he yells out,
Horrible sight! Now, I see, 'tis true;

A defeated Macbeth sees Banquo poking fun at him, and he points to his descendants and smiles at Macbeth. Macbeth is in disbelief at what's happening, and he exclaims, "What, is this so?"
It's as though he is resigned to his fate. The witches do a triumphant dance, because they have achieved what they had set out to do: destroy Macbeth. First Witch says "Our duties did his welcome pay"

MACBETH **TEXT**	**ACT 4 scene 1** **EXPLANATION**

Enter LENNOX

LENNOX
What's your grace's will?

MACBETH
Saw you the weird sisters?

LENNOX
No, my lord.

MACBETH
Came they not by you?

LENNOX
No, indeed, my lord.

MACBETH
Infected be the air whereon they ride;
And damn'd all those that trust them! I did hear
The galloping of horse: who was't came by?

LENNOX
'Tis two or three, my lord, that bring you word
Macduff is fled to England!

MACBETH
Fled to England!

LENNOX
Ay, my good lord.

MACBETH
Time, thou anticipatest my dread exploits:
The flighty purpose never is o'ertook
Unless the deed go with it; from this moment
The very firstlings of my heart shall be
The firstlings of my hand. And even now,
To crown my thoughts with acts, be it thought and don
The castle of Macduff I will surprise;
Seize upon Fife; give to the edge o' the sword
His wife, his babes, and all unfortunate souls
That trace him in his line. No boasting like a fool;
This deed I'll do before this purpose cool.
But no more sights!–Where are these gentlemen?
Come, bring me where they are.

Exeunt

Lennox [*to Macbeth*]: **Macduff is fled to England**

A confused Macbeth asks Lennox if he saw the witches. Paranoid, Macbeth now regrets trusting the witches:

damn'd all those that trust them!

He knows they have sent him to his doom.

At this time in the play the many dramatic events that follow unnerves Macbeth even further, and the audience sees him plunge further into darkness.

Lennox tells Macbeth

Macduff is fled to England!

Note the exclamation mark denoting Macbeth's shock.

Macbeth is all emotional and desperate in this scene. He is going to act without reason – he is going to let his heart rule his head.

He personifies time and says that time knows the terrible deed that he is about to carry out: killing MacDuff's family.

Time, thou anticipatest my dread exploits.

Hastily, Macbeth decides that he is going to go to Fife and kill MacDuff's wife and kids

give to the edge o' the sword
His wife, his babes

He is serious; there will be

No boasting like a fool

The simile gives him an air of confidence and bravery.

Macbeth is now on a killing spree, and he wants the deed to be done before he changes his mind

This deed I'll do before this purpose cool

Although very bold and brave Macbeth sees Macduff as a potential threat who must be eliminated. He reveals to the audience his intentions to murder Macbeth and his family.

He is sinking to such low depths to actually slaughter a child to achieve his aim for the crown.

This dreadful act of his will have serious consequences for him later on because Macduff becomes incensed, and he is bent on taking revenge on Macbeth for his foul deeds.

Ross tells lady Macduff that her husband has fled to England because he may be afraid. She is alone with her son and Lady MacDuff accuses her husband of cowardice because he deserted her and their son.

"He loves us not"

Ironically Macduff's son asks his mother what the word 'traitor' means. He is just about to become the victim of a traitor.

Ross warns Lady MacDuff of danger and leaves because he does not want to be present when the murders take place.

However, she is surrounded by Macbeth's men, and they brutally kill her son.

We learn later that she is also killed, and we hear her scream off stage.

Soldiers approach Macduff's castle at Fife

Inside Macduff's castle with his children playing

MACBETH TEXT

ACT 4 scene 2 EXPLANATION

Macduff's castle at Fife

ENTER Lady MACDUFF, her Son, and Thane ROSS

LADY MACDUFF
What had he done, to make him fly the land?
ROSS
You must have patience, madam.
LADY MACDUFF
He had none:
His flight was madness: when our actions do not,
Our fears do make us traitors.
ROSS
You know not
Whether it was his wisdom or his fear.
LADY MACDUFF
Wisdom! to leave his wife, to leave his babes,
His mansion and his titles in a place
From whence himself does fly? He loves us not;
He wants the natural touch: for the poor wren,
The most diminutive of birds, will fight,
Her young ones in her nest, against the owl.
All is the fear and nothing is the love;
As little is the wisdom, where the flight
So runs against all reason.

Lady MacDuff is confused and angry at MacDuff's disappearance,

What has he done to make him fly the land?

Ross tries to defend him by trying to convince Lady MacDuff by explaining that MacDuff's flight to England may have been the result of his fear or wisdom.

Lady MacDuff's spontaneous utterance was "Wisdom!" with an exclamation mark suggesting her fury, that MacDuff had left them so vulnerable and alone, exposed to the danger by the tyrant Macbeth. She declares,

He loves us not

It's a very emotive statement, and the audience gets emotionally involved; we empathise with Lady MacDuff's plight. At this point, she is desperate.

Shakespeare gives us a beautiful imagery of the wren who will fight to protect her young in her nest against the owl. The owl is a bird of prey, and it can symbolically represent Macbeth's ruthless behaviour; he is, after all, prepared to kill an innocent woman and her child.

Lady MacDuff accuses MacDuff of being a coward. She says it was merely fear and not love that made MacDuff to leave.

All is fear and nothing is the love

She says that he was afraid for himself and did not have any love for them.

Lady Macduff [*to Ross*]**: What had he done, to make him** [Macduff] **fly the land?**

Lady Macduff [*to Ross*]**: Wisdom! to leave his wife, to leave his babes,**

MACBETH TEXT

ACT 4 scene 2 EXPLANATION

ROSS
My dearest coz,
I pray you, school yourself: but for your husband,
He is noble, wise, judicious, and best knows
The fits o' the season. I dare not speak much further;
But cruel are the times, when we are traitors
And do not know ourselves, when we hold rumour
From what we fear, yet know not what we fear,
But float upon a wild and violent sea
Each way and move. I take my leave of you:
Shall not be long but I'll be here again:
Things at the worst will cease, or else climb upward
To what they were before. My pretty cousin,
Blessing upon you!
LADY MACDUFF
Father'd he is, and yet he's fatherless.
ROSS
I am so much a fool, should I stay longer,
It would be my disgrace and your discomfort:
I take my leave at once.
Exit

Ross says goodbye to Macduff's son and wife

Ross once again tries to defend MacDuff by saying that;

He is noble, wise, judicious

and that he understands the troubles that are plaguing the country at present,

The fits o' the season

Ross expresses his fear, saying

But cruel are the times, when we are traitors

that times are dangerous, 'cruel', and that they all feel like traitors though they don't know why

And do not know ourselves, when we hold rumour
From what we fear, yet know not what we fear,

They fear, and they don't know what they are afraid of. It is clearly evident here how Macbeth has created an atmosphere of tyrannical political upheaval and fear.

He gives us a visual imagery of someone floating aimlessly,

upon a wild and violent sea

to show the extent of his fear. Once again, the 'wild and violent sea' symbolises Macbeth and his violent actions.

Ross leaves. Maybe he is afraid of Macbeth's wrath if he leans towards or helps his enemies.

He believes that maybe the current terrible political situation will stop

Things at the worst will cease

or will get worse

climb upward
To what they were before

MACBETH
TEXT

LADY MACDUFF
Sirrah, your father's dead;
And what will you do now? How will you live?
SON
As birds do, mother.
LADY MACDUFF
What, with worms and flies?
SON
With what I get, I mean; and so do they.
LADY MACDUFF
Poor bird! thou'ldst never fear the net nor lime,
The pitfall nor the gin.
SON
Why should I, mother? Poor birds they are not set for.
My father is not dead, for all your saying.
LADY MACDUFF
Yes, he is dead; how wilt thou do for a father?
SON
Nay, how will you do for a husband?
LADY MACDUFF
Why, I can buy me twenty at any market.
SON
Then you'll buy 'em to sell again.
LADY MACDUFF
Thou speak'st with all thy wit: and yet, i' faith,
With wit enough for thee.
SON
Was my father a traitor, mother?
LADY MACDUFF
Ay, that he was.
SON
What is a traitor?
LADY MACDUFF
Why, one that swears and lies.
SON
And be all traitors that do so?
LADY MACDUFF
Every one that does so is a traitor, and must be hanged.
SON
And must they all be hanged that swear and lie?
LADY MACDUFF
Every one.
SON
Who must hang them?
LADY MACDUFF
Why, the honest men.

ACT 4 scene 2

EXPLANATION

Lady MacDuff tells her son that his father is dead, and she asks him how he will live without him.

your father's dead;
And what will you do now? How will you live?

The child very cleverly replies,

As birds do, mother

His reply parallels his mother's earlier speech about the wren's motherly instincts to protect her young.

We can conclude that maybe Lady MacDuff knew her impending fate and was worried about her son's survival. Little did she realise that her son will also meet the same fate she will.

This scene is very emotive, and it foreshadows Lady MacDuff and her son's fate. Even her reply to her son is ominous. She even calls him a bird deserted

Poor bird! thou'ldst never fear the net nor lime,

Her son is confident that his father is still alive

My father is not dead, for all your saying.

She insists MacDuff is dead and says that she can

buy me twenty at any market

We can detect her anger and her frustration here, implying that MacDuff was insignificant when it came to caring for his family.
She spits these words out with a bitter tone. Her son is very witty and questions whether his father is a traitor,

Was my father a traitor, mother?

She is very angry and declares her husband a traitor,

one that swears and lies

and insists that all traitors

must be hanged by 'honest men'.

MACBETH
TEXT

SON
Then the liars and swearers are fools,
for there are liars and swearers enough to beat
the honest men and hang up them.
LADY MACDUFF
Now, God help thee, poor monkey!
But how wilt thou do for a father?
SON
If he were dead, you'ld weep for him:
if you would not, it were a good sign
that I should quickly have a new father.
LADY MACDUFF
Poor prattler, how thou talk'st!

ENTER a Messenger
MESSENGER
Bless you, fair dame! I am not to you known,
Though in your state of honour I am perfect.
I doubt some danger does approach you nearly:
If you will take a homely man's advice,
Be not found here; hence, with your little ones.
To fright you thus, methinks, I am too savage;
To do worse to you were fell cruelty,
Which is too nigh your person. Heaven preserve you!
I dare abide no longer.
Exit

LADY MACDUFF
Whither should I fly?
I have done no harm. But I remember now
I am in this earthly world; where to do harm
Is often laudable, to do good sometime
Accounted dangerous folly: why then, alas,
Do I put up that womanly defence,
To say I have done no harm?

Lady Macduff debates with her son about traitors

ACT 4 scene 2
EXPLANATION

The messenger tells Lady MacDuff that he came to warn her that

some danger does approach you nearly

She was ordered to take herself and her children to safety

Be not found here; hence, with your little ones

It seems as though the messenger had some inkling or ominous prediction about the murders of Lady MacDuff and her son, because he uses biblical imagery prematurely

Heaven preserve you!

as though he was already welcoming her to heaven. The exclamation mark can suggest a finality, an end to their lives.

The messenger leaves. Notice how both Ross and this messenger, knowing full well that Lady MacDuff and her son are in mortal danger, but they both deserted them.

This clearly shows the toxic atmosphere of fear that Macbeth has created.

Obviously, they are fearful of him and the consequences of his actions; otherwise, they would help Lady MacDuff and her son. Note what Ross says previously in this scene: "From what we fear, yet know not what we fear."

Lady MacDuff declares her innocence:

I have done no harm

She draws a contrast here and explains that people who do harm is praised: "To do harm, Is often laudable", while doing good is "Accounted dangerous folly". Lady MacDuff asks a rhetorical question: "Why then, alas, do I put up that womanly defence, To say, I have done no harm?" She has given up the fight.
She knows her fate is sealed because her innocence doesn't count. The audience empathises with her situation, and they get emotionally involved. Shakespeare creates a very tense atmosphere here.

MACBETH
TEXT

ENTER the Murderers
What are these faces?

FIRST MURDERER
Where is your husband?
LADY MACDUFF
I hope, in no place so unsanctified
Where such as thou mayst find him.
FIRST MURDERER
He's a traitor.
SON
Thou liest, thou shag-hair'd villain!
FIRST MURDERER
What, you egg!
Stabbing him
Young fry of treachery!
SON
He has kill'd me, mother:
Run away, I pray you!
Dies

Exit LADY MACDUFF, crying 'Murder!'
Exeunt Murderers, following her

Lady Macduff and son about to be Murdered

ACT 4 scene 2
EXPLANATION

We can cut the tension with a knife, and he creates suspense because the audience is on tenter hooks, wondering what's going to happen next.

The First Murderer demands to know where MacDuff is, and he labels MacDuff a traitor. The son boldly challenges him, calling him a liar:

Thou liest, thou shag-hair'd villain!

Shakespeare presents us with an imagery of an egg

What you egg!
Young fry of treachery!

The First Murderer yells at the son. This implies that the son is the offspring of a traitor. MacDuff is now seen as a traitor. We revert back to Lady MacDuff's speech about protecting "Her young ones in her nest, against the owl". The imagery has become a reality now. Her son is now against the owl; the murderer represents the owl, and the young child is defenceless against the cruel tyrant who stabs and kills him.

The end of the scene is very emotional, and the audience is left spellbound by the sheer horror of it. As the child dies, he shows his bravery and resilience to the end because he sees to the welfare of his mother as he is dying:

Run away, I pray you

Lady MacDuff exits *"crying, "Murder"*, as she is pursued by the murderers. The tension is palpable here, and the audience becomes nervous; this scene ends with suspense.

The audience was wondering what happened to Lady MacDuff. This is a very clever ending that Shakespeare created. He deliberately didn't allow Lady MacDuff to be killed on stage so that he can create maximum impact on his audience.

He wants us to pause and empathise with the child's brutal death; then he slowly unravels the horror that is unfolding. It is only then that he tells us about Lady MacDuff's death in the next scene.

MACBETH SUMMARY | **ACT 4 scene 3**

Malcolm is suspicious and he tests Macduff's loyalty. In doing so he can gage whether Macduff is still loyal to Macbeth.

Malcolm speaks very bitterly about Macbeth, and he pretends to be a tyrant like Macbeth.

MacDuff convinces him that he is loyal to Scotland

"I am not treacherous"

and tells him about Macbeth's atrocities. He is furious with Macbeth and calls him,

"An untitled tyrant"

MacDuff labels Macbeth a tyrant who has caused chaos in Scotland with all his killings:

This tyrant whose sole name blisters our tongues

'Blisters' are associated with sickness.

Malcolm says that the mere mention of Macbeth's name will cause sores on their tongues.
It refers to the people's anger and hatred for Macbeth.

Sadly, Ross informs Macduff of the brutal slaying of his family. He is furious and vows to avenge the death of his innocent family.

English Court moving into Scotland

Malcolm and Macduff survey English Court

MACBETH TEXT

The English Court in England

Enter MALCOLM and MACDUFF

MALCOLM
Let us seek out some desolate shade, and there
Weep our sad bosoms empty.
MACDUFF
Let us rather
Hold fast the mortal sword, and like good men
Bestride our down-fall'n birthdom: each new morn
New widows howl, new orphans cry, new sorrows
Strike heaven on the face, that it resounds
As if it felt with Scotland and yell'd out
Like syllable of dolour.
MALCOLM
What I believe I'll wail,
What know believe, and what I can redress,
As I shall find the time to friend, I will.
What you have spoke, it may be so perchance.
This tyrant, whose sole name blisters our tongues,
Was once thought honest: you have loved him well.
He hath not touch'd you yet. I am young; but
something
You may deserve of him through me, and wisdom
To offer up a weak poor innocent lamb
To appease an angry god.
MACDUFF
I am not treacherous.

ACT 4 scene 3 EXPLANATION

Malcolm reveals that he has support from England to gather their forces to invade Scotland.

He tells MacDuff that Macbeth

This tyrant,
Was once thought honest: you have loved him well.

Malcolm uses the dative 'once' to show that Macbeth is no longer decent and honest. He was also once loved, but not anymore.

Malcolm tells MacDuff,

He hath not touched you yet, but something
You may deserve of him through me

Malcolm is sceptical about MacDuff, specifically whether he is working for Macbeth. He goes further to use an imagery of a lamb to the slaughter

To offer up a weak, poor, innocent lamb

This can be compared to Christ's crucifixion on the cross and how he was like a sacrificial lamb (like Duncan, Banquo, Lady MacDuff and the other innocent people Macbeth has killed).

Malcolm refers to Macbeth as "an angry God". Malcolm is wondering whether MacDuff is trying to trick him to satisfy Macbeth's lust for killing.

MacDuff reassures Malcolm that he is not evil and "not treacherous".

English Court on the move

Malcolm [*to Macduff*]**: This tyrant**

MACBETH — ACT 4 scene 3

TEXT

MALCOLM
But Macbeth is.
A good and virtuous nature may recoil
In an imperial charge. But I shall crave your pardon;
That which you are my thoughts cannot transpose:
Angels are bright still, though the brightest fell;
Though all things foul would wear the brows of grace,
Yet grace must still look so.
MACDUFF
I have lost my hopes.
MALCOLM
Perchance even there where I did find my doubts.
Why in that rawness left you wife and child,
Those precious motives, those strong knots of love,
Without leave-taking? I pray you,
Let not my jealousies be your dishonours,
But mine own safeties. You may be rightly just,
Whatever I shall think.

Macduff [*to Malcolm*]**: I have lost my hopes.**

EXPLANATION

Malcolm highlights the fact that Macbeth is "good and virtuous" by nature but can turn or "recoil" into treachery.

The verb "recoil" is associated with a snake. Macbeth can be compared to a snake with a forked tongue; he pretends to be good but is actually deadly. Clearly, Macbeth adheres to Lady Macbeths stern advice (Act 1 scene 5) for him to

look like th' innocent flower,
But be the serpent under't

Shakespeare uses a biblical imagery here:

Angels are bright still, though the brightest fell.

Malcolm refers to the "brightest that fell", meaning Satan, who tried to challenge God and was expelled from Heaven. Macbeth is compared to the devil who was once an angel and fell out of favour with God.

Shakespeare also uses a personification to present the theme of appearance versus reality:

Though all things foul wear brows of grace.

This means that people like Macbeth with an evil character will pretend to be good and virtuous.

Malcolm is still suspicious of MacDuff, and he questions him about leaving his wife and son, whom he loves, under such dangerous conditions to come to England.

The use of dramatic irony is evident here because the audience already knows that MacDuff's family has been murdered.

Let not my jealousies be your dishonours

Malcolm reassures MacDuff that his suspicions should be seen as his own safety and that he is not viewing MacDuff as dishonourable.

MACBETH
TEXT

MACDUFF
Bleed, bleed, poor country!
Great tyranny! lay thou thy basis sure,
For goodness dare not cheque thee:
Wear thou thy wrongs;
The title is affeer'd! Fare thee well, lord:
I would not be the villain that thou think'st
For the whole space that's in the tyrant's grasp,
And the rich East to boot.
MALCOLM
Be not offended:
I speak not as in absolute fear of you.
I think our country sinks beneath the yoke;
It weeps, it bleeds; and each new day a gash
Is added to her wounds: I think withal
There would be hands uplifted in my right;
And here from gracious England have I offer
Of goodly thousands: but, for all this,
When I shall tread upon the tyrant's head,
Or wear it on my sword, yet my poor country
Shall have more vices than it had before,
More suffer and more sundry ways than ever,
By him that shall succeed.
MACDUFF
What should he be?

Malcolm [*to Macduff*]**: When I shall tread upon the tyrant's head, Or wear it on my sword**

ACT 4 scene 3
EXPLANATION

MacDuff gives out a painful cry.

Bleed, bleed poor country!

This refers to the bloodshed and chaos that Macbeth has caused in Scotland.

He bemoans the fact that the tyrant Macbeth has robbed the country of its goodness like the virtuous Duncan and replaced it with villainy and wrongdoing

For goodness does not check thee

Macbeth's title as king is creating fear among everyone

The title is affeer'd!

MacDuff finally manages to convince Malcolm that he is not the 'villain' that Malcolm thinks he is. Malcolm uses some strong verbs like 'sinks', 'weeps' and 'bleed' to describe, in despair how their country has sunk into anarchy.

Malcolm is pouring out his fury when he cries out,

each new day a gash
Is added to her wounds

In the onomatopoeia 'gash' and 'wounds', we can feel Malcolm's anger and fury towards Macbeth because he has crippled the country with his tyrannical control.

Malcolm confirms that he has got a huge, strong army to fight against Macbeth.

Shakespeare gives us a visual imagery of Malcolm's determination when Malcolm says that,

When I shall tread upon the tyrant's head,
Or wear it on my sword

This is a very violent, graphic imagery of the suffering that Malcolm is going to heap upon Macbeth. The audience can actually visualise Macbeth's head on Malcolm's sword.

MACBETH
TEXT

ACT 4 scene 3
EXPLANATION

MALCOLM
It is myself I mean: in whom I know
All the particulars of vice so grafted
That, when they shall be open'd, black Macbeth
Will seem as pure as snow, and the poor state
Esteem him as a lamb, being compared
With my confineless harms.
MACDUFF
Not in the legions
Of horrid hell can come a devil more damn'd
In evils to top Macbeth.
MALCOLM
I grant him bloody,
Luxurious, avaricious, false, deceitful,
Sudden, malicious, smacking of every sin
That has a name: but there's no bottom, none,
In my voluptuousness: your wives, your daughters,
Your matrons and your maids, could not fill up
The cistern of my lust, and my desire
All continent impediments would o'erbear
That did oppose my will: better Macbeth
Than such an one to reign.
MACDUFF
Boundless intemperance
In nature is a tyranny; it hath been
The untimely emptying of the happy throne
And fall of many kings. But fear not yet
To take upon you what is yours: you may
Convey your pleasures in a spacious plenty,
And yet seem cold, the time you may so hoodwink.
We have willing dames enough: there cannot be
That vulture in you, to devour so many
As will to greatness dedicate themselves,
Finding it so inclined.

Macduff [*to Malcolm*]**: Of horrid hell can come a devil more damn'd In evils to top Macbeth.**

Malcolm uses a planting imagery "grafted" and "open'd" to describe his vengeance against " black Macbeth".

Note the dark imagery that describes evil Macbeth. Malcolm talks about how Macbeth planted the seeds of evil and destruction, which opened into a flower.

Malcolm reveals that his evil against Macbeth will be so great that people will see him as being "pure as snow" and as meek as a lamb.

Once again, we are faced with the sacrificial lamb scenario, but Macbeth is not as innocent and good as the sacrificial lamb; his death can't be interpreted as innocent as Duncan's.

MacDuff's use of biblical imagery "hell", "devil", "damn'd", and "evil" indicating that Macbeth is associated with the devil, and he is damned to hell.

Remember his utterance after he killed Duncan; he was terrified he couldn't say "amen". We knew then that he was already a damned man heading straight to hell.

MacDuff confirms that Macbeth is the "devil incarnate" and that no one is as evil as he is
Of horrid hell can come a devil more damn'd
In evils to top Macbeth.
Malcolm vents his frustrations and curses Macbeth granting him
bloody,
Luxurious, avaricious, false

He wants violence to be heaped upon Macbeth. Malcolm says that he is lustful in his quest for revenge, that it is
The cistern of my lust

MacDuff once again labels Macbeth a tyrant and bemoans the fact that Macbeth had killed Duncan to occupy the happy throne and throw the country into chaos
The untimely emptying of the happy throne

MacDuff encourages Malcolm to fight and take back his crown,
To take upon you that is yours

MACBETH TEXT

ACT 4 scene 3 EXPLANATION

MALCOLM
With this there grows
In my most ill-composed affection such
A stanchless avarice that, were I king,
I should cut off the nobles for their lands,
Desire his jewels and this other's house:
And my more-having would be as a sauce
To make me hunger more; that I should forge
Quarrels unjust against the good and loyal,
Destroying them for wealth.
MACDUFF
This avarice
Sticks deeper, grows with more pernicious root
Than summer-seeming lust, and it hath been
The sword of our slain kings: yet do not fear;
Scotland hath foisons to fill up your will.
Of your mere own: all these are portable,
With other graces weigh'd.
MALCOLM
But I have none: the king-becoming graces,
As justice, verity, temperance, stableness,
Bounty, perseverance, mercy, lowliness,
Devotion, patience, courage, fortitude,
I have no relish of them, but abound
In the division of each several crime,
Acting it many ways. Nay, had I power, I should
Pour the sweet milk of concord into hell,
Uproar the universal peace, confound
All unity on earth.

Malcolm [*to Macduff*]**: had I power, I should Pour the sweet milk of concord into hell**

Malcolm shows his disgust for Macbeth and how he usurped the crown. Does status mean freedom from the consequences of choice?

He can rob "the nobles of their land", jewels, and houses and his greed will rise so much

to make me hunger more", that he will pick "unjust fights against the good and loyal" people to take their possessions for himself. This hints at what Macbeth did once he became king. He misused his power and destroyed Scotland.

MacDuff uses an imagery of a plant saying that Macbeth's greed,

grows with more pernicious root

It grows more deadly, and it's not just a passing lust. He uses a metaphor:

it hath been
The sword of our slain kings

Macbeth's greed was responsible for the killing of Scotland's kings.

MacDuff tells Malcolm that he has got enough support from Scotland to carry out your revenge

Scotland hath foisons to fill up your will.

Malcolm gives us a long list of good characteristics and accuses himself of not having them,

the king-becoming graces,
As justice, verity, temperance, stableness

Referring to Macbeth, he says that

had I power, I should
Pour the sweet milk of concord into hell

Let us draw a juxtaposition here: "pour the sweet milk of concord into hell". In Act 1 scene 5, Lady Macbeth says she fears Macbeth's nature is "too full of the milk of human kindness".

MACDUFF
O Scotland, Scotland!
MALCOLM
If such a one be fit to govern, speak:
I am as I have spoken.
MACDUFF
Fit to govern?
No, not to live. O nation miserable!
With an untitled tyrant bloody-scepter'd,
When shalt thou see thy wholesome days again,
Since that the truest issue of thy throne
By his own interdiction stands accursed,
And does blaspheme his breed? Thy royal father
Was a most sainted king: the queen that bore thee,
Oftener upon her knees than on her feet,
Died every day she lived. Fare thee well!
These evils thou repeat'st upon thyself
Have banish'd me from Scotland. O my breast,
Thy hope ends here!

Macduff [*to Malcolm*]**: O nation miserable!**

Milk here refers to Macbeth's innocence and purity untainted by any evil. But in Act4 scene 3, Malcolm says that he will "pour the sweet of concord into hell".

In this way, Malcolm accuses Macbeth of robbing the country of its innocence and goodness, hence creating hell. By now, Macbeth has descended into anarchy and disrupted the peace.

Note the contrast and how Macbeth has changed from innocence to evil; at first in Act 1 scene 7, he said, "We will proceed no further in this business". Yet, now in Act 4 acene 3, he has degenerated, and he is surely dancing with the devil because of all his atrocious killings, heading straight to 'hell'.

Macduff's earlier cry, "Bleed, bleed, poor country!" can be echoed again with his desperate cry now,

O Scotland, Scotland!

Macduff's painful cries and despair for his country shows a deep sense of helplessness for Scotland. This sad tone is endearing to the audience, and they get emotionally involved and empathise with his sad situation.

Macduff is furious and tells Malcolm he is not "Fit to govern?" and laments "O nation Miserable!"

Macduff once again gives vent to his frustration about how miserable the nation has become because Macbeth is a tyrant with a crown that is bloody and murderous: "bloody-scepter'd.

Macduff demands to know when Malcolm will inherit the throne and enjoy the fruits of his inheritance, enjoying better days

see thy wholesome days again

Duncan is praised as a saint, pure, and akin to God

Thy royal father
Was a most sainted king

MACBETH
TEXT

ACT 4 scene 3
EXPLANATION

MALCOLM
Macduff, this noble passion,
Child of integrity, hath from my soul
Wiped the black scruples, reconciled my thoughts
To thy good truth and honour. Devilish Macbeth
By many of these trains hath sought to win me
Into his power, and modest wisdom plucks me
From over-credulous haste: but God above
Deal between thee and me! for even now
I put myself to thy direction, and
Unspeak mine own detraction, here abjure
The taints and blames I laid upon myself,
For strangers to my nature. I am yet
Unknown to woman, never was forsworn,
Scarcely have coveted what was mine own,
At no time broke my faith, would not betray
The devil to his fellow and delight
No less in truth than life: my first false speaking
Was this upon myself: what I am truly,
Is thine and my poor country's to command:
Whither indeed, before thy here-approach,
Old Siward, with ten thousand warlike men,
Already at a point, was setting forth.
Now we'll together; and the chance of goodness
Be like our warranted quarrel! Why are you silent?

MACDUFF
Such welcome and unwelcome things at once
'Tis hard to reconcile.

Enter a Doctor

MALCOLM
Well; more anon.–
Comes the king forth, I pray you?

DOCTOR
Ay, sir; there are a crew of wretched souls
That stay his cure: their malady convinces
The great assay of art; but at his touch–
Such sanctity hath heaven given his hand–
They presently amend.

MALCOLM
I thank you, doctor.
Exit Doctor

MACDUFF
What's the disease he means?

Malcolm is satisfied with MacDuff's loyalty and passion for revenge, calling him a "child of integrity". Malcolm is happy that his doubts about MacDuff have now disappeared

hath from my soul
Wiped the black scruples

There's a juxtaposition here between the devilish Macbeth and God. Malcolm associates Macbeth to the devil; he was patient, because Macbeth's tricks prevented him from taking revenge sooner

many of these trains hath sought to win me

He puts his faith in God to help both him and MacDuff be victorious over Macbeth

God above
Deal between thee and me!

Malcolm wants to be guided by MacDuff, and a new relationship and bond has now developed between these two

I put myself in thy direction

Malcolm retracts

The taints and blames I laid upon myself

All the negative things he said about himself is alien to him; it doesn't apply to his nature

For strangers to my nature

Malcolm never lost faith in taking what was his own: the crown. Siward has now prepared ten thousand men set to fight. They are joining forces and hope that their success will match the true justice that they are going to fight for.

MACBETH TEXT

ACT 4 scene 3 EXPLANATION

MALCOLM
'Tis call'd the evil:
A most miraculous work in this good king;
Which often, since my here-remain in England,
I have seen him do. How he solicits heaven,
Himself best knows: but strangely-visited people,
All swoln and ulcerous, pitiful to the eye,
The mere despair of surgery, he cures,
Hanging a golden stamp about their necks,
Put on with holy prayers: and 'tis spoken,
To the succeeding royalty he leaves
The healing benediction. With this strange virtue,
He hath a heavenly gift of prophecy,
And sundry blessings hang about his throne,
That speak him full of grace.

Enter ROSS

MACDUFF
See, who comes here?

MALCOLM
My countryman; but yet I know him not.

MACDUFF
My ever-gentle cousin, welcome hither.

MALCOLM
I know him now. Good God, betimes remove
The means that makes us strangers!

ROSS
Sir, amen.

MACDUFF
Stands Scotland where it did?

ROSS
Alas, poor country!
Almost afraid to know itself. It cannot
Be call'd our mother, but our grave; where nothing,
But who knows nothing, is once seen to smile;
Where sighs and groans and shrieks that rend the air
Are made, not mark'd; where violent sorrow seems
A modern ecstasy; the dead man's knell
Is there scarce ask'd for who; and good men's lives
Expire before the flowers in their caps,
Dying or ere they sicken.

Malcolm and MacDuff suspect Ross of being a traitor. Remember he left Lady MacDuff and her son to be killed. He did not protect them but disappeared instead. There is a very uncomfortable exchange between Ross and MacDuff.

Malcolm greets Ross,

I know him not

implying that Ross is become now a stranger.

Ross gives information about Scotland, saying that

It cannot
Be call'd our mother, but our grave

Mothers are generally nurturing and protective; yet Scotland, their mother country, cannot protect them; instead, it is sending them to their graves.

Nobody smiles anymore and Shakespeare uses a series of verbs like "sighs", "groans", and "shrieks" to highlight the peoples' anguish and pain.

Ross explains that so many people are dying, that

good men's lives
Expire before the flowers in their caps

Nobody bothers to enquire for which death the bell knells. The tone changes here.

It is very emotive and sombre because MacDuff enquires about his family, and the audience get emotional.

Macduff greets Ross who joins Malcolm's cause

MACBETH
TEXT

ACT 4 scene 3
EXPLANATION

MACDUFF
O, relation
Too nice, and yet too true!
MALCOLM
What's the newest grief?
ROSS
That of an hour's age doth hiss the speaker:
Each minute teems a new one.
MACDUFF
How does my wife?
ROSS
Why, well.
MACDUFF
And all my children?
ROSS
Well too.
MACDUFF
The tyrant has not batter'd at their peace?
ROSS
No; they were well at peace when I did leave 'em.
MACDUFF
But not a niggard of your speech: how goes't?
ROSS
When I came hither to transport the tidings,
Which I have heavily borne, there ran a rumour
Of many worthy fellows that were out;
Which was to my belief witness'd the rather,
For that I saw the tyrant's power a-foot:
Now is the time of help; your eye in Scotland
Would create soldiers, make our women fight,
To doff their dire distresses.
MALCOLM
Be't their comfort
We are coming thither: gracious England hath
Lent us good Siward and ten thousand men;
An older and a better soldier none
That Christendom gives out.
ROSS
Would I could answer
This comfort with the like! But I have words
That would be howl'd out in the desert air,
Where hearing should not latch them.
MACDUFF
What concern they?
The general cause? or is it a fee-grief
Due to some single breast?

MacDuff doesn't know that his family is killed.
He enquires about his wife and children,

"How does my wife and all my children.

Shakespeare creates suspense here because the audience will want to see MacDuff's reaction. There is pain in Ross's reply:

No; they were well at peace when I did leave 'em.

He is trying to ease in the information that MacDuff's family is dead.
He says that they were well knowing full well that they were going to be killed just after he left.

He beats about the bush about giving Macduff the dreadful news about his family's slaughter by Macbeth.

He says that he had news that will grieve them, and it is weighing very heavily on him.

When I came hither to transport the tidings,
Which I have heavily borne

Macduff is curious and asks;

What concern they?
The general cause? or is it a fee-grief
Due to some single breast?

Macduff,Ross,Malcolm discuss Macbeth's treachery

MACBETH TEXT	ACT 4 scene 3 EXPLANATION

ROSS
No mind that's honest
But in it shares some woe; though the main part
Pertains to you alone.
MACDUFF
If it be mine,
Keep it not from me, quickly let me have it.
ROSS
Let not your ears despise my tongue for ever,
Which shall possess them with the heaviest sound
That ever yet they heard.
MACDUFF
Hum! I guess at it.
ROSS
Your castle is surprised; your wife and babes
Savagely slaughter'd: to relate the manner,
Were, on the quarry of these murder'd deer,
To add the death of you.
MALCOLM
Merciful heaven!
What, man! ne'er pull your hat upon your brows;
Give sorrow words: the grief that does not speak
Whispers the o'er-fraught heart and bids it break.
MACDUFF
My children too?
ROSS
Wife, children, servants, all
That could be found.
MACDUFF
And I must be from thence!
My wife kill'd too?
ROSS
I have said.
MALCOLM
Be comforted:
Let's make us medicines of our great revenge,
To cure this deadly grief.
MACDUFF
He has no children. All my pretty ones?
Did you say all? O hell-kite! All?
What, all my pretty chickens and their dam
At one fell swoop?

Ross tells MacDuff that his castle was invaded and,

your wife and babes
Savagely slaughter'd

The alliteration, "savagely slaughter'd" brings a sense of revulsion in the audience because we can visualise the brutality of the killing of an innocent woman and her child. Shakespeare uses a hunting imagery:

on the quarry of these murdered deer

They were hunted down like animals and murdered. Malcolm's exclamation at the horrific news,

Merciful heaven!

shows his horror and disgust. MacDuff is in shock. He can't believe that his wife and child are killed, and Malcolm is determined to take revenge now more than ever

Let's make us medicines of our great revenge,
To cure this deadly grief.

MacDuff is in so much of grief, he asks many rhetorical questions like,

All my pretty ones?
Did you say all? O hell-kite! All?

This clearly shows MacDuff's shock and disbelief. Shakespeare uses bird imagery again

all my pretty chickens and their dam
At one fell swoop?

Ross [*to Macduff as he turns to Malcolm in horror*]**: your wife and babes Savagely slaughter'd**

MACBETH TEXT

ACT 4 scene 3 EXPLANATION

MALCOLM
Dispute it like a man.
MACDUFF
I shall do so;
But I must also feel it as a man:
I cannot but remember such things were,
That were most precious to me. Did heaven look on,
And would not take their part? Sinful Macduff,
They were all struck for thee! naught that I am,
Not for their own demerits, but for mine,
Fell slaughter on their souls. Heaven rest them now!
MALCOLM
Be this the whetstone of your sword: let grief
Convert to anger; blunt not the heart, enrage it.
MACDUFF
O, I could play the woman with mine eyes
And braggart with my tongue! But, gentle heavens,
Cut short all intermission; front to front
Bring thou this fiend of Scotland and myself;
Within my sword's length set him; if he 'scape,
Heaven forgive him too!
MALCOLM
This tune goes manly.
Come, go we to the king; our power is ready;
Our lack is nothing but our leave; Macbeth
Is ripe for shaking, and the powers above
Put on their instruments. Receive what cheer you may:
The night is long that never finds the day.

Exeunt

Macolm [*to Macduff*]**: let grief Convert to anger**

Once again, just as the wren will fight the owl to protect its young, MacDuff's children should have been protected by their father. Macbeth's act of violence against the innocent child is unspeakable and disgusting.

MacDuff says that Macbeth doesn't have children so he cannot exact proper revenge on Macbeth. Malcolm urges MacDuff to

Dispute it like a man.

and take your revenge

MacDuff is so angry and bitter that he questions why God doesn't step in and save them:

Did heaven look on,
And would not take their part?

He blames himself and believes that they all died because of him:

Sinful MacDuff, They were all struck for thee!

Malcolm eggs MacDuff on to take revenge. He is forceful and urges him to

let grief
Convert to anger

MacDuff is now furious and is bent on killing Macbeth

Bring thou this fiend of Scotland and myself;
Within my sword's length set him

The scene closes when Malcolm and MacDuff are going to the English king for assistance, and they are ready for revenge. They pray that

the powers above
Put on their instruments

meaning God must help them to eliminate Macbeth.

MACBETH SUMMARY | **ACT 5 scene 1** |

We can juxtapose Lady Macbeth's behaviour from that of the beginning.

There is a huge contrast and a shift in her character traits from being the cold, ruthless woman at the beginning to a disorientated, broken women in Act 5.

This is the famous sleepwalking scene where the doctor and a waiting gentlewoman discuss Lady Macbeth's strange behaviour.

They then witness Lady Macbeth sleepwalking and admitting her guilt, and her desperate attempts to wash her hands to remove the blood.

She is mentally and psychologically affected, no more that strong, bold woman ("Unsex me").
We see a broken, defeated Lady Macbeth on the brink of death.

The doctor concludes that she does not need medical help but spiritual help. She is a psychological wreck. She says that she couldn't believe that Duncan could have so much blood.

We can also draw a juxtaposition here between Lady Macbeth's earlier advice to Macbeth when he killed Duncan and her futile attempt to wash the blood from her hands.

"A little water clears us of this deed"

Now she will share Macbeth's fear that Duncan's murder has stained them with blood and guilt. Here she is tries to wash out the blood and her guilt with water. "Out damn spot! Out, I say!"

Now she realises that all the water in the world cannot erase the guilt of her dirty deed. Hence, she contemplates suicide.

Doctor and Gentlewoman assessing Lady Macbeth's state of mind inside her apartment

Lady Macbeth sleep walking

MACBETH **TEXT**	**ACT 5 scene 1** **EXPLANATION**

Dunsinane. Lady's Macbeth's apartments in the castle.

Enter a DOCTOR of Physic and a Waiting-GENTLEWOMAN

DOCTOR
I have two nights watched with you, but can perceive no truth in your report. When was it she last walked?

GENTLEWOMAN
Since his majesty went into the field, I have seen her rise from her bed, throw her night-gown upon her, unlock her closet, take forth paper, fold it, write upon't, read it, afterwards seal it, and again return to bed; yet all this while in a most fast sleep.

DOCTOR
A great perturbation in nature, to receive at once the benefit of sleep, and do the effects of watching! In this slumbery agitation, besides her walking and other actual performances, what, at any time, have you heard her say?

GENTLEWOMAN
That, sir, which I will not report after her.

DOCTOR
You may to me: and 'tis most meet you should.

GENTLEWOMAN
Neither to you nor any one; having no witness to confirm my speech.

Enter Lady MACBETH, with a taper
Lo you, here she comes! This is her very guise; and, upon my life, fast asleep. Observe her; stand close.

DOCTOR
How came she by that light?

GENTLEWOMAN
Why, it stood by her: she has light by her continually 'tis her command.

The doctor has waited for two nights to see Lady Macbeth's strange behaviour and concludes that there is no truth in what the gentlewoman said

can perceive
no truth in your report

The Gentlewoman goes on to explain to the doctor that she definitely witnessed Lady Macbeth behave strangely since Macbeth went "into the field", i.e. to war.

Shakespeare gives us a list of the events that can be seen as Lady Macbeth's mental deterioration

rise from her bed, throw her night-gown upon
her, unlock her closet

Once again, mention is made of the clothing imagery; Lady Macbeth is wearing a "night-gown", which can be associated with death and foreshadows Lady Macbeth's death later on.

The gentlewoman is afraid for her life, and she refuses to reveal what she has heard Lady Macbeth say

Neither to you nor any one; having no witness to
confirm my speech.

She tells the doctor to observe Lady Macbeth and the doctor wonders why she has light around her

How came she by that light?

The use of light can suggest that Lady Macbeth is trying, in her fallen state, to bring light and redemption into her life.

The gentlewoman replies that

she has light by her continually

In Act 1, Scene 5, Lady Macbeth says, "Come thick night." However, now, she wants light.

One can connote that it's a sign of seeking redemption for her sins before she dies. Lady Macbeth is trying to wash the blood off her hands.

MACBETH
TEXT

DOCTOR
You see, her eyes are open.

GENTLEWOMAN
Ay, but their sense is shut.

DOCTOR
What is it she does now? Look, how she rubs her hands.

GENTLEWOMAN
It is an accustomed action with her, to seem thus washing her hands: I have known her continue in this a quarter of an hour.

LADY MACBETH
Yet here's a spot.

DOCTOR
Hark! she speaks: I will set down what comes from her, to satisfy my remembrance the more strongly.

LADY MACBETH
Out, damned spot! out, I say!–One: two: why, then, 'tis time to do't.–Hell is murky!–Fie, my lord, fie! a soldier, and afeard? What need we fear who knows it, when none can call our power to account?–Yet who would have thought the old man to have had so much blood in him.

DOCTOR
Do you mark that?

LADY MACBETH
The thane of Fife had a wife: where is she now?– What, will these hands ne'er be clean?–No more o' that my lord, no more o' that: you mar all with this starting.

DOCTOR
Go to, go to; you have known what you should not.

GENTLEWOMAN
She has spoke what she should not, I am sure of that: heaven knows what she has known.

ACT 5 scene 1
EXPLANATION

The play was written in blank verse, yet Lady Macbeth speaks in prose here.

This can suggest that she is remorseful and wants to be redeemed of her sins. Shakespeare's continuous use of punctuation like exclamation marks and rhetorical questions can suggest Lady Macbeth's desperation.

Now she tries desperately to wash her hands and rid them of the blood and her guilt;

Out damned spot! Out, I say!

Once again, she references hell like she did in Act 1, Scene 5: "And pull thee in the dunnest smoke of hell."

She is obviously afraid of her fate for she remarks that "Hell is murky". In this sleepwalking scene, she reveals that they had killed Duncan.

Yet who would have thought the old man
to have had so much blood in him.

At this point, we see a broken, distraught Lady Macbeth as compared to her strength and boldness in Act 2, Scene 2, "That which had made them drunk had made me bold".

We can draw a parallel here when Macbeth feels guilty after he had killed Duncan. Lady Macbeth reassures him by saying, in Act 2, "A little water clears as of this deed." And yet, here, she is struggling to clean her hands:

What will these hands ne'er be clean?

Notice that she is blaming Macbeth for killing Duncan.

No more o' that,
my lord, no more o' that.

She is trying to shelve the blame onto Macbeth to ease her conscience.

MACBETH
TEXT

LADY MACBETH
Here's the smell of the blood still: all the
perfumes of Arabia will not sweeten this little hand
Oh, oh, oh!
DOCTOR
What a sigh is there! The heart is sorely charged.
GENTLEWOMAN
I would not have such a heart in my bosom for the
dignity of the whole body.
DOCTOR
Well, well, well,–
GENTLEWOMAN
Pray God it be, sir.
DOCTOR
This disease is beyond my practise: yet I have known
those which have walked in their sleep who have died
holily in their beds.
LADY MACBETH
Wash your hands, put on your nightgown;
look not so pale.–
I tell you yet again, Banquo's buried;
He cannot come out on's grave.

ACT 5 scene 1
EXPLANATION

She is clearly delusional and hallucinating, and the motif of blood once more surfaces in this scene. Shakespeare uses sensory imagery here:

Here's the smell of the blood still.

She is feeling so guilty that she imagines the smell of the blood is so strong that

all the
perfumes of Arabia will not sweeten this little hand

This can be compared to what Macbeth says in Act 2, Scene 2, when he asks, "Will all great Neptune's ocean wash this blood from my hand?" Just like Lady Macbeth's guilt, Macbeth felt guilty then for killing Duncan, and Lady Macbeth belittled him by saying, "My hands are of your colour, but I shame to wear a heart so white", accusing him of being a coward.

The doctor is quite alarmed at Lady Macbeth's behaviour and declares that he cannot cure her sickness, because her sickness is more of a mental and psychological nature.

It's obvious that Lady Macbeth is paranoid because she is addressing herself and commanding herself:

Wash your hands, put on your nightgown

The clothing imagery is, once again, repeated in the play; putting on the "night-gown" can symbolise the heralding of death. She is trying to convince herself that Banquo will not come alive again and haunt her:

I tell you yet again Banquo's buried

Doctor:This disease is beyond my practise: yet have known those which have walked in their sleep

Lady Macbeth [*to herself in a trance*]**: Wash your hands, put on your nightgown**

DOCTOR
Even so?
LADY MACBETH
To bed, to bed! there's knocking at the gate:
come, come, come, come, give me your hand.
What's done cannot be undone.–
To bed, to bed, to bed!
Exit

DOCTOR
Will she go now to bed?
GENTLEWOMAN
Directly.
DOCTOR
Foul whisperings are abroad: unnatural deeds
Do breed unnatural troubles: infected minds
To their deaf pillows will discharge their secrets:
More needs she the divine than the physician.
God, God forgive us all! Look after her;
Remove from her the means of all annoyance,
And still keep eyes upon her. So, good night:
My mind she has mated, and amazed my sight.
I think, but dare not speak.
GENTLEWOMAN
Good night, good doctor.

Exeunt

Lady Macbeth [*to Gentlewoman and Doctor*]: **What's done cannot be undone**

Lady Macbeth's final speech suggests it's the end for her. She's delusional, she's hallucinating, and she imagines that Macbeth is with her.

In Act 3, Scene 2, she says to Macbeth, "What's done is done". This refers to Duncan's death, and she repeats it just before her death:

come, come, come, come, give me your hand.
What's done cannot be undone

This means that they cannot bring the dead ones back to life. We see a very regrettable and distraught Lady Macbeth. The repetition of

To bed, to bed, to bed?

suggests her death.

The doctor says that

unnatural deeds
Do breed unnatural troubles

Killing was against the law of God and of nature and is punishable by God.

The doctor says that people who are mentally disturbed "infected minds" will tell their secrets to their 'deaf pillows' because pillows are inanimate objects and cannot divulge what it had heard.

He goes on to say that she needs God more than she needs a doctor's cure. Shakespeare uses biblical imagery

God, God forgive us all!

suggesting that Lady Macbeth should be pardoned because both the doctor and the audience tend to sympathise with Lady Macbeth's plight; we want her to be forgiven. Her desperation here tugs at our heartstrings.

MACBETH SUMMARY	**ACT 5 scene 2**	p132

This battle scene can be juxtaposed with the beginning when Macbeth was a celebrated war hero, and King Duncan praised him

"My worthy Cawdor!

But now, we see that he has become a tragic hero because of a flaw in his personality: greed.

Lennox, Menteith, Angus, and Caithness, four Scottish Lords, joined Malcolm and the English forces, moved north and marched into Scotland.

They are determined to overthrow Macbeth and are planning an attack on him.

The forces set up camp at Birnam Wood, very close to Macbeth's castle at Dunsinane.

Shakespeare accelerates the pace here. For example, there are rapid preparations for war, plans, moves, and advances.

These movements add to the desperate pace and accelerate the fury and determination of Malcolm's army to defeat Macbeth.

Macbeth has lost all credibility and respect as a king. People are terrified of him and obey his commands out of sheer fear.

The lords are determined to get rid of Macbeth and rid Scotland of this illness.

Countryside near Dunsinane castle

Rebel Army amassing against Macbeth

MACBETH
TEXT

Countryside near Dunsinane. Drum and colours.

ENTER Thane MENTEITH, Thane CAITHNESS, Thane ANGUS, Thane LENNOX, and soldiers

MENTEITH
The English power is near, led on by Malcolm,
His uncle Siward and the good Macduff:
Revenges burn in them; for their dear causes
Would to the bleeding and the grim alarm
Excite the mortified man.
ANGUS
Near Birnam wood
Shall we well meet them; that way are they coming.
CAITHNESS
Who knows if Donalbain be with his brother?
LENNOX
For certain, sir, he is not: I have a file
Of all the gentry: there is Siward's son,
And many unrough youths that even now
Protest their first of manhood.
MENTEITH
What does the tyrant?
CAITHNESS
Great Dunsinane he strongly fortifies:
Some say he's mad; others that lesser hate him
Do call it valiant fury: but, for certain,
He cannot buckle his distemper'd cause
Within the belt of rule.

ACT 5 scene 2
EXPLANATION

The scene opens with a very angry army ready to take revenge on Macbeth ("Revenges burn in them").

They discuss how uncomfortable Macbeth will be with this sudden turn of events. They refer to him as "grim" and say that he is a "mortified man" so they meet near Birnam Wood. Caithness enquires whether Donalbain is fighting with Malcolm, and Lennox said that he was not. Mentheith enquires what Macbeth is doing

What does the tyrant?

Caithness says that Macbeth is turning his castle into a fortress in order to protect himself.

They once again discuss his state of mind:

Some say he's mad; others that lesser hate him

It's obvious that he has lost control of his faculties, and his subjects hate him.

He is furious and trying to act brave:

Do call it valiant fury

He has lost control of his subjects and his passions:

He cannot buckle his distemper'd cause
Within the belt of rule

Lennox and Angus leaders of rebel army

Thanes Caithness and Menteith joining rebel army

MACBETH
TEXT

ANGUS
Now does he feel
His secret murders sticking on his hands;
Now minutely revolts upbraid his faith-breach;
Those he commands move only in command,
Nothing in love: now does he feel his title
Hang loose about him, like a giant's robe
Upon a dwarfish thief.
MENTEITH
Who then shall blame
His pester'd senses to recoil and start,
When all that is within him does condemn
Itself for being there?
CAITHNESS
Well, march we on,
To give obedience where 'tis truly owed:
Meet we the medicine of the sickly weal,
And with him pour we in our country's purge
Each drop of us.
LENNOX
Or so much as it needs,
To dew the sovereign flower and drown the weeds.
Make we our march towards Birnam.

Exeunt, marching

ACT 5 scene 2
EXPLANATION

Angus talks about Macbeth's guilt:
Now does he feel
His secret murders sticking on his hands

This means Macbeth has blood on his hands. Once again, we notice the clothing imagery that Shakespeare very often repeats,

now does he feel his title
Hang loose about him

Macbeth is not big enough to hold the crown. The simile like a giant's robe

suggests that the title doesn't fit him and is falling off him like a loose robe.

Menteith comments on Macbeth's state of mind once again and says that we can't blame him for his reactions because he is now very troubled "pester'd senses".

Caithness is determined to fight until they shed their last drop of blood and purge his country of its evil

pour we in our country's purge
Each drop of us.

This scene ends with a flower imagery:

To dew the sovereign flower and drown the weeds

They are referring to bringing Macbeth down just like how the weeds are destroyed, and they march to fulfil their wishes to kill Macbeth.

Angus: Now does he feel His secret murders sticking on his hands

Lennox: To dew the sovereign flower and drown the weeds. Make we our march towards Birnam.

MACBETH SUMMARY	**ACT 5 scene 3**	

The witches predicted that,

"Macbeth shall never vanquished be
Until Great Birnam Wood to high Dunsinane hill
Shall come against him"

Having heard this prediction, Macbeth was convinced that nobody can hurt him.

How misguided he was. He dismisses reports of an invasion. He was angry at the servant who delivered the news that the army was approaching, and he very bravely asked for his armour.

He acts bravely, still convinced that he can never be defeated because of the witches' prophecy. He brands the other lords and the servant as cowards, "cream-faced and lily-livered".

The doctor delivers his message to Macbeth saying that he is unable to cure

"a mind diseased",

referring to Lady Macbeth's affected state of mind and her paranoia.

Macbeth is desperate, and he gives vent to his frustration by being very unkind to the doctor.

Macbeth is now doomed, and he constantly thinks about the witches' prophecies.

Macbeth on the Dunsinane's battlements

Seyton inside Dunsinane castle

MACBETH TEXT

ACT 5 scene 3 EXPLANATION

Dunsinane, Macbeth's castle

Enter MACBETH, DOCTOR and Attendants

MACBETH
Bring me no more reports; let them fly all:
Till Birnam wood remove to Dunsinane,
I cannot taint with fear. What's the boy Malcolm?
Was he not born of woman? The spirits that know
All mortal consequences have pronounced me thus:
'Fear not, Macbeth; no man that's born of woman
Shall e'er have power upon thee.' Then fly false thanes,
And mingle with the English epicures:
The mind I sway by and the heart I bear
Shall never sag with doubt nor shake with fear.

Enter a Servant
The devil damn thee black, thou cream-faced loon!
Where got'st thou that goose look?
SERVANT
There is ten thousand–
MACBETH
Geese, villain!
SERVANT
Soldiers, sir.
MACBETH
Go prick thy face, and over-red thy fear,
Thou lily-liver'd boy. What soldiers, patch?
Death of thy soul! those linen cheeks of thine
Are counsellors to fear. What soldiers, whey-face?
SERVANT
The English force, so please you.

At the beginning of this scene, we see a very agitated and irate Macbeth

Bring me no more reports

Shakespeare's use of short, snappy sentences gives us an indication of Macbeth's confused state and his racing mind.

Notice the similarity between Macbeth and Lady Macbeth's reaction when they are about to die. Both of them speak to themselves:

'Fear not, Macbeth; no man that's born of woman
Shall e'er have power upon thee.'

At the point, he is still adamant that the witches' prophecies will help him

the heart I bear
Shall never sag with doubt nor shake with fear.

He is delusional and has developed a false sense of confidence.

The vicious attack on the servant shocks the audience, and Macbeth's brutality and desperation is evident here;

The devil damn thee black

His use of the biblical imagery with reference to the devil is ironic here because he is damned by the devil for all his vicious deeds.

Macbeth: Bring me no more reports

Servant [*to Macbeth*]**: There is ten thousand–**

MACBETH TEXT

MACBETH
Take thy face hence.
Exit Servant

Seyton!–I am sick at heart,
When I behold–Seyton, I say!–This push
Will cheer me ever, or disseat me now.
I have lived long enough: my way of life
Is fall'n into the sear, the yellow leaf;
And that which should accompany old age,
As honour, love, obedience, troops of friends,
I must not look to have; but, in their stead,
Curses, not loud but deep, mouth-honour, breath,
Which the poor heart would fain deny, and dare not.
Seyton!

Enter SEYTON
SEYTON
What is your gracious pleasure?
MACBETH
What news more?
SEYTON
All is confirm'd, my lord, which was reported.
MACBETH
I'll fight till from my bones my flesh be hack'd.
Give me my armour.
SEYTON
'Tis not needed yet.
MACBETH
I'll put it on.
Send out more horses; skirr the country round;
Hang those that talk of fear. Give me mine armour.
How does your patient, doctor?
DOCTOR
Not so sick, my lord,
As she is troubled with thick coming fancies,
That keep her from her rest.

ACT 5 scene 3 EXPLANATION

When Macbeth talks to Seyton, Shakespeare uses several dashes and exclamation marks highlighting Macbeth's fear and loss of words. The dashes suggest that he is pondering his desperate situation. His outbursts are beyond reasoning.

He says,

I am sick at heart"

implying that he is now going crazy with fear and worry about losing his crown

disseat me now

Macbeth asks Seyton about news that's coming in about the invasion. Macbeth says that he is determined to fight to the death:

I'll fight till from my bones my flesh be hack'd.

He uses graphic death imagery here, suggesting his paranoia and fear. He orders preparation for war and is rather ruthless when he says,

Hang those that talk of fear.

We see how far both his mind and his fears have degenerated. He enquires about Lady Macbeth's health:

The doctor tells him that she is not sick but troubled

As she is troubled with thick-coming fancies

This means that she is mentally and not physically ill.

Macbeth: I am sick at heart

Doctor: As she is troubled with thick coming fancies

MACBETH TEXT	ACT 5 scene 3 EXPLANATION
MACBETH Cure her of that. Canst thou not minister to a mind diseas'd, Pluck from the memory a rooted sorrow, Raze out the written troubles of the brain And with some sweet oblivious antidote Cleanse the stuff'd bosom of that perilous stuff Which weighs upon the heart? **DOCTOR** Therein the patient Must minister to himself. **MACBETH** Throw physic to the dogs; I'll none of it. Come, put mine armour on; give me my staff. Seyton, send out. Doctor, the thanes fly from me. Come, sir, dispatch. If thou couldst, doctor, cast The water of my land, find her disease, And purge it to a sound and pristine health, I would applaud thee to the very echo, That should applaud again.–Pull't off, I say.– What rhubarb, cyme, or what purgative drug, Would scour these English hence? Hear'st thou of them? **DOCTOR** Ay, my good lord; your royal preparation Makes us hear something. **MACBETH** Bring it after me. I will not be afraid of death and bane, Till Birnam forest come to Dunsinane. *Exeunt all but Doctor* **DOCTOR** *[Aside]* Were I from Dunsinane away and clear, Profit again should hardly draw me here. *Exeunt*	Macbeth insists that the doctor cures her of her diseased mind: Cans't thou not minister to a mind diseas'd? He wants the doctor to help to cure her problems: Which weighs upon the heart? When the doctor told Macbeth that he cannot help his wife, he was furious and implied that physics was useless: Throw physic to the dogs, I'll none of it. Macbeth is still trying to be confident and says, I will not be afraid of death and bane, Till Birnam forest come to Dunsinane. We notice that he still has faith on the witches' prediction because he still believes that he will never be defeated. He is soon about to learn of the witches' treachery albeit too late. He is prepared to go to war now! The doctor is nervous and afraid at these turn of events, and he vows that all the money in the world will not entice him to come here again; Profit again should hardly draw me here.
 **Macbeth: Throw physic to the dogs; I'll none of it.**	 **Macbeth: I will not be afraid of death**

MACBETH SUMMARY	**ACT 5 scene 4**	p139

The English and Scottish armies, led by Malcolm, meet in Birnam Wood.

The bough's of Birnam Wood was cut down and used as a camouflage and each soldier carried a branch in front of them.

Malcolm orders this, so that the size of the army can be hidden. Once again, we see the witches' prophecy coming true in a reference to Birnam Wood moving towards Dunsinane, but it is clear here that they speak in half-truths because they didn't specify that the trees were a camouflage. Making Macbeth believe that it is impossible for the trees to move.

Macbeth has made his castle into a fortress in order to withstand a siege.

His troops are afraid of him and only fight because they have to, and not out of love or patriotism. Now Macbeth has cause to be nervous because he is about to be the victim of a deadly battle.

Malcolm is trying to rid Scotland of Macbeth's atrocities by claiming the crown and rid his diseased country from the vile treachery that pervades it.

They are now ready for the battle.

Soldiers cut trees from Birnam Wood

Menteith, Siward, Malcolm, Macduff lead the army

MACBETH
TEXT

Birnam Wood.
Soldiers marching, Drum beating, and Colours fluttering.

Enter MALCOLM son of murdered King DUNCAN,
Enter SIWARD Earl of Northumberland and his son,
Enter Thane Macduff, Thane Menteith, Thane Caithness
Enter Thane Angus, Thane LENNOX, and Thane ROSS

MALCOLM
Cousins, I hope the days are near at hand
That chambers will be safe.
MENTEITH
We doubt it nothing.
SIWARD
What wood is this before us?
MENTEITH
The wood of Birnam.
MALCOLM
Let every soldier hew him down a bough
And bear't before him: thereby shall we shadow
The numbers of our host and make discovery
Err in report of us.
SOLDIER
It shall be done.
SIWARD
We learn no other but the confident tyrant
Keeps still in Dunsinane, and will endure
Our setting down before 't.
MALCOLM
'Tis his main hope:
For where there is advantage to be given,
Both more and less have given him the revolt,
And none serve with him but constrained things
Whose hearts are absent too.
MACDUFF
Let our just censures
Attend the true event, and put we on
Industrious soldiership.
SIWARD
The time approaches
That will with due decision make us know
What we shall say we have and what we owe.
Thoughts speculative their unsure hopes relate,
But certain issue strokes must arbitrate:
Towards which advance the war.
Exeunt, marching

ACT 5 scene 4

EXPLANATION

In this scene, Malcolm says he hopes

That chambers will be safe

to protect Macbeth. Ironically, Macbeth's chamber wasn't as safe as Duncan thought because Macbeth killed him there! Now Macbeth wants his room to protect him from the invading army.

Siward says that the "tyrant" is holed up in his castle

Keeps still in Dunsinane

Macbeth will wait there until the army besieges it. Malcolm remarks that great and ordinary men alike have rebelled against him.

Both more and less have given him the revolt.

MacDuff wants to go and fight with all his might, and he encourages everyone to do the same:

Let our just censures
Attend the true event, and put we on
Industrious soldiership

Siward is wise when he says that speculation can only amount to uncertain hopes, but the only way that they can test their success is by fighting

Thoughts speculative their unsure hopes relate

They then advance towards war.

Birnam Wood outside the walls of Dunsinane castle

MACBETH SUMMARY	ACT 5 scene 5	p141

Macbeth had gathered his army, and he is pretty certain that his strong castle will shield him against the advancing army.

He appears to be brave saying that he had

"almost forgot the taste of fears".

All of his wretched behaviour has made him hard and cold. He doesn't feel the pangs of fear.
A scream is heard and Seyton informs Macbeth that Lady Macbeth has committed suicide, and she is dead.

When he is told that she is dead, he gives a very cold response saying,

"She should have died hereafter".

His nonchalant attitude to lady Macbeth's death is surprising indicating to us that he knows that his death is inevitable.

We can juxtapose this to his earlier praise, when he called Lady Macbeth,

"His partner in greatness"

Macbeth learns that the Birnam Wood is advancing towards Dunsinane, and he can't believe it.

Then he thinks about the witches' prophecies about Birnam Wood coming to Dunsinane. He is furious; out of desperation, he changes his plans, and he orders a direct attack on the advancing army.

Dunsinane castle with Macbeth and his army inside

Lady Macbeth is in a troubled state of mind

MACBETH
TEXT

Dunsinane. Inside Macbeth's castle.

Enter Macbeth with his servant SEYTON.
Enter Soldiers with drum and colours.

MACBETH
Hang out our banners on the outward walls;
The cry is still 'They come:' our castle's strength
Will laugh a siege to scorn: here let them lie
Till famine and the ague eat them up:
Were they not forced with those that should be ours,
We might have met them dareful, beard to beard,
And beat them backward home.

A cry of women within
What is that noise?
SEYTON
It is the cry of women, my good lord.
Exit

MACBETH
I have almost forgot the taste of fears;
The time has been, my senses would have cool'd
To hear a night-shriek; and my fell of hair
Would at a dismal treatise rouse and stir
As life were in't: I have supp'd full with horrors;
Direness, familiar to my slaughterous thoughts
Cannot once start me.

Macbeth [*to Seyton*]**: our castle's strength**
Will laugh a siege to scorn

ACT 5 scene 5
EXPLANATION

Macbeth's arrogance is shocking here. Shakespeare uses a personification to highlight this:

our castle's strength
Will laugh a siege to scorn

He is boasting that no one can harm him because his castle is strong and can withstand any army.

Macbeth is certain that the army cannot penetrate his castle and that they will have to wait for a very long time to be successful, even

Till famine and the ague eat them up:

Macbeth is angry, and he believes that if so many of his men hadn't defected to Malcolm's army, he would have won the battle

And beat them backward home.

[A CRY OF A WOMAN WITHIN]

We see a defeated Macbeth, and he is immune to any fears

almost forgot the taste of fears

He finally admits that he had created so much horror, saying,

I have supp'd full with horrors;
Direness, familiar to my slaughterous thoughts

but that he is not afraid anymore

Cannot once start me

MACBETH
TEXT

Re-enter SEYTON
Wherefore was that cry?
SEYTON
The queen, my lord, is dead.
MACBETH
She should have died hereafter;
There would have been a time for such a word.
To-morrow, and to-morrow, and to-morrow,
Creeps in this petty pace from day to day
To the last syllable of recorded time,
And all our yesterdays have lighted fools
The way to dusty death. Out, out, brief candle!
Life's but a walking shadow, a poor player
That struts and frets his hour upon the stage
And then is heard no more: it is a tale
Told by an idiot, full of sound and fury,
Signifying nothing.

Seyton [*to Macbeth*]**: The queen, my Lord, is dead**

ACT 5 scene 5
EXPLANATION

[RE-ENTER SEYTON]

Macbeth enquires about the noise:

Wherefore was that cry?

Macbeth learns that Lady Macbeth is dead.

She should have died hereafter.

There are several ways that you can interpret his answer. One can infer that he does not care for Lady Macbeth anymore; another interpretation is that he knows he is about to be killed by the army and that she will shortly follow.

This can be revenge for the killing of Lady MacDuff or revenge for her role in the killing of Duncan. Here, we see that Macbeth's mental state is fast deteriorating.

The repetition of "to-morrow" can show his mounting fear and confusion. We can draw a parallel to the bold, confident behaviour of Macbeth earlier in the play to a fallen, dejected, weak Macbeth.

Shakespeare uses a biblical imagery here whilst Macbeth is in the last throes of death.

The way to dusty death

refers to God's creation of man ("Ashes to ashes, dust to dust"). God created man out of dust, and man becomes dust when he dies. Macbeth is about to die and become dust. Furthermore, the use of the light imagery
Out, out, brief candle!

can suggest that Macbeth's life is about to be snuffed out like the candle. The use of the adjective 'brief' can suggest Macbeth's short reign on the throne. The fact that he wants the candle to go out means that his life was so full of "darkness" that he doesn't want the light to infiltrate.

He talks about life being played on a stage, and he was a very poor actor and how his time on the stage is over. He is afraid, because he is about to die:
Life's but a walking shadow, a poor player
That struts and frets his hour upon the stage

MACBETH
TEXT

Enter a Messenger

Thou comest to use thy tongue; thy story quickly.

MESSENGER

Gracious my lord,
I should report that which I say I saw,
But know not how to do it.

MACBETH

Well, say, sir.

MESSENGER

As I did stand my watch upon the hill,
I look'd toward Birnam, and anon, methought,
The wood began to move.

MACBETH

Liar and slave!

MESSENGER

Let me endure your wrath, if't be not so:
Within this three mile may you see it coming;
I say, a moving grove.

MACBETH

If thou speak'st false,
Upon the next tree shalt thou hang alive,
Till famine cling thee: if thy speech be sooth,
I care not if thou dost for me as much.
I pull in resolution, and begin
To doubt the equivocation of the fiend
That lies like truth: 'Fear not, till Birnam wood
Do come to Dunsinane:' and now a wood
Comes toward Dunsinane. Arm, arm, and out!
If this which he avouches does appear,
There is nor flying hence nor tarrying here.
I gin to be aweary of the sun,
And wish the estate o' the world were now undone.
Ring the alarum-bell! Blow, wind! come, wrack!
At least we'll die with harness on our back.

Exeunt

ACT 5 scene 5

EXPLANATION

The messenger tells Macbeth that he saw the wood of Birnam move. Macbeth was furious and he yelled at the messenger calling him

Liar and slave!

It's obvious that Macbeth is shocked because the witches prophesy is now coming true. He now realises that the witches had lied to him and spoke half-truths the fiend that lies like truth

He is shocked that what they said is now happening

'Fear not, till Birnam wood
Do come to Dunsinane:'

He realises that he cannot stay holed up in the castle anymore:

There is nor flying hence nor tarrying here.

He has to change his plans. He prepares for war:

Ring the alarum-bell! Blow, wind! come, wrack!

The use of the repeated exclamation mark can suggest Macbeth's panic, confusion, and mounting fear. He has accepted his fate and promised to die with

harness on our back

meaning that he will die with full armour instead of being slaughtered in his castle. Note that the use of his armour at the beginning of the play signified honour and bravery, which Macbeth hopes to achieve now in death.

Macbeth sees Birnam Wood move towards him

MACBETH SUMMARY	**ACT 5 scene 6**	

The witches' prophecy has come true, and Macbeth is now in mortal danger.

Camouflaged as trees, Malcolm and his army now reached Dunsinane:

"Macbeth shall never vanquished be
Until great Birnam Wood to High Dunsinane hill
Shall come against him".

Malcolm's rebel army outside Dunsinane castle

Macduff: Make all our trumpets speak

MACBETH TEXT

Dunsinane. Surrounding the Macbeth's castle.
Drums and colours

Enter MALCOLM, SIWARD, MACDUFF, and their army.

MALCOLM
Now near enough: your leafy screens throw down.
And show like those you are. You, worthy uncle,
Shall, with my cousin, your right-noble son,
Lead our first battle: worthy Macduff and we
Shall take upon 's what else remains to do,
According to our order.
SIWARD
Fare you well.
Do we but find the tyrant's power to-night,
Let us be beaten, if we cannot fight.
MACDUFF
Make all our trumpets speak; give them all breath,
Those clamorous harbingers of blood and death.

Exeunt

ACT 5 scene 6 EXPLANATION

Blow all the trumpets. Malcolm orders his army to throw their camouflage away and reveal themselves

your leafy screens throw down

They are now ready for the assault. Malcolm gives orders, ironically, he addresses Macduff as

your right-noble son,
Lead our first battle

In the same way that king Duncan addressed Macbeth when he was victorious in war. One can conclude that Malcolm is ready to be the king and assume the crown and restore his country to its former glory just, like his father did.

Shakespeare creates a very tense atmosphere here. MacDuff personifies the trumpets

Make all our trumpets speak; give them all breath,

He is eager to have the trumpets announce their arrival with its booming sound and take revenge on Macbeth.
Note Shakespeare's uses of auditory imagery here.
He wants the trumpets to come alive with power. He says that the trumpets have the power to announce,

blood and death

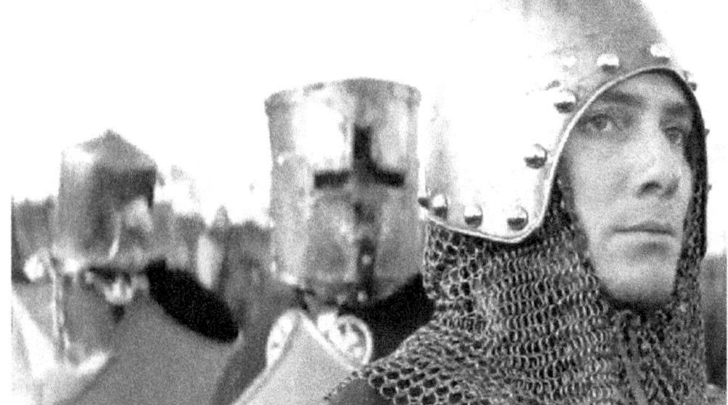

Malcolm [*to Siward*]: your right noble son, Lead our first battle

Young Siward and Macduff inside Dunsinane castle searching for Macbeth

MACBETH SUMMARY	**ACT 5 scene 7**	p147

CLIMAX AND RESOLUTION

We can conclude by saying that the play is cyclical because it starts with Macbeth being the war hero, and now, he dies a tragic hero.

Macbeth kills young Siward, who tried to challenge him.

MacDuff is determined to kill Macbeth, and the two meet. They began to fight, and Macbeth mocks MacDuff, telling him the witches' prophecy,

"for none of woman born shall harm Macbeth".

Then, MacDuff reveals to him that he was not born of a woman but was delivered through caesarean section.

Macbeth is horrified at this revelation. He is also shocked at the way he had been tricked by the witches and calls them "juggling fiends", devils who toyed with his life and destroyed him.

At first, Macbeth refused to fight MacDuff but decided that he will fight to the bitter end.

MacDuff kills him and brings Macbeth's severed head on stage.

Malcolm has won the war, and he becomes the new king of Scotland, restoring the natural order of things.

Macduff searches Dunsinane's courtyard

Young Siward searches Dunsinane's chambers

MACBETH
TEXT

ACT 5 scene 7
EXPLANATION

Inside Dunsinane castle
A call to Arms [Alarums]
Enter Macbeth

MACBETH
They have tied me to a stake; I cannot fly,
But, bear-like, I must fight the course. What's he
That was not born of woman? Such a one
Am I to fear, or none.

Enter YOUNG SIWARD
YOUNG SIWARD
What is thy name?
MACBETH
Thou'lt be afraid to hear it.
YOUNG SIWARD
No; though thou call'st thyself a hotter name
Than any is in hell.
MACBETH
My name's Macbeth.
YOUNG SIWARD
The devil himself could not pronounce a title
More hateful to mine ear.
MACBETH
No, nor more fearful.
YOUNG SIWARD
Thou liest, abhorred tyrant; with my sword
I'll prove the lie thou speak'st.
They fight and YOUNG SIWARD is slain

MACBETH
Thou wast born of woman
But swords I smile at, weapons laugh to scorn,
Brandish'd by man that's of a woman born.
Exit with Young Siward's body

In this last scene, we see the climax and resolution. We see Macbeth has suffered retribution for all his evil deeds. The reader becomes emotionally involved in this scene because we tend to empathise with him a bit. He is like a trapped animal in this scene:

They have tied me to a stake; I cannot fly.

He is determined to fight to the end like a bear. His bravery right to the end is displayed as he insists that no man who wasn't born of woman should terrify him.

[ENTER YOUNG SIWARD]

Young Siward asks Macbeth who he was, and he makes reference to hell. It's ironic, because that's where Macbeth would be heading to soon

thou call'st thyself a hotter name
Than any is in hell.

When Macbeth reveals who he is, young Siward once again calls Macbeth a "devil" and a "abhorred tyrant". They fight, and young Siward is killed.

Even at the end he still didn't heed the fact that young Seward was just a youth, he was prepared to kill him just the way he had Macduff's child killed. Macbeth's ruthlessness knows no bounds even to the very end. This shows that he is remorseless for all the atrocities that he has caused. Hence, we tend to show him no pity like the way we softened to Lady Macbeth in the end because she showed signs of being remorseful just before she died.

Young Siward slain by Macbeth

Macbeth confronts the invaders lead by Malcolm

MACBETH TEXT

ACT 5 scene 7 EXPLANATION

Alarums.
Enter MACDUFF

MACDUFF
That way the noise is. Tyrant, show thy face!
If thou be'st slain and with no stroke of mine,
My wife and children's ghosts will haunt me still.
I cannot strike at wretched kerns, whose arms
Are hired to bear their staves: either thou, Macbeth,
Or else my sword with an unbatter'd edge
I sheathe again undeeded. There thou shouldst be;
By this great clatter, one of greatest note
Seems bruited. Let me find him, fortune!
And more I beg not.
Exit. Alarums

Enter MALCOLM and SIWARD

SIWARD
This way, my lord; the castle's gently render'd:
The tyrant's people on both sides do fight;
The noble thanes do bravely in the war;
The day almost itself professes yours,
And little is to do.

MALCOLM
We have met with foes
That strike beside us.

SIWARD
Enter, sir, the castle.

Alarums
Exeunt

MacDuff is following the sounds to find Macbeth:

Tyrant, show thy face!

He wants to kill Macbeth; otherwise, he will feel guilty for not doing justice to his family

If thou be'st slain and with no stroke of mine

He is determined to take revenge for the death of his family

My wife and children's ghost will haunt me still

Siward tells Malcolm that the castle has surrendered, and that Macbeth's people are fighting on both sides

The tyrant's people on both sides do fight

The castle is handed over to Malcolm:

The day almost itself professes yours.

Macbeth surveys the invaders daring them to fight

Macduff finds Macbeth

MACBETH SUMMARY	**ACT 5 scene 8**	

Macbeth questions why he should play the Roman fool and die by his own sword. Better to fight, and live!

Enter Macduff exclaiming.

"Turn, hell-hound, turn"

They fight, each trading insults.

Macbeth declares,

"I bear a charmed life which must not yield
To one of woman born"

But Macduff counters,

"Despite thy charm,
Macduff was from his mother's womb
Untimely ripp'd"

Macbeth

"Accursed be that tongue that tells me so"

Macbeth refuses to yield and is killed by Macduff.

Macduff [*to Macbeth*]**: Turn, hell-bound, turn!**

Macbeth [*to Macduff*]**: Of all men else I have avoided thee**

MACBETH **TEXT**	**ACT 5 scene 8** **EXPLANATION**
Dunsinane, Another part of the field. *Enter Macbeth* **MACBETH** Why should I play the Roman fool, and die On mine own sword? whiles I see lives, the gashes Do better upon them. *Enter MACDUFF* **MACDUFF** Turn, hell-hound, turn! **MACBETH** Of all men else I have avoided thee: But get thee back; my soul is too much charged With blood of thine already. **MACDUFF** I have no words: My voice is in my sword: thou bloodier villain Than terms can give thee out! *They fight* **MACBETH** Thou losest labour: As easy mayst thou the intrenchant air With thy keen sword impress as make me bleed: Let fall thy blade on vulnerable crests; I bear a charmed life, which must not yield, To one of woman born. **MACDUFF** Despair thy charm; And let the angel whom thou still hast served Tell thee, Macduff was from his mother's womb Untimely ripp'd.	Macbeth refuses to commit suicide. When an honourable Roman soldier is facing defeat, he will commit suicide, but Macbeth refuses to play the Roman fool, and die On mine own sword? MacDuff once again uses the imagery of hell to address Macbeth. Note the alliteration: Turn, hell-bound, turn! showing MacDuff's fury Macbeth taunts MacDuff: Thou losest labour. This means that MacDuff is wasting his time. Macbeth is also confident when he says, I bear a charmed life, which must not yield, To one of woman born. He is repeating the witches' prophecy to MacDuff. We can see how Macbeth has put his full faith on the witches' predictions. MacDuff then reveals to him that he was not of woman born but caesarean section Macduff was from his mother's womb Untimely ripp'd.
 **Macbeth** [*to Macduff*]**: I bear a charmed life, which must not yield, To one of woman born.**	 **Macduff** [*to Macbeth*]**: Macduff was from his mother's womb Untimely ripp'd.**

MACBETH TEXT

MACBETH
Accursed be that tongue that tells me so,
For it hath cow'd my better part of man!
And be these juggling fiends no more believed,
That palter with us in a double sense;
That keep the word of promise to our ear,
And break it to our hope. I'll not fight with thee.
MACDUFF
Then yield thee, coward,
And live to be the show and gaze o' the time:
We'll have thee, as our rarer monsters are,
Painted on a pole, and underwrit,
'Here may you see the tyrant.'
MACBETH
I will not yield,
To kiss the ground before young Malcolm's feet,
And to be baited with the rabble's curse.
Though Birnam wood be come to Dunsinane,
And thou opposed, being of no woman born,
Yet I will try the last. Before my body
I throw my warlike shield. Lay on, Macduff,
And damn'd be him that first cries, 'Hold, enough!'

Alarums
Exeunt, fighting

Enter MACBETH and MACDUFF, fighting
MACBETH slain

Exit MACDUFF with MACBETH's body.

ACT 5 scene 8 EXPLANATION

Macbeth is furious because he now realises that the witches had tricked him, and he calls them,

juggling fiends no more believed

the devils who played with his mind. He goes on to rant about how they spoke half-truths and words with double-meaning

That palter with us in a double sense

Macbeth then decides that he is in serious danger, and he refuses to fight MacDuff

I'll not fight with thee

MacDuff urges Macbeth to give up:

Then yield thee, coward.

But Macbeth's strength is admirable here because he doesn't yield to MacDuff's demand

I will not yield

He challenges MacDuff to a fair duel:

Lay on, Macduff,
And damn'd be him that first cries, 'Hold, enough!'

Macbeth died courageously and fought until his death. He protected his manhood, something that Lady Macbeth accused him of lacking at in the beginning of the play "But I shame to wear a heart so white".

Macbeth [*aside*]: juggling fiends no more believed That palter with us in a double sense;

Macbeth slain by Macduff
Witches' prophecy fulfilled: Macbeth will not be harmed unless by unnatural birth

MACBETH SUMMARY	**ACT 5 scene 9**	

Malcolm, Siward, Ross and Thanes return to Malcom's headquarters, not sure if Macduff had survived the battle.

Ross informs Siward

"Your son, my lord, has paid a soldier's debt"

Siward is proud of his son's valour,

"Had I as many sons as I have hairs,
I would not wish them to a fairer death"

As to other who died, Siward exclaims with humility,

"He's worth no more"

Enter the missing Macduff with Macbeth's head, exclaiming Malcolm as the new king,

"Hail, king, for so thou art. Behold where stands
Th' usurper's cursed head."

ALL proclaim Malcolm,

"Hail, King of Scotland"

Macduff stands triumphant having slain Macbeth

Malcolm [*to Siward on his fallen son Young Siward*]: **He's worth more sorrow**

MACBETH **TEXT**	**ACT 5 scene 9** **EXPLANATION**

Dunsinane, Malcolm's headquarters.
Macbeth's army sounds Retreat
Malcolm's army sounds Victory

ENTER with drum and colours, MALCOLM, SIWARD, ROSS
ENTER other Thanes with Soldiers

MALCOLM
I would the friends we miss were safe arrived.
SIWARD
Some must go off: and yet, by these I see
So great a day as this is cheaply bought.
MALCOLM
Macduff is missing, and your noble son.
ROSS
Your son, my lord, has paid a soldier's debt:
He only lived but till he was a man;
The which no sooner had his prowess confirm'd
In the unshrinking station where he fought,
But like a man he died.
SIWARD
Then he is dead?
ROSS
Ay, and brought off the field: your cause of sorrow
Must not be measured by his worth, for then
It hath no end.
SIWARD
Had he his hurts before?
ROSS
Ay, on the front.
SIWARD
Why then, God's soldier be he!
Had I as many sons as I have hairs,
I would not wish them to a fairer death:
And so, his knell is knoll'd.

Malcolm is concerned that Macduff hasn't arrived, and he hopes he'll return safely.

Ross tells Siward that his son

has paid a soldier's debt

He was brave and "like a man he died".

Siward is proud of his son's bravery, and he accepted his death and says that he fought with determination and patriotism.

Why then, God's soldier be he!"

In conclusion, we see the motif of the knelling of the bell heralding death surfacing once again.

And so, his knell is knoll'd.

When Duncan died, we also saw the knelling of the bells.

Ross removes the crown from Macbeth's head

Ross takes the crown to its rightful owner Malcolm

MACBETH TEXT	ACT 5 scene 9 EXPLANATION

MALCOLM
He's worth more sorrow,
And that I'll spend for him.
SIWARD
He's worth no more
They say he parted well, and paid his score:
And so, God be with him! Here comes newer comfort.

Re-enter MACDUFF, with MACBETH's head
MACDUFF
Hail, king! for so thou art: behold, where stands
The usurper's cursed head: the time is free:
I see thee compass'd with thy kingdom's pearl,
That speak my salutation in their minds;
Whose voices I desire aloud with mine:
Hail, King of Scotland!
ALL
Hail, King of Scotland!
Flourish

MALCOLM
We shall not spend a large expense of time
Before we reckon with your several loves,
And make us even with you. My thanes and kinsmen,
Henceforth be earls, the first that ever Scotland
In such an honour named. What's more to do,
Which would be planted newly with the time,
As calling home our exiled friends abroad
That fled the snares of watchful tyranny;
Producing forth the cruel ministers
Of this dead butcher and his fiend-like queen,
Who, as 'tis thought, by self and violent hands
Took off her life; this, and what needful else
That calls upon us, by the grace of Grace,
We will perform in measure, time and place:
So, thanks to all at once and to each one,
Whom we invite to see us crown'd at Scone.

Flourish. Exeunt.

END OF PLAY

Malcolm is hailed king of Scotland, and he is crowned. He rewards his thanes and kinsman with titles of earls.

Malcolm also decides to bring all the people who fled

the snares of watchful tyranny

back home.

Malcolm is determined, now that he is king, to restore Scotland to its former glory and put right all the wrongs during Macbeth's reign.

Macduff hails Malcolm as king,

"Hail, King of Scotland!"

There is obvious joy in their voices because they got rid of the tyrant Macbeth and can once again be blessed with a loyal, honest king like Duncan.

Malcolm refers to Macbeth and lady Macbeth as;

"Dead butcher and his fiend-like queen."

These harsh verbs can denote his hate and anger.

He thanked everyone for their support and invites them to his coronation at Scone.

ALL exclaim [*to Malcolm, son of Duncan*]:
Hail, King of Scotland

MACBETH

Macbeth is the protagonist turned antagonist in the play. He is a tragic hero, because, at first, he was a celebrated war hero in Act 1, Scene 2 and was described as "brave Macbeth" by the Sergeant. However, he fell from grace because of a flaw in his character, and that flaw was greed.

Sadly, at the beginning of the play, he is portrayed as being very innocent. Lady Macbeth says that he is "too fall o' th' milk of human kindness". Although Lady Macbeth thinks that Macbeth is weak and innocent, if we look carefully at Act 1, Scene 2, we notice that Macbeth possessed a hidden trait of brutality in him.

The Sergeant gives us a visual description of this brutality when Macbeth killed a man in battle:
"Till he unseamed him from the nave to the chops."

This foreshadows his murderous actions later in the play. Duncan called him "valiant cousin! Worthy gentleman". His burning desire to become king leads him to kill King Duncan. This leads him further into a series of killings, which is the catalyst for his ultimate destruction and death. He is confronted by the witches at the beginning of the play.

He was enamoured by their prediction that he will become the Thane of Cawdor and, ultimately, king. To his surprise, these predictions materialized, and he became hooked on the witches' words to the end.

In Act 1, Scene 1, the witches say, "Fair is foul, and foul is fair", and Macbeth actually echoed these words himself: "So foul and fair a day I have not seen." Hence, we can link him to the witches. He has now begun to evolve into a dark creature like the witches. He later expresses his intentions of killing Duncan as "black and deep desires".

In Act 1, Scene 7, we see a very troubled Macbeth suffering an inner conflict: "Must I do it or not." He decides against killing King Duncan and tells Lady Macbeth, "We will proceed no further in this business."

However, Lady Macbeth's manipulation and goading persuades him to kill Duncan. In Act 2, Scene 1, the audience experiences what is known as the dagger scene; Macbeth hallucinates and asks,
"Is this a dagger which I see before me?" Macbeth hallucinates, and he imagines a bloody dagger hovering in the air and pointing towards Duncan's room. He takes that as a sign that the dagger is guiding him into killing King Duncan.

The evil in him prepares him to carry out the deed: "I am settled and bend up." After he kills Duncan, he becomes paranoid and imagines hearing voices.

He is disturbed by his actions, and his conscience plagues him. As the witches predicted, he has become king; his next victim is Banquo and his son. He is now acting independently of Lady Macbeth.

The audience is shocked at how Macbeth has descended into anarchy, because he is consorting with murderers whom he hired to kill Banquo and his sons. In the banquet scene, he is terrified when he imagines seeing the ghost of Banquo. Once again, he is hallucinating, and we see a very disturbed and troubled Macbeth. Now he sees MacDuff as a threat ("Beware MacDuff") and decides to eliminate his family. While MacDuff fled, Macbeth ruthlessly slaughtered MacDuff's wife and son.

The killing of an innocent woman and child creates untold revulsion amongst the audience. The callous action of his infuriates MacDuff, and he is bent on taking revenge on Macbeth. In the end, we learn that the witches' prophecies have come true, and Macbeth realized, too late, that the "juggling fiends", known as the witches, had tricked him. When a messenger tells him that he saw the "woods moving", he was furious and angrily dismisses him. In Act 1, Scene 7, Macbeth kills young Siward, and, ultimately, his tragic downfall is climaxed when he is killed by MacDuff. MacDuff beheads him and brings his served head onto the stage fulfilling his desire for revenge.

LADY MACBETH

During the Jacobean period and the reign of James of England (1603 – 1625), women had little status. They were under the control of men and were not allowed to voice their opinions. Surprisingly, Lady Macbeth does not fit the stereotypical women of this period, because she is portrayed as having dominance over her husband ("Leave this night's business in my care"). Lady Macbeth is seen as a very controversial, unconventional character, especially to a contemporary audience. She is associated to the witches and can be seen as the 'fourth witch' because she consults with the supernatural in Act 1, Scene 5. She is a deeply ambitious woman who lusts after power and status.

Macbeth's letter tells her of his encounter with the witches and their prediction that he will become king; this fires up her zest to become queen. She will stop at nothing to achieve her ambition and urges Macbeth to kill Duncan and seize the crown. She uses persuasive adjectives like "worthy" and "my husband" to entice him, but, when she sees that he is reluctant to yield to her demands

"We will proceed no further in this business"

She becomes furious and belittles him, targeting his manhood

"And live a coward in thine own esteem."

She is ruthless in her attack of him. "When you durst do it, then you are a man". Shakespeare gives us a visual imagery of Lady Macbeth's speech when she ruthlessly says that if she had "given sucker" she would "pluck her baby while it was smiling and dash the brains out".

Here, her devious and ruthless personality is clearly visible, and the onomatopoeia "dash" gives the audience a sense of revulsion for her cruelty. Finally, Lady Macbeth manages to convince Macbeth to kill Duncan, and he relents: "I am settled and bend up." She prepares to kill Duncan, and she consults the supernatural for guidance. In Act 1, Scene 5, she says, "Unsex me." She wants to shed off her womanly wiles and become more like a man. Losing her femineity will enable her to be more cold and ruthless like a man ("Make thick my blood").

Shakespeare presents Lady Macbeth as close to being supernatural, and we see her very dark toned soliloquy where she is cavorting with the supernatural. Her desperation for power has become great. She is also presented as being bold and confident, because, when Macbeth asks, "If we should fail?", she tell him to

"screw your courage to the sticking place and we'll not fail".

Her evil intentions and immense power over Macbeth is clearly visible here.

She also tells him in Act 1 Scene 7 to "look like the innocent flower but be a serpent under it".

She wants him to pretend to be kind and sweet like a beautiful flower but maintain murderous intent when Duncan comes to the castle. After Macbeth kills Duncan and refuses to re-enter the scene of the crime, she is bold enough to go and place the bloody daggers on the sleeping guards. In the banquet scene, although, by now, she is quite isolated from Macbeth, she still dominates the scene. She knows exactly how to draw attention away from Macbeth, who feared the ghost of Banquo. She tells their guests to leave when she recognises that the situation was getting out of control. She very skilfully makes excuses for him, telling the guests that his reaction is borne from a sickness he has had since his youth and begs them to save him the embarrassment.

Earlier in the play, Macbeth is so surprised at Lady Macbeth's cold, calculating nature that he says, "Bring forth men children only."

Here, he is referring to her ruthless nature devoid of any feminine characteristics

"Take my milk for gall"

In Act 1, Scene 5, Lady Macbeth asks the supernatural to make her milk bitter as gall. This can be seen as mirroring Act 5, Scene 1. The gallbladder produces bile to break down fats, and, in the aforementioned scene, we can see a broken Lady Macbeth on the verge of death. She is hallucinating and this strong, ironclad lady is now a mere shadow of her former self. She is sleepwalking and ultimately reveals her guilt and torment since Duncan's death

"Yet who would have thought the old man to have so much blood?"

It is ironic, because, in Act 2, she tells Macbeth that "a little bit of water shall clear us of this deed". This can be compared to when she says "out damn spot, out," as she tries desperately to wash Duncan's bloodstains from her hands. She then commits suicide. When Macbeth was told that she has died, he shows acceptance and says, "She should have died hereafter."

We tend to sympathise with Lady Macbeth here, because she was able to redeem herself and show some remorse, "all the perfumes of Arabia will not sweeten this little hand." (Act 5 scene 1)

We can juxtapose her behaviour and attitude to her sins to Macbeth's. Macbeth was cold and ruthless right to the end, especially when he killed young Siward. He showed no remorse for his actions and fought to the end.

BANQUO

Banquo does not feature so prominently as Macbeth and Lady Macbeth. However, his role in the play is a vital one. Looking at the theme of good versus evil in the play, Banquo is seen as the opposite of Macbeth. He is good, loyal, and virtuous, whereas Macbeth represents the evil in the play.

Since both men had a supernatural experience with the witches, although with differing reactions to them, we can say that they are gothic doubles. These reactions to the prophecies provide a stark contrast between Macbeth and Banquo. Macbeth is immediately taken in by the witches' prophecies, and he is intrigued by them. However, Banquo is sceptical of them, and he challenges them:

"You should be woman and yet your beards forbid me to interpret that you are so."

Banquo was quite shocked at Macbeth's reaction to the witches and asks why he was "so rapt withal" at the witches' prophecies:

"Why do you start and seem to fear things that that do sound so fair?"

Banquo was said to be King James 1 ancestor, and that is why Shakespeare portrays him as a loyal and virtuous character. At the beginning of the play, he is presented as a courageous, noble character alongside Macbeth, receiving accolades from the king. He was shocked to learn that Macbeth has been awarded the title of Thane of Cawdor and says,

"What can the devil speak true?"

He associates the witches to the devil and evil. Although they prophesied that his sons will be kings, he was not overwhelmed by this revelation. Unlike Macbeth, who was mesmerized by the witches' prediction that he will be king, Banquo is cautious and warns Macbeth that

"the instruments of darkness tells us truths".

Banquo is a man of integrity and wisdom and resisted the temptation of the witches, thereby juxtaposing Macbeth's behaviour to his. He is loyal and honourable to the king, and he distances himself from Macbeth when he suspects that Macbeth will be overcome with greed for power

"thou playest most foully for it".

Banquo uses the clothing imagery when referring to Macbeth's success. He says,

"New honours come upon him, like our strange garments",

suggesting that Macbeth is not fit to be king, and he compares this to clothes that does not fit.

Ironically, Macbeth also uses the clothing imagery when he asks, "Why do you dress me in borrowed robes?" It's obvious that these garments do not belong to him but was forcefully taken from Duncan.

When Banquo and Duncan visit Macbeth's castle, Banquo remarks,

"Heaven's breath smells wooingly here."

He uses a biblical imagery, praising the castle's atmosphere, stating that "the air is delicate". Sadly, it was here, in these innocent looking surroundings, that Duncan was murdered. Banquo was too naïve and good to see the danger and deception that was lurking.

When Banquo tells Macbeth, "I dreamt last night of the three weird sisters", Macbeth lied to him saying, "I think not of them."

By now, Macbeth sees Banquo as a threat to his throne. When he asks Banquo to help him, promising he will reward him, Banquo refuses and says that he is loyal to the king. Banquo has now become a target for Macbeth. Macbeth is desperate to get rid of Banquo, so he hires two murderers to kill him.

He tells the murderers that Banquo is their enemy, and he needs to be eliminated:

"Both of you know Banquo was your enemy."

Macbeth also tells the murderers that Fleance,

"whose absence is no less material to me than his father's, must embrace the fate of that dark hour."

Shakespeare uses dark imagery reflecting Macbeth's dark thoughts about killing Banquo and Fleance.

The witches prophesied that Banquo's descendants will be king, and Macbeth, viewing this as a threat, decides to kill him. Banquo very gracefully agrees to go to the banquet at Macbeth's castle with his son Fleance.

Fleance is holding a torch, and the use of light image can suggest that Banquo wants Macbeth to see the light. Unfortunately, that torch was extinguished during the scuffle between the murderers and Banquo.

The extinguished torch can symbolise that Macbeth is left in the dark and is now doomed. Banquo is killed, and he shows his fatherly love to Fleance when he asks him to flee

"O, treachery! Fly, good Fleance, Fly, Fly, Fly! Thou mayest revenge. O Slave!".

Once again, Macbeth has violated the Divine Right of Kings by killing Banquo.

This scene ends with a distinct rhyming couplet:

"Banquo, thy soul's flight, if it finds heaven must find it out tonight".

Macbeth's ruthlessness is evident here when he tells Banquo to find heaven tonight.

The rhyming couplet "flight" and "night" suggest a finality to end Banquo's life. After Banquo's murder, Macbeth raises a toast at the banquet to Banquo, but he begins to hallucinate. He imagines the ghost of Banquo. One can infer that Banquo's last words before he died was

"Thou mayst revenge",

in part, done by taunting Macbeth with his ghostly appearance.

WITCHES

One of Shakespeare's greatest character creations in Macbeth is that of the witches. These mysterious, gothic creatures not only add spice and enigma to the play but also helps to develop the plot. They are responsible for much of the action, and their wit intrigues the readers. They appear at strategic points in the play creating much suspense and tension and always talking in rhymes and half-truths to trap Macbeth. The play was written during the reign of King James the first, and he had a particular interest in witches. He believed in them. Surprisingly, he wrote a book on witches in 1597. He firmly believed that witches existed and that they possessed supernatural powers.

Witches were used as scapegoats and they were always blamed for any malady in nature like the bad weather and ironically, they always appear in thunder and lightning. King James was a big fan of Shakespeare's plays, and he may have been inspired by the witches in King James' book Daemonologie, because they were similar to the witches in the play.

The play opens with the appearance of the witches in "thunder and lightning". Note Shakespeare's use of pathetic fallacy and the witches always appearing in boisterous, ferocious weather. This can tie up to the fact that they were always blamed for the bad weather in King James' rule. They also appear in the barren, wild heathland. Shakespeare creates an eerie and mysterious atmosphere that sets the tone and the pace of the dark events of death to follow.

To the Elizabethan audience, witches were seen as evil; they were condemned and executed. They were seen as "withered and so wild in their attire". They are responsible for the reversal of the normal order in both nature and man. They cause havoc and disruptions in nature; for example, they were responsible for Macbeth violating the divine right of kings by killing King Duncan. When Duncan was murdered, Ross and the old man talk about the reversal of the normal order and the disruption of nature:

"A falcon towering in her pride of place was by a mousing owl hawked and killed."

Lady Macbeth also mentions that the raven croaked "the fatal entrance of Duncan".

She also calls on the witches to "unsex" her, to make her more like a man.

The witches speak in blank verse, and their speeches have a certain rhythm and rhyme scheme to it ("done", "won"). This denotes a certain excitement to their tone; remember, their aim is to destroy Macbeth. They also speak in riddles and half-truths, which Macbeth only realises at the end. One can infer that they are singing a jubilant song because they are about to trick Macbeth

"Double, double toil and trouble. Fire burn and cauldron bubble".

When we look at the concoctions of the witches' brew, we can detect the extent of their evil

"Finger of birth strangled babe, scale of dragon, tooth of wolf."

Their famous song is a juxtaposition, "Fair is foul and foul is fair".

The evil witches rejoice in making mischief by making good things bad and bad things good. Ironically, these words were echoed by Macbeth: "So fair and foul a day I have not seen." It's obvious that this mirroring can be attributed to the fact that Macbeth is connected to the witches and eventually becomes evil like them. He thrusts his faith wholly on the witches' predictions from the beginning to the end, which culminates in his death.

He was not the "worthy Macbeth", as Duncan lovingly called him after all. When he goes to meet the witches, they say, "Something wicked this way comes." The witches have now certainly taken Macbeth into their fold and made him one of them. They knew that their predictions would fire up his greed and ambition, because they could "look into the seeds of time".

The evil of the witches can also be seen when one of them destroyed the sailor, because his wife refused to give her chestnuts. Banquo is very sceptical of the witches when he meets them

"look not like the inhabitants of the earth".

He says that they look like creatures from another world; they look like women

"yet your beards forbid me to interpret that you are so".

He cannot decipher which sex they belong to because they look like women, but they had beards.

These supernatural creatures certainly had a gothic air about them. Banquo was shocked at Macbeth's reaction to the witches' prophecies, and he says that he seems "rapt withal", meaning he is fascinated with the witches and their prophecies. Banquo further goads Macbeth about his reaction:

"Why do you start and seem to fear things that do sound so fair?"

When Macbeth was appointed the Thane of Cawdor, Banquo calls them the devil:

"What can the devil speak true?"

He does not trust the witches and knows that they are evil.

Although they predicted that his descendants would become kings, he was not impressed by their predictions as much as Macbeth was. Banquo warns Macbeth and says that,

"The instruments of darkness tells us truths."

The witches gave them many predictions

"All hail Macbeth! Thou shalt be king hereafter...Great Glamis! Worthy Cawdor".

When he visits them again in Act 4, Scene 1, they show him an armed head, a bloody child, a crowned child with a tree in his hand, and a row of eight kings with Banquo's ghost following. Since all their predictions after their first meeting came true, Macbeth puts his full faith on the witches' predictions. They tell him

"for none of woman born shall harm Macbeth";

unknown to him, MacDuff was born by Caesarean section. They also tell him that

"Macbeth shall never vanquished be
Until Great Birnam wood to high Dunsinane hill shall come against him".

In Act 5, Scene 5, when the messenger tells Macbeth,

"I looked toward Birnam methought the wood began to move",

Macbeth becomes furious, because the witches' prophecy was coming true. He yells at the messenger in fury "Liar and slave". At the end in Act 5, Scene 7, when MacDuff reveals that he

"was from his mother's womb untimely ripped"

Macbeth was shocked, and he curses the witches for telling him half-truths. He calls them "juggling fiends" and fights bravely to the very end.

AMBITION

The theme of ambition dominates the play, and it is the main contributory factor for Macbeth's rise and fall. Macbeth became a tragic hero. He fell from grace because of a flaw in his character; that flaw was his greed to fulfil his ambition to be king. During King James rule, kings were seen as next to God. It was believed that they were chosen by God and had a divine right to rule. If this right is violated, as Macbeth did by killing King Duncan, then there are serious consequences like death. Because of his vaulting ambition, Macbeth descended from a celebrated war hero to a serial murderer. Despite him summing up the good qualities Duncan had and the titles he gave him

"This Duncan hath borne his faculties so meek", Macbeth still decided to kill him.

Macbeth also suffered from an inner conflict at this stage ("Must I or must'nt I"), but his greed and ambition overruled that judgement, and he carried out his heinous crime of killing Duncan. One can argue that both Lady Macbeth and the witches had a huge influence on his decision. He told Lady Macbeth, "We will proceed no further in this business."

After much goading and manipulation from her ("If thou was man thou dost do it"), sadly, he finally relents to her wishes. The witches played with his mind and told him half-truths, but their prophecies spurred him on, and he believed them until his death. The question of free will kicks in here, and we think that he should be much stronger in a male dominated world.

These women ignited his ambition and his greed for power. At the beginning, he urges the witches to stay because he became excited with their prophecies ("Stay you imperfect creatures"). He even goes back to visit them in Act 4, and he begs them to tell him

"shall Banquo's issue ever reign in this kingdom".

He obviously saw Banquo as threat and decided to kill Banquo and his son. He became very bold and resolute, and he even worked independently of Lady Macbeth. He even stooped so low as to liaise with murderers who ruthlessly killed Banquo. Macbeth even lied to the murderers that "Banquo was an enemy of mine".

Macbeth was afraid that the witches had predicted that Banquo's sons will be king

"They placed a fruitless crown and put a barren sceptre in my gripe"

Now we can see how far his ambitious desires had made him sink to have his own friend Banquo killed.

Worse still, he has turned into a tyrant, cold and unfeeling, when he ordered the killing of Lady MacDuff and her innocent child. This "vaulting" ambition of his has reached levels of insanity because he goes on to kill right to the very end for ambitions sake. He also saw MacDuff as a threat because the witches told him to

"beware MacDuff, beware the thane of Fife".

Lady Macbeth plays a vital role in triggering the actions of greed and ambition. Ever since she received the letter from Macbeth, her burning desire to become queen can make her akin to the witches. She calls on the supernatural to "unsex me" and "make thick my blood" so that she will not feel any remorse or sympathy. She goads and manipulates Macbeth: "Was hope so drunk" to convince him into killing Duncan? She took the lead role and meticulously planned the murder of Duncan and succeeded.

TRAGIC HERO

Most of the action is concentrated on one character: Macbeth. Shakespeare traces his rise and fall. Hence, the play has a twofold structure. Lady Macbeth plays a pivotal role in moving the plot along because of the evil she concocts. Her character is spellbinding, and she intrigues the audience from Act 1, Scene 5 to the beginning of Act 3. The witches too move the plot along with their actions. They set the tone and the pace for the play.

They are also responsible for creating suspense and tension in the play. They also create the complication leading to the rising action in the play.

In Act 1 we see the exposition when they tell Macbeth that he will be king hence spurring on the rising action which adds to the complication. The climax of the play takes place in Act 2 when Macbeth kills Duncan. The rising tension here is palpable gripping the audience's attention and keeping them riveted. Lady Macbeth spurs on the action adding to the crisis in Act 2 because she skilfully plans the murder of Duncan.

We can trace Macbeth's guilt and his suspicions of Banquo, and this crisis leads him to kill Banquo. The focus moves onto the witches in Act 4 where Macbeth tries to resolve the situation by visiting the witches to ease his doubts. They give him several predictions, which leads to a catastrophe when MacDuff and Malcolm prepare to attack Macbeth. The climax is in Act 5, when Macbeth is killed and good overcame evil. Shakespeare writes in iambic pentameter. Most of the play is written in blank verse, which is unrhyming iambic pentameter because it is in a poetic form with rhyme schemes like the witches' speeches "When the hurlyburly's done, when the battle's lost and won".

Shakespeare also uses prose in his speeches, which is often spoken by the lower social classes like the porter

"Here's a knocking indeed! If a man were porter of hell-gate, he should have turning the key".

Compare the porter's speech to that of the witches, which have a distinct rhyme scheme. Shakespeare uses prose in other important scenes like the killing of MacDuff's family and Lady Macbeth's sleepwalking scene. In each of these scenes, something dramatic happens so the writer wants to get the audience emotionally involved because those are rather emotional scenes. Shakespeare also adds rhyming couplets to the end of each scene, perhaps to get the audience guessing about the plot.

APPEARANCE and Reality

Shakespeare makes use of appearance as a mask to contradict reality thus creating falsehoods to mask truth. This creates a schism where true actions are not revealed until the deed is done. The witches proclaim prophecies which appear to favour Macbeth but instead bring about his downfall.

Shakespeare is portraying what the audience knows is practiced in every day life: people deceive to gain an advantage. Macbeth is based on this, and it is reflected again and again in the language and imagery of the play.

In Act 1 scene 5, Lady Macbeth instructs her husband Macbeth in the deadly art of Appearance and reality

"look like th' innocent flower,
But be the serpent under't"

As Macbeth is deceived by the witches, so is King Duncan by Macbeth and his wife Lady Macbeth. In Act 1 scene 6. King Duncan arrives at Dunsinane castle, unaware that the hostess Lady Macbeth is the instigator in motivating Macbeth to murder. The appearance of hospitality masks the reality of murder to gain the crown.

Yet again, appearance in the form of illusions is real to Macbeth but not to Lady Macbeth or the guests at the Banquet in Act 3 scene 4.

Having deceived Duncan, in Act 4 scene 1 Macbeth is uncertain as to whether the prophecies are reality or not. He declares on being told Great Birnam Wood shall come against him,

"Who can impress the forest, bid the tree
Unfix his earthbound root?"

However, by Act 5 scene 5, Macbeth realises the truth that he has been deceived by the fiendish witches. Great Birnam Wood can come against him in the form of men camouflaged as trees! To the Messenger he replies,

"To doubt th' equivocation of the fiend
That lies like truth"

Reality is invariable hidden by appearance!

MACBETH

In the play Macbeth, many characters have many controversial aspects associated with them. A prime example is Lady Macbeth. In this essay, I will be covering how Lady Macbeth changes throughout the play. In Act 1, Scene 5, Lady Macbeth is seen as an unconventional character, especially to a contemporary audience. This is displayed when she says, "Unsex me here." This connects Lady Macbeth to the witches as, at that time, witches were seen as vindictive characters.

This is reinforced when she says she wants no "remorse", no "compunctious visitings of nature" to shake her "fell purpose". This shows her immediate dominance and ambition. In addition, the phrase 'crown to the toe' is effective as it presents Lady Macbeth as determined that she is practically the queen already. Furthermore, the use of the quotes "dunnest smoke of hell" and "keen blade" tell the reader that she wants "hell" to hide her "knife" as if guiding Macbeth. Additionally, the use of the silent "k" is "knife" reinforces the idea of secrecy, ultimately foreshadowing Duncan's death when they escape the blame. However, this contrasts to Act 5, Scene 1, where she uses a candle to protect her from "murky Hell".

In addition, the use of the phrase "take my milk for gall" foreshadows the state of Lady Macbeth in Act 5, Scene 1, as "gall" means bile. Bile is used for breaking things down, much like how Lady Macbeth was broken down.

In Act 2, Scene 2, Lady Macbeth is portrayed as a character unaffected by emotion and like a controller of Macbeth. For example, "Go get some water and wash this filthy witness from your hand." The use of the imperative verbs "go", "get", and "wash" are effective as it shows that Lady Macbeth is calm and resolute as well as firmly in control. In addition, the phrase "A foolish thought to say "a sorry sight"' conveys her nerves of steel; nothing can affect her emotions. Furthermore, this is reinforced by her statement "but I shame to wear a heart so white", meaning she is ashamed that she did not go through with the deed.

This contradicts Act 5, Scene 1, when she asks, "Will this hand ne'er be clean?" There is also a small flaw in her resolute mind, saying, "Had he not... I had done't." This creates a little element of guilt in Lady Macbeth's mind.

Lady Macbeth is portrayed as a protective yet reprimanding character in Act 3, Scene 4. For example, when she says "sit, worthy friends...regard him not". This paragraph is very effective as it removes some suspicion from the lords and thanes at the banquet.

However, when just with Macbeth, Lady Macbeth is as brutal as ever, targeting his manhood by saying, “Are you a man?” and “Oh proper… her grandam.” This scene reflects the first Act, particularly one moment in Act 1, Scene 5 when Lady Macbeth says, “Look like the innocent flower, but be the serpent under’t.”

In Act 5, Scene 1, Lady Macbeth appears as frail as well as a shadow of her former self. For example, her sleepwalking. Shakespeare’s use of sleepwalking is effective; in Jacobean society, sleepwalking was a sign of a guilty conscience. It is accurately described as ‘a great perturbation’. Furthermore, this scene is quite ironic as she is re-enacting Duncan’s murder; “will all great…from my hand” in Act 2, Scene 2 is a reflection of “all the great perfumes of … little hand”, showing she has turned into a guilty mess. Later, the quote ‘[t]he thane of fife had a wife:” is effective as the caesura ‘:’ is used very wisely.

One can imply that, through the use of the caesura, Lady Macbeth is reflecting on all those whose lives have been cut off during the play (as a caesura is used for to cut a sentence /line in half), reflecting her immediate guilt. This also foreshadows Act 5, Scene 5, when her life ends. In addition, the use of the phrase ‘knocking at the gate! Is effective as it relates back to Act 2, Scene 3, when the porter acted as the gatekeeper of Hell.

This shows her fear of hell, much like Macbeth in Act 1, Scene 5. Another connotation can be made about structure, which is that the repeated use of question marks is very effective as the shape of the question mark is very twisted, mirroring Lady Macbeth’s state of mind. This is reinforced by her recollections and speeches being disjointed and in non-chronological order.

SHAKESPEARE'S LADY MACBETH

Shakespeare presents Lady Macbeth as a power hungry and vindictive woman, whose character is against the stereotypes of a Jacobean woman. Shakespeare creates this unique character by changing Lady Macbeth's tone through carefully choosing her language choices and her line structure. Shakespeare presents Lady Macbeth as persuasive and as wanting more power. As soon as Macbeth is informed of the prophecy that he will be king, he tells Lady Macbeth. Lady Macbeth starts persuading Macbeth to kill the current king, King Duncan, and rule Scotland, with Lady Macbeth by his side. Macbeth opposes the idea of killing Duncan at first, but, at the end, he is broken, and Lady Macbeth's will be done.

This implies that Lady Macbeth is very persuasive and can control Macbeth. In the Jacobean era, the wife would not be able or allowed to argue with her husband; however, Lady Macbeth made Macbeth kill the king, which suggests that she wants to be powerful and doesn't care how she gets it. The theme in this scene is power and the hunger for it. Power is the fuel that Lady Macbeth craves and is the reason for many deaths.

Shakespeare presents Lady Macbeth as a deceptive woman, who uses the fact that she is a woman as a weapon ("Why, worthy thane, you do unbend your noble strength to think"). Lady Macbeth is talking to Macbeth. She begins by praising him ("worthy"); however, she ends the speech with orders and telling Macbeth that he did things wrong. She also accuses him of being "infirm of purpose". Macbeth would be proud of himself, because Lady Macbeth is his wife, and her opinion means a lot to him.

Lady Macbeth is skilful with words, such as 'worthy' and 'my husband'. Macbeth is the man in the relationship, but he still needs Lady Macbeth's praise and acceptance, which is against the stereotype, which is that the wife is to watch the kids, at home, and her husband succeeds in his chosen career, which implies Lady Macbeth is more than the normal Jacobean woman. This would intrigue the audience because they probably would never have thought that a woman would be as powerful to act like Lady Macbeth. The audience of males will be surprised and uncomfortable because this character is unusual. They would dislike and distrust her.

Shakespeare presents Lady Macbeth as close to being supernatural or a woman who wants to be a man. He does this by carefully choosing her language choices ("Unsex me here", "make thick my blood"). Lady Macbeth knows about the prophecy and the quotes are taken out of a soliloquy. The entire tone of the soliloquy is dark because of the vocabulary choices. Lady Macbeth is alone, which implies that anything she says and does is the true Lady Macbeth. "Come you spirits", she calls the spirits and asks them to "unsex" her; Lady Macbeth wants to be stripped of her feminine spirit and stereotypes. If you are a man, you can kill; kill King Duncan, and Macbeth will be king. This implies that she is desperate for power.

The second point is that she is talking to greater beings. This suggests that Lady Macbeth has some business with the supernatural, maybe the witches or that she is a witch. She could be mad and be talking to herself. "Smoke of hell" is a metaphor, referring to covering up whatever she might do. We can take it literally, as if this was a spell. We link hell to the devil; in the Jacobean era, women would give their souls and have intercourse with the devil in trade for their powers that will make them a witch. Therefore, the theory that Lady Macbeth is a witch is likely.

The theme is this scene is supernatural. This theme is important in the play because, without the witches, there would be no story. The audiences will be uncomfortable and quite scared of her because witches can kill people. They would be immersed into the play because of the plot. Shakespeare creates the impression that Lady Macbeth is more powerful and dominant in her relationship by changing the line structure and iambic pentameter.

When Lady Macbeth and Macbeth have a discussion in Act 3, Scene 2, Shakespeare allows Lady Macbeth to interrupt or end Macbeth's iambic pentameter, twice. This suggests that she is overpowering, which is against the stereotype. You must leave this' Lady Macbeth says to Macbeth. This is imperative, which you can link to wanting more power.

In conclusion, Lady Macbeth is a mysterious character, which leaves many questions for the audience. What is clear is that she is not a normal Jacobean woman; she wants power and the ability to control. The audience will dislike the character because she would not fit into society.

LADY MACBETH AS A POWERFUL CHARACTER?

The Macbeth scenes are generally intended to express tragedy in the play. Much of Act 1, Scene 5 is concentrated on Lady Macbeth, because she has dominance over her husband. The scene commences with Lady Macbeth in solitude. She receives a letter from Macbeth, informing her that he had been awarded the title Thane of Cawdor after a victorious battle. Macbeth also wrote that the witches predict he will replace Duncan as King. After reading the letter, Lady Macbeth learns that the King would come and stay at her palace. She immediately evokes spirits to "unsex" her by removing all traces of her femininity and sympathy. She later encourages Macbeth to develop their plan to murder King Duncan.

In the first scene, Shakespeare informed the audience of "thunder and lightning"; this provides a stereotypical view of something evil and sinister. This fits in with the conventions of tragedy, because we see that evil has immense power conveyed by the weather. Even more sinister, "three witches" appear suddenly; this is a traditional number of witches, resembling powerfulness, linking it in to the supernatural world of sinful spells.

Lady Macbeth seems more committed to the murder of King Duncan than Macbeth, because she is wholehearted in her actions, and Macbeth very much doubts the murder. He asks, "If we should fail", and she responds, "we fail?". This is an indication of her devotion to the murder, and she attempts to convince Macbeth it is inevitable. These quotes also tell us that Lady Macbeth has fated Macbeth to become a sinful murderer.

There is other evidence that Lady Macbeth is possessed by guilt in Act 5, Scene 1, there is a scene of her sleepwalking which in Elizabethan times was seen as a sign of a guilty conscience and the words she muttered had tormented her since the death of Duncan. "Banquo's buried; he cannot come out on's grave." Shakespeare has portrayed Lady Macbeth as a stereotypical villain. She invokes spirits to "unsex" her as femininity is often judged as a weakness. This collaborates with witchcraft, although femininity does not mix with the images she had created when drawing out spirits: "the raven himself is hoarse" and "take my milk for gall".

This is a distinct trade of femininity for power. Instead of suckling new life with mother's milk, she will trade it for the power to do what must be done, even if that is only in the form of an emotional numbness.

She provokes evil to control Macbeth, as she responds to him after reading his letter: "Look like the innocent flower but be the serpent under't". This is part of her malicious plan to degrade Macbeth's masculinity until he follows her commands. As she recognises Macbeth's weakness, Lady Macbeth gains confidence and power.

Macbeth - Macbeth is a Scottish general and the thane of Glamis who is led to wicked thoughts by the prophecies of the three witches, especially after their prophecy that he will be made thane of Cawdor comes true. Macbeth is a brave soldier and a powerful man, but he is not a virtuous one. He is easily tempted into murder to fulfil his ambitions to the throne, and, once he commits his first crime and is crowned King of Scotland, he embarks on further atrocities with increasing ease.

Ultimately, Macbeth proves himself better suited to the battlefield than to political intrigue, because he lacks the skills necessary to rule without being a tyrant. His response to every problem is violence and murder. Unlike Shakespeare's great villains, such as lago in Othello and Richard III in Richard III, Macbeth is never comfortable in his role as a criminal. He is unable to bear the psychological consequences of his atrocities.

Lady Macbeth - Macbeth's wife, a deeply ambitious woman who lusts for power and position. Early in the play, she seems to be the stronger and more ruthless of the two, as she urges her husband to kill Duncan and seize the crown. After the bloodshed begins, however, Lady Macbeth falls victim to guilt and madness to an even greater degree than her husband. Her conscience affects her to such an extent that she eventually commits suicide.

Interestingly, she and Macbeth are presented as being deeply in love, and many of Lady Macbeth's speeches imply that her influence over her husband is primarily sexual. Their joint alienation from the world, occasioned by their partnership in crime, seems to strengthen the attachment that they feel to each another.

The **Three Witches** - Three "black and midnight hags" who plot mischief against Macbeth using charms, spells, and prophecies. Their predictions prompt him to murder Duncan, to order the deaths of Banquo and his son, and to blindly believe in his own immortality. The play leaves the witches' identity unclear; aside from the fact that they are servants of Hecate, we know little about their place in the cosmos.

In some ways, they resemble the mythological Fates, who impersonally weave the threads of human destiny. They clearly take a perverse delight in using their knowledge of the future to toy with and destroy human beings.

Banquo - The brave, noble general whose children, according to the witches' prophecy, will inherit the Scottish throne. Like Macbeth, Banquo thinks ambitious thoughts, but he does not translate those thoughts into actions.

RESOLUTION OF MACBETH'S CONFLICT (ACT 2 scene 1)

Macbeth is one of Shakespeare's most popular plays. In Act 2, Scene 1, Macbeth's conflict varies from whether or not he should kill Duncan. The witch's prophecies and Lady Macbeth's pushiness are two vital ingredients that contribute to Macbeth's conflict. Macbeth resolves his inner conflict in Act 2, Scene 1 by killing the king. On the other hand, in Act 1, Scene 7, Lady Macbeth, who belittles Macbeth and attacks his man hood, persuades him to kill King Duncan. By the end of the scene, he looks convinced because she targets his soft spot: his bravery. "But screw your courage to the sticking place"; Lady Macbeth tells Macbeth to suck it up and be a man. From this point on, Macbeth is determined to fulfil his promise.

In addition, Lady Macbeth said she would dash the brains out of her newborn baby "had I so sworn as you have done to this". She tells him if she had made a promise as big as his, she would go through with it. I don't think any woman is capable of killing her own baby. However, Lady Macbeth says this to show her strength and that she shows no mercy. This is to hide her cold, calculative, and manipulative motives. However, deep down, she's weak and vulnerable like any other woman back in Shakespeare's day.

Shakespeare's purpose of this scene is to show Macbeths inner conflict through dramatic irony. This scene shows the doubt and emotional struggle Macbeth is still having just before he kills Duncan. The dramatic irony is useful for the audience, because they get to see the vivid image inside Macbeth's head (the worry, guilt, and doubt he is having). This soliloquy helps Macbeth think about what he hasn't already thought about, 'bloody business' Macbeth doesn't think about how messy and bloody the murders going to be, but during this dramatic irony he realises how atrocious it will be.

The Shakespearean audience are captured by magical imagery from the theme of witchcraft because it was so common back then. However, now people don't think witches exist, they would say its superstitions. We aren't supposed to like Macbeth because what he is doing is wrong, but we should understand him. Macbeth isn't naturally evil, but he has a breaking point that leads to his choices in Act 2.

The Shakespearean audience wouldn't have liked Macbeth at all because plotting or thinking about killing the king was consider a treasonous thought and they would hate anyone who tried to harm the "rightful king". But a modern-day audience would understand how he's feeling inside; we would feel sorry for him, although what he's doing is wrong.

It's partly because we don't believe in the supernatural and treason now is not as big as back then. Someone won't get arrested for saying they hate the king in public, whereas, back then, there was a big chance you would have. When Macbeth enters in Act 2, Scene 1, he is given a diamond ring by Banquo. Banquo tells him that it is a gift for Lady Macbeth from King Duncan for her boundless hospitality. This is ironic, because she is plotting against him ("This diamond he greets your wife"). At this point, Macbeth feels guilty because he is about to commit a horrendous crime and the king has just sent a ring for his wife. How can he go through with this? After all, he has been awarded the title Thane of Cawdor for being a brave and heroic soldier. Banquo mentions he had a dream about the "three weird sisters", that they have shown "some truth" to Macbeth, specifically about him becoming Thane of Cawdor. This hits a soft spot in Macbeth, and he tries to edge away from the topic by saying, "I think not of them." He's not pleased Banquo has mentioned this. He doesn't like the fact that Banquo still thinks of them, especially because he is about to commit regicide.

Macbeth's soliloquy is very important. It starts with Macbeth hallucinating, as he sees a floating dagger, its handle towards Macbeth and the tip pointing towards Duncan's chamber. He tries to clutch the handle but doesn't succeed 'let me clutch thee', this is a clear indication of the emotional conflict Macbeth suffers as he tries to clutch an invisible dagger, and later on in we see this conflict resolved as Macbeth goes to kill the king.

Macbeth can interpret the 'dagger' in different ways; it could be used as a guide to Duncan's chamber.

The dagger can be a warning, telling Macbeth that what he is about to do is wrong, or it could be a representative of the supernatural, taunting Macbeth to kill Duncan. Shakespeare lets the audience interpret this in whatever manner they want; he doesn't specifically say Macbeth uses the dagger as a guide to Duncan's chamber. He says, "The handle toward my hand? Come, let me clutch thee." It is up to us, the audience, to decide how Macbeth uses his distinct imagination of the dagger.

Macbeth's second emotional change is when he sees thick drops of blood on the blade of the dagger; as a symbol, this imagined blood has the biggest impact. Macbeth moves towards the dagger, but, when blood appears on it, he pauses to rethink his course of action ("And on thy blade and dudgeon gouts of blood").

He doesn't realise that murder is a messy crime. Although it's a silly thing to think, of course stabbing requires the presence of blood; this is how Macbeth's inner conflict is shown. Blood gives Macbeth a jolt of unease; he doesn't like the fact that his hands will be covered in the blood of a man who trusted him. This gives him a guilty conscious.

Another interpretation could be that he understands "it is the bloody business which informs", but he is not horrified, nor does he feel guilty. Actually, he wants attempt to be as deadly and bloody as that dagger. I disagree with this, because when blood appears on the dagger Macbeth is taken aback; he realises how messy the murder is going to be and therefore feels guilty.

The third emotional change Macbeth has is the supernatural ("Pale Hecate's offerings; and wither'd Murder"). Macbeth blames the supernatural for what he is seeing; he believes the witches are tampering with his head in order to compel him to evil. The dagger encourages Macbeth to commit the crime; at the same time, it shows the audience that what Macbeth is about to do is evil. Shakespeare uses the supernatural to show the audience what evil is. Through the play, you begin to notice that the supernatural is used in all instances where evil is present. Macbeth's conflict is resolved at the end of the scene after the bell has rung; Shakespeare uses witchcraft to set the mood for the scene and the bell symbolises Macbeth's strength ("I go, and it is done; the bell invites me"). The sound of the bell gives Macbeth the power and courage to complete his ambition; it's as if he's forgotten what just happened and started a new chapter.

In Macbeth's soliloquy, Shakespeare uses personification when Macbeth talks to the dagger, as if it were a person ("I have thee not, and yet I see thee still"). He becomes obsessed and possessed, horrified by what he is about to do. He uses repetition ("bloody business" and "gouts of blood") to emphasise and draw attention to the word blood. A metaphor is presented in Macbeth's soliloquy ("A dagger of the mind"); it foreshadows what happens after Duncan's death. The dagger is like Duncan, no longer present but always in Macbeth's mind. Antithesis is used at the end; "heaven" and "hell" are deliberately chosen to contrast the options in front of Macbeth; this highlights his inner conflict. Duncan is likely to go to heaven, but could he go to hell?

The bell is a form of auditory imagery and an offstage theatrical device to indicate a passing of time. In addition, it had a double meaning; it is a signal telling Macbeth that the guards have been drugged and is summoning King Duncan to his grave. Shakespeare doesn't use any other murder weapon apart from a dagger. He uses this because "dagger" is the only word that would fit in iambic pentameter. The dagger represents the bloody course on which Macbeth is about to embark.

Another perspective would be that Shakespeare uses the word "dagger" because it's not as commonly used as knife. Macbeth sees a dagger as a symbol of his own betrayal of Duncan.

Shakespeare uses many semi colons and colons in Macbeth's soliloquy to show his emotional change. Semi colons are very important, because they are interpreted by an actor on stage. This allows them to make either long or short pauses where they are needed ("I see thee still;"). The semi colon is a long pause; it is there because Macbeth has just seen blood on the dagger, and he's in denial, showing how taken aback he is and that he's got a lot on his mind. You can tell by the way someone speaks when they have a lot on their mind; they have frequent long pauses, and they speak quite slowly. Long pauses help the audience think about what's going on, giving them time to reflect.

If Macbeth was calm, Shakespeare wouldn't have used semicolons and colon because they're used when somebody is rethinking, in doubt, or when confused or shocked. If Macbeth was calm, there would be no need of them. However, Shakespeare would use commas to make a brief pause and help the speech flow. The atmosphere for this scene would be calm and airy as Banquo, Fleance, and Macbeth stand in Macbeth's courtyard. On stage, the scene would be dark, and there would be no props apart from the floating dagger if the director chooses to have one.

Shakespeare uses "thou marshall'st me the way that I was going to be"; if interpreted by the actor, this line is an indication that Macbeth is moving toward the floating dagger whilst having his drawn. Macbeth doesn't gracefully walk towards the dagger; he moves slowly with frequent pauses. This is because he's confused, and he doesn't know if he should follow the dagger; this reveals his inner turmoil to the audience. In this scene, Macbeth suffers from a lot of inner conflict; this begins when Banquo gives him the ring through his third emotional change about the supernatural. At the end of this scene, we feel gutted, because Macbeth didn't change his mind, but we also understand that his ambition took the best of him.

By the end of the scene, Macbeth's conflict is resolved, but not in the manner the audience would have liked it. The Shakespearean audience would be furious at Macbeth as he goes to kill the king. In their head, Macbeth is truly evil, and they would hate Macbeth even more after this scene.

EXAM STYLE QUESTIONS

Macbeth

Read the following extract from **Act 1 Scene 3** of Macbeth and then answer the question that follows.

At this point in the play, Macbeth is speaking to Banquo. Macbeth and Banquo meet the witches on their way home from war.

MACBETH So foul and fair a day I have not seen.
BANQUO How far is't call'd to Forres? What are these
So wither'd and so wild in their attire,
That look not like the inhabitants o' the earth,
And yet are on't? Live you? or are you aught
That man may question? You seem to understand me,
By each at once her choppy finger laying
Upon her skinny lips: you should be women,
And yet your beards forbid me to interpret
That you are so.
MACBETH Speak, if you can: what are you?
First Witch All hail, Macbeth! hail to thee, thane of Glamis!
Second Witch All hail, Macbeth, hail to thee, thane of Cawdor!
Third Witch All hail, Macbeth, thou shalt be king hereafter!
BANQUO Good sir, why do you start; and seem to fear
Things that do sound so fair?

Starting with this speech, explain how far you think Shakespeare presents the Witches in Macbeth to be evil.
Write about:

- How Shakespeare presents the Witches in this extract
- How far you think Shakespeare presents the Witches as evil in the play as a whole.

Macbeth

Read the following extract from **Act 1 Scene 3** of Macbeth and then answer the question that follows.

At this point in the play, Ross and Angus greet Macbeth. They tell him that he is now Thane of Cawdor and that Macdonald has been put to death for treason.

ROSS And, for an earnest of a greater honour,
He bade me, from him, call thee thane of Cawdor:
In which addition, hail, most worthy thane!
For it is thine.
BANQUO What, can the devil speak true?
MACBETH The thane of Cawdor lives: why do you dress me
In borrow'd robes?
ANGUS Who was the thane lives yet;
But under heavy judgment bears that life
Which he deserves to lose. Whether he was combined
With those of Norway, or did line the rebel
With hidden help and vantage, or that with both
He labour'd in his country's wrack, I know not;
But treasons capital, confess'd and proved,
Have overthrown him.
MACBETH *Aside.*
Glamis, and Thane of Cawdor:
The greatest is behind.

Starting with this speech, explain how Shakespeare presents ambition in Macbeth.
Write about:

- How Shakespeare presents ambition in this speech
- How Shakespeare presents ambition in the play as a whole.

Macbeth

Read the following extract from **Act 1 Scene 3** of Macbeth and then answer the question that follows.

At this point in the play, Macbeth is speaking. He has just received news that he is now the Thane of Cawdor and he is considering what the Witches have said.

MACBETH *Aside.*
This supernatural soliciting
Cannot be ill, cannot be good: if ill,
Why hath it given me earnest of success,
Commencing in a truth? I am thane of Cawdor:
If good, why do I yield to that suggestion
Whose horrid image doth unfix my hair
And make my seated heart knock at my ribs,
Against the use of nature? Present fears
Are less than horrible imaginings:
My thought, whose murder yet is but fantastical,
Shakes so my single state of man that function
Is smother'd in surmise, and nothing is
But what is not.
BANQUO Look, how our partner's rapt.
MACBETH *Aside.*
If chance will have me king, why, chance may crown me,
Without my stir.
BANQUO New honours come upon him,
Like our strange garments, cleave not to their mould
But with the aid of use.

Starting with this speech, explain how far you think Shakespeare presents the witches and supernatural events to influence Macbeth's decisions.
Write about:
- How Shakespeare presents Macbeth's reaction to the witches in this scene
- How Shakespeare presents the effect of the Witches on Macbeth in the play as a whole.

Macbeth

Read the following extract from **Act 1 Scene 5** of Macbeth and then answer the question that follows.

At this point in the play, Lady Macbeth is speaking. She has received a letter from Macbeth who has told her about the witches.

LADY MACBETH *Reads Macbeth's letter*

Glamis thou art, and Cawdor; and shalt be
What thou art promised: yet do I fear thy nature;
It is too full o' the milk of human kindness
To catch the nearest way: thou wouldst be great;
Art not without ambition, but without
The illness should attend it: what thou wouldst highly,
That wouldst thou holily; wouldst not play false,
And yet wouldst wrongly win: thou'ldst have, great Glamis,
That which cries 'Thus thou must do, if thou have it;
And that which rather thou dost fear to do
Than wishest should be undone.' Hie thee hither,
That I may pour my spirits in thine ear;
And chastise with the valour of my tongue
All that impedes thee from the golden round,
Which fate and metaphysical aid doth seem
To have thee crown'd withal

Starting with this speech, explain how far you think Shakespeare presents Lady Macbeth as a powerful woman.

Write about:

- How Shakespeare presents Lady Macbeth in this speech
- How Shakespeare presents Lady Macbeth as a powerful woman in the play as a whole.

Macbeth

Read the following extract from **Act 1 Scene 5** of Macbeth and then answer the question that follows.

At this point in the play, Macbeth and Lady Macbeth are talking. Lady Macbeth is informing Macbeth of her plans for King Duncan who will be visiting.

LADY MACBETH O, never
Shall sun that morrow see!
Your face, my thane, is as a book where men
May read strange matters.To beguile the time,
Look like the time; bear welcome in your eye,
Your hand, your tongue: look like the innocent flower,
But be the serpent under't. He that's coming
Must be provided for: and you shall put
This night's great business into my dispatch;
Which shall to all our nights and days to come
Give solely sovereign sway and masterdom.
MACBETH We will speak further.
LADY MACBETH Only look up clear;
To alter favour ever is to fear:
Leave all the rest to me

Starting with this speech, explain how Shakespeare presents the relationship of Macbeth and Lady Macbeth.
Write about:

- How Shakespeare presents their relationship in this speech
- How Shakespeare presents their relationship in the play as a whole

Macbeth

Read the following extract from **Act 1 Scene 7** of Macbeth and then answer the question that follows.

At this point in the play, Macbeth is speaking. He is considering whether or not to murder King Duncan who sleeps at his castle that night.

MACBETH
He's here in double trust;
First, as I am his kinsman and his subject,
Strong both against the deed; then, as his host,
Who should against his murderer shut the door,
Not bear the knife myself. Besides, this Duncan
Hath borne his faculties so meek, hath been
So clear in his great office, that his virtues
Will plead like angels, trumpet-tongued, against
The deep damnation of his taking-off;
And pity, like a naked new-born babe,
Striding the blast, or heaven's cherubim, horsed
Upon the sightless couriers of the air
Shall blow the horrid deed in every eye,
That tears shall drown the wind. I have no spur
To prick the sides of my intent, but only
Vaulting ambition, which o'erleaps itself
And falls on the other.

Starting with this speech, explain how far you think Shakespeare presents Macbeth to be uncertain of his decisions.

Write about:

- How Shakespeare presents Macbeth's feelings of uncertainty in this speech
- How Shakespeare presents Macbeth to be uncertain of his decisions in the play as a whole.

Macbeth

Read the following extract from **Act 1 Scene 7** of Macbeth and then answer the question that follows.

At this point in the play, Macbeth and Lady Macbeth are talking. Lady Macbeth is persuading Macbeth to agree to the plan to kill King Duncan.

MACBETH
Prithee, peace:
I dare do all that may become a man;
Who dares do more is none.
LADY MACBETH
What beast was't, then,
That made you break this enterprise to me?
When you durst do it, then you were a man;
And, to be more than what you were, you would
Be so much more the man. Nor time nor place
Did then adhere, and yet you would make both:
They have made themselves, and that their fitness now
Does unmake you. I have given suck, and know
How tender 'tis to love the babe that milks me:
I would, while it was smiling in my face,
Have pluck'd my nipple from his boneless gums,
And dash'd the brains out, had I so sworn as you
Have done to this.
MACBETH
If we should fail?
LADY MACBETH
We fail!
But screw your courage to the sticking-place,
And we'll not fail

Starting with this speech, explain how far you think Shakespeare presents Macbeth as a brave man.
Write about:

- How Shakespeare presents attitudes to bravery in this speech
- How Shakespeare presents bravery in the play as a whole.

Macbeth

Read the following extract from **Act 2 Scene 1** of Macbeth and then answer the question that follows.

At this point in the play, Macbeth is speaking. He is planning to murder King Duncan and he sees a dagger.

MACBETH
Is this a dagger which I see before me,
The handle toward my hand? Come, let me clutch thee.
I have thee not, and yet I see thee still.
Art thou not, fatal vision, sensible
To feeling as to sight? Or art thou but
A dagger of the mind, a false creation,
Proeeding from the heat-oppressed brain?
I see thee yet, in form as palpable
As this which now I draw.
Thou marshall'st me the way that I was going;
And such an instrument I was to use.
Mine eyes are made the fools o' the other senses,
Or else worth all the rest; I see thee still,
And on thy blade and dudgeon gouts of blood,
Which was not so before. There's no such thing:
It is the bloody business which informs
Thus to mine eyes.

Starting with this speech, explain how Shakespeare presents death in Macbeth.
Write about:
- How Shakespeare presents attitudes to death in this speech
- How Shakespeare presents death in the play as a whole.

Macbeth

Read the following extract from **Act 2 Scene 2** of Macbeth and then answer the question that follows.

At this point in the play, Macbeth and Lady Macbeth are speaking. They have murdered King Duncan as he slept in the castle.

MACBETH [Within]Who's there? what, ho!
LADY MACBETH Alack, I am afraid they have awaked,
And 'tis not done. The attempt and not the deed
Confounds us. Hark! I laid their daggers ready;
He could not miss 'em. Had he not resembled
My father as he slept, I had done't.
Enter MACBETH
My husband!
MACBETH I have done the deed. Didst thou not hear a noise?
LADY MACBETH I heard the owl scream and the crickets cry.
Did not you speak?
MACBETH When?
LADY MACBETH Now.
MACBETH As I descended?
LADY MACBETH Ay.
MACBETH Hark!
Who lies I' the second chamber?
LADY MACBET Donalbain.
MACBETH This is a sorry sight.
Looking on his hands
LADY MACBETH A foolish thought, to say a sorry sight

Starting with this speech, explain how Shakespeare presents the effects of guilt in Macbeth.
Write about:

- How Shakespeare presents guilt in this speech
- How Shakespeare presents the effects of guilt in the play as a whole.

Macbeth

Read the following extract from **Act 2 Scene 2** of Macbeth and then answer the question that follows.

At this point in the play, Macbeth and Lady Macbeth are speaking. Macbeth is discussing the murder of King Duncan with Lady Macbeth.

MACBETH
One cried 'God bless us!' and 'Amen' the other;
As they had seen me with these hangman's hands.
Listening their fear, I could not say 'Amen,'
When they did say 'God bless us!'
LADY MACBETH
Consider it not so deeply.
MACBETH
But wherefore could not I pronounce 'Amen'?
I had most need of blessing, and 'Amen'
Stuck in my throat.
LADY MACBETH
These deeds must not be thought
After these ways; so, it will make us mad.
MACBETH
Methought I heard a voice cry 'Sleep no more!
Macbeth does murder sleep', the innocent sleep,
Sleep that knits up the ravell'd sleeve of care,
The death of each day's life, sore labour's bath,
Balm of hurt minds, great nature's second course,
Chief nourisher in life's feast,-

Starting with this speech, explain how far you think Shakespeare presents Macbeth and Lady Macbeth to regret their actions.
Write about:
- How Shakespeare presents regret in this speech
- How Shakespeare presents regret in the play as a whole.

Macbeth

Read the following extract from **Act 2 Scene 2** of Macbeth and then answer the question that follows.

At this point in the play, Macbeth and Lady Macbeth are speaking. Macbeth has just murdered Duncan at his castle.

MACBETH I'll go no more:
I am afraid to think what I have done;
Look on't again I dare not.
LADY MACBETH Infirm of purpose!
Give me the daggers: the sleeping and the dead
Are but as pictures: 'tis the eye of childhood
That fears a painted devil. If he do bleed,
I'll gild the faces of the grooms withal;
For it must seem their guilt.
[*Exit. Knocking within*]
MACBETH Whence is that knocking?
How is't with me, when every noise appals me?
What hands are here? ha! they pluck out mine eyes.
Will all great Neptune's ocean wash this blood
Clean from my hand? No, this my hand will rather
The multitudinous seas in incarnadine,
Making the green one red.
[*Re-enter LADY MACBETH*]
LADY MACBETH My hands are of your colour; but I shame
To wear a heart so white

Starting with this speech, explain how far you think Shakespeare presents Macbeth to have troubled thoughts.
Write about:

- How Shakespeare presents Macbeth's troubled thoughts in this speech
- How Shakespeare presents troubled thoughts in the play as a whole.

Macbeth

Read the following extract from **Act 3 Scene 1** of Macbeth and then answer the question that follows.

At this point in the play, Macbeth is speaking. He is discussing his fear of Banquo who was with him when he met the witches.

MACBETH

To be thus is nothing;
But to be safely thus.--Our fears in Banquo
Stick deep; and in his royalty of nature
Reigns that which would be fear'd: 'tis much he dares;
And, to hat dauntless temper of his mind,
He hath a wisdom that doth guide his valour
To act in safety. There is none but he
Whose being I do fear: and, under him,
My Genius is rebuked; as, it is said,
Mark Antony's was by Caesar. He chid the sisters
When first they put the name of king upon me,
And bade them speak to him: then prophet-like
They hail'd him father to a line of kings:
Upon my head they placed a fruitless crown,
And put a barren sceptre in my gripe,
Thence to be wrench'd with an unlineal hand,
No son of mine succeeding

Starting with this speech, explain how far you think Shakespeare presents Macbeth to have troubled thoughts.
Write about:
- How Shakespeare presents Macbeth's troubled thoughts in this speech
- How Shakespeare presents troubled thoughts in the play as a whole.

Macbeth

Read the following extract from **Act 3 Scene 2** of Macbeth and then answer the question that follows.

At this point in the play, Macbeth and Lady Macbeth are speaking. They are discussing their feelings after the murder of Duncan and Macbeth's fear now that he is King.

LADY MACBETH Nought's had, all's spent,
Where our desire is got without content:
'Tis safer to be that which we destroy
Than by destruction dwell in doubtful joy.
Enter MACBETH
How now, my lord! why do you keep alone,
Of sorriest fancies your companions making,
Using those thoughts which should indeed have died
With them they think on? Things without all remedy
Should be without regard: what's done is done.
MACBETH We have scotch'd the snake, not kill'd it:
She'll close and be herself, whilst our poor malice
Remains in danger of her former tooth.
But let the frame of things disjoint, both the worlds suffer,
Ere we will eat our meal in fear and sleep
In the affliction of these terrible dreams
That shake us nightly: better be with the dead,
Whom we, to gain our peace, have sent to peace,
Than on the torture of the mind to lie
In restless ecstasy. Duncan is in his grave;
After life's fitful fever he sleeps well;
Treason has done his worst: nor steel, nor poison,
Malice domestic, foreign levy, nothing,
Can touch him further.

Starting with this speech, explain how far you think Shakespeare presents Macbeth and Lady Macbeth to be unhappy.
Write about:

- How Shakespeare presents unhappiness in this extract
- How Shakespeare presents unhappiness in the play as a whole.

Macbeth

Read the following extract from **Act 3 Scene 4** of Macbeth and then answer the question that follows.

At this point in the play, Macbeth is speaking. At the banquet, he has just seen the ghost of Banquo who has been murdered.

MACBETH Thou canst not say I did it: never shake
Thy gory locks at me.
ROSS Gentlemen, rise: his highness is not well.
LADY MACBETH Sit, worthy friends: my lord is often thus,
And hath been from his youth: pray you, keep seat;
The fit is momentary; upon a thought
He will again be well: if much you note him,
You shall offend him and extend his passion:
Feed, and regard him not. Are you a man?
MACBETH Ay, and a bold one, that dare look on that
Which might appal the devil.
LADY MACBETH O proper stuff!
This is the very painting of your fear:
This is the air-drawn dagger which, you said,
Led you to Duncan. O, these flaws and starts,
Impostors to true fear, would well become
A woman's story at a winter's fire,
Authorized by her grandam. Shame itself!
Why do you make such faces?
When all's done,
You look but on a stool.

Starting with this speech, explain how Shakespeare presents the effect of betrayal.
Write about:
- How Shakespeare presents betrayal in this speech
- How Shakespeare presents betrayal in the play as a whole.

Macbeth

Read the following extract from **Act 4 Scene 1** of Macbeth and then answer the question that follows.

At this point in the play, Macbeth visits the Witches to demand answers to his questions.

Second Witch	By the pricking of my thumbs, Something wicked this way comes. Open, locks, Whoever knocks!
Enter MACBETH	
MACBETH	How now, you secret, black, and midnight hags! What is't you do?
ALL	A deed without a name.
MACBETH	I conjure you, by that which you profess, Howe'er you come to know it, answer me: Though you untie the winds and let them fight Against the churches; though the yesty waves Confound and swallow navigation up; Though bladed corn be lodged and trees blown down; Though castles topple on their warders' heads; Though palaces and pyramids do slope Their heads to their foundations; though the treasure Of nature's germens tumble all together, Even till destruction sicken; answer me To what I ask you.
First Witch	Speak.
Second Witch	Demand.
Third Witch	We'll answer

Starting with this speech, explain how far you think Shakespeare presents Macbeth as a changed man.
Write about:

- How Shakespeare presents Macbeth in this speech
- How Shakespeare presents Macbeth as a changed man in the play as a whole.

In **Act 5 scene 3**, how does Shakespeare present paranoia and obsession?

Macbeth

Read the following extract from **Act 4 Scene 2** of Macbeth and then answer the question that follows.

At this point in the play, Lady Macduff has found out that her husband Macduff has fled Scotland to join the rebel army in England.

LADY MACDUFF What had he done, to make him fly the land?
ROSS You must have patience, madam.
LADY MACDUFF He had none:
His flight was madness: when our actions do not,
Our fears do make us traitors.
ROSS You know not
Whether it was his wisdom or his fear.
LADY MACDUFF Wisdom! to leave his wife, to leave his babes,
His mansion and his titles in a place
From whence himself does fly? He loves us not;
He wants the natural touch: for the poor wren,
The most diminutive of birds, will fight,
Her young ones in her nest, against the owl.
All is the fear and nothing is the love;
As little is the wisdom, where the flight
So runs against all reason

Starting with this speech, explain how Shakespeare presents fear and bravery in the play.
Write about:

- How Shakespeare presents fear and bravery in this speech
- How Shakespeare presents fear and bravery in the play as a whole.

In **Act 3 scene 2**, how does Shakespeare present deceitfulness in the play?

Macbeth

Read the following extract from **Act 4 Scene 3** of Macbeth and then answer the question that follows.

At this point in the play, Macduff is in England and Malcolm is testing Macduff's loyalty to Scotland.

MACDUFF
Fit to govern!
No, not to live. O nation miserable,
With an untitled tyrant bloody-scepter'd,
When shalt thou see thy wholesome days again,
Since that the truest issue of thy throne
By his own interdiction stands accursed,
And does blaspheme his breed? Thy royal father
Was a most sainted king: the queen that bore thee,
Oftener upon her knees than on her feet,
Died every day she lived. Fare thee well!
These evils thou repeat'st upon thyself
Have banish'd me from Scotland. O my breast,
Thy hope ends here!

MALCOLM
Macduff, this noble passion,
Child of integrity, hath from my soul
Wiped the black scruples, reconciled my thoughts
To thy good truth and honour. Devilish Macbeth
By many of these trains hath sought to win me
Into his power, and modest wisdom plucks me
From over-credulous haste: but God above
Deal between thee and me!

Starting with this speech, explain how Shakespeare presents the importance of trust in the play.
Write about:

- How Shakespeare presents the importance of trust in this speech
- How Shakespeare presents the importance of trust in the play as a whole.

Macbeth

Read the following extract from **Act 4 Scene 3** of Macbeth and then answer the question that follows.

At this point in the play, Macduff has found out that his wife and children have been killed.

MALCOLM Be comforted:
Let's make us medicines of our great revenge,
To cure this deadly grief.
MACDUFF He has no children.All my pretty ones?
Did you say all? O hell-kite! All?
What, all my pretty chickens and their dam
At one fell swoop?
MALCOLM Dispute it like a man.
MACDUFF I shall do so;
But I must also feel it as a man:
I cannot but remember such things were,
That were most precious to me. Did heaven look on,
And would not take their part? Sinful Macduff,
They were all struck for thee! naught that I am,
Not for their own demerits, but for mine,
Fell slaughter on their souls. Heaven rest them now!
MALCOLM Be this the whetstone of your sword: let grief
Convert to anger; blunt not the heart, enrage it.
MACDUFF O, I could play the woman with mine eyes
And braggart with my tongue! But, gentle heavens,
Cut short all intermission; front to front
Bring thou this fiend of Scotland and myself;
Within my sword's length set him; if he 'scape,
Heaven forgive him too!

Starting with this speech, explain how far you think Shakespeare presents Macduff as a hero.
Write about:
- How Shakespeare presents Macduff in this speech
- How Shakespeare Macduff as a hero in the play as a whole.

Macbeth

Read the following extract from **Act 5 Scene 1** of Macbeth and then answer the question that follows.

At this point in the play, the Doctor and Gentlewoman are watching Lady Macbeth as she sleepwalks.

LADY MACBETH Out, damned spot! out, I say!—
One: two: why, then, 'tis time to do't.—
Hell is murky!—
Fie, my lord, fie! a soldier, and afeard?
What need we fear who knows it,
when none can call our power to account?—
Yet who would have thought
the old man to have had so much blood in him.
Doctor Do you mark that?
LADY MACBETH The thane of Fife had a wife: where is she now?—
What, will these hands ne'er be clean?—
No more o' that, my lord, no more o' that:
you mar all with this starting.
Doctor Go to, go to; you have known what you should not.
Gentlewoman She has spoke what she should not, I am sure of that:
heaven knows what she has known.
LADY MACBETH Here's the smell of the blood still:
all the perfumes of Arabia
will not sweeten this little hand.
Oh, oh, oh!
Doctor What a sigh is there! The heart is sorely charged.
Gentlewoman I would not have such a heart in my bosom
for the dignity of the whole body

Starting with this speech, explain how far you think Shakespeare presents Lady Macbeth as a changed woman.
Write about:
- How Shakespeare presents Lady Macbeth in this speech
- How Shakespeare presents Lady Macbeth in the play as a whole.

Macbeth

Read the following extract from **Act 5 Scene 3** of Macbeth and then answer the question that follows.

At this point in the play, Macbeth is preparing for battle against Malcom and the English army.

MACBETH Bring me no more reports; let them fly all:
Till Birnam wood remove to Dunsinane,
I cannot taint with fear. What's the boy Malcolm?
Was he not born of woman? The spirits that know
All mortal consequences have pronounced me thus:
'Fear not, Macbeth; no man that's born of woman
Shall e'er have power upon thee.' Then fly, false thanes,
And mingle with the English epicures:
The mind I sway by and the heart I bear
Shall never sag with doubt nor shake with fear.
Enter a Servant
The devil damn thee black, thou cream-faced loon!
Where got'st thou that goose look?
Servant There is ten thousand—
MACBETH Geese, villain!
Servant Soldiers, sir.
MACBETH Go prick thy face, and over-red thy fear,
Thou lily-liver'd boy. What soldiers, patch?
Death of thy soul! those linen cheeks of thine
Are counsellors to fear. What soldiers, whey-face?

Starting with this speech, explain how far you think Shakespeare presents Macbeth as a hero.
Write about:

- How Shakespeare presents Macbeth in this speech
- How Shakespeare presents Macbeth as a hero in the play as a whole.

In **Act 3 scene 4**, how does Shakespeare present Macbeth as a man who is in control?

Macbeth

Read the following extract from **Act 5 Scene 5** of Macbeth and then answer the question that follows.

At this point in the play, Macbeth is facing the English army and has just found out that Lady Macbeth has died.

MACBETH I have almost forgot the taste of fears;
The time has been, my senses would have cool'd
To hear a night-shriek; and my fell of hair
Would at a dismal treatise rouse and stir
As life were in't: I have supp'd full with horrors;
Direness, familiar to my slaughterous thoughts
Cannot once start me.
Re-enter SEYTON
Wherefore was that cry?

SEYTON The queen, my lord, is dead.

MACBETH She should have died hereafter;
There would have been a time for such a word.
To-morrow, and to-morrow, and to-morrow,
Creeps in this petty pace from day to day
To the last syllable of recorded time,
And all our yesterdays have lighted fools
The way to dusty death. Out, out, brief candle!
Life's but a walking shadow, a poor player
That struts and frets his hour upon the stage
And then is heard no more: it is a tale
Told by an idiot, full of sound and fury,
Signifying nothing

Starting with this speech, explain how far you think Shakespeare presents regret.
Write about:

- How Shakespeare presents Macbeth in this speech
- How Shakespeare presents regret in the play as a whole.

Macbeth

ACT 1 scene 3

Macbeth [aside]: Two truths are told, ...

Discuss how Shakespeare presents witchcraft and the supernatural.

ACT 1 scene 5

Lady Macbeth [soliloquy]: yet do I fear thy nature, ...

Explain how far Shakespeare presents Lady Macbeth as a powerful woman.

Lady Macbeth: The raven himself is hoarse, ...

How does Shakespeare present Lady Macbeth as an ambitious woman?

Lady Macbeth [to Macbeth]: O never shall sun that morrow see, ...

Lady Macbeth [to Macbeth]: Leave all the rest to me.

How does Shakespeare use imagery in the play?

ACT 1 scene 7

Macbeth [soliloquy]: If it were done when 'tis done, then ....

How does Shakespeare present the character of Macbeth

- focusing on a man
- who struggles with a guilty conscience?
- suffering from an inner conflict?

Lady Macbeth: Was the hope drunk, ...

Macbeth: Prithee, peace ....

How does Shakespeare present masculinity in the play?

ACT 2 scene 1

Macbeth [soliloquy]: Is this a dagger which I see before me, ….

Discuss how Shakespeare present hallucination in the play?

ACT 2 scene 2

Lady Macbeth: Who was it, that thus cried? ….

Macbeth: I'll go no more, ….

Lady Macbeth: Infirm of purpose!

How does Shakespeare present the relationship between Macbeth and Lady Macbeth?

ACT 3 scene 1

Banquo: Thou hast it now, King, Cawdor, Glamis,all, ….

Explain how Shakespeare presents the relationship between Banquo and Macbeth.

Macbeth [soliloquy]: He chid the sisters, ….

How does Shakespeare present ambition in the play?

ACT 3 scene 2

Macbeth [to Lady Macbeth]: We have scorch'd the snake, not kill'd it, ….

Discuss how Shakespeare present

- deceitfulness in the play
- Macbeth as a troubled character?

Macbeth [to Lady Macbeth]: Duncan is in his grave, ….

Lady Macbeth: You must leave this

Discuss how Shakespeare present paranoia and obsession.

Macbeth [to Lady Macbeth]: So shall I, love, ….

Macbeth [to Lady Macbeth]: A deed of dreadful note.

Discuss the themes of Appearance and Reality in the play.

ACT 3 scene 4

Lady Macbeth [to Macbeth]: Are you not a man?, ….

Macbeth [to Banquo's Ghost]: Shall be the mews of kites.

How does Shakespeare present Macbeth as a man who is in control?

ACT 4 scene 1

Macbeth [to Witches]: I conjure you by which you profess, ...
Third Witch: We'll answer.
How does Shakespeare present chaos and disorder in the play?

ACT 4 scene 2

Lady Macduff [to Ross]: Wisdom? To leave his wife, to leave his babes, ...
Ross: The fits o'th' season.
How does Shakespeare present women in the play?

ACT 4 scene 3

Malcolm [to Macduff]: Macduff, this noble passion, ...
Macduff: 'Tis hard to reconcile
How does Shakespeare present the themes of good and evil?

ACT 5 scene 1

Doctor [to Gentlewoman]: What is it she does now? ....
Lady Macbeth [to Doctor]: You mar all with this starting
How does Shakespeare explore guilt in the play?

ACT 5 scene 3

Macbeth [to Servant]: Bring me no more reports, let them fly all; ....
Macbeth [to Servant]: Take thy face hence!
How does Shakespeare present heroism in the play?

ACT 5 scene 5

Macbeth [to Seyton]: She should have died hereafter; ....
Messenger [to Macbeth]: I say, a moving grove.
How does Shakespeare present Macbeth's state of mind?

ACT 5 scene 8

Macbeth [to Macduff]: I bear a charmed life which must not yield ....
Macbeth [to Macduff]: And damn'd be him that first cries, 'Hold, enough!'.
How does Shakespeare present bravery in the play?

ACT 5 scene 9

Malcolm [to all]: What more to do ....
Malcolm [to all]: We will perform in measure, time, and place.
How does Shakespeare present Malcolm's loyalty and leadership?

SUMMARY – MACBETH

Macbeth is one of Shakespeare's most compelling and alluring plays. It reflects the rise and fall of a tragic hero, Macbeth. He meets the witches and receives a prophecy that he will become King. Consumed by ambition and his wife prods him into action, he decides to kill King Duncan. When Duncan visits him, Macbeth kills him with a dagger, and becomes King.

Macbeth is restless about the witches' prophecy that Banquo's heirs will be kings. He hires three murderers to kill Banquo and his son Fleance. Luckily, Fleance escapes but sadly Banquo dies. He then goes back to the witches who tell him to beware Macduff. Now, this revelation sets him off again. He becomes threatened by Macduff and he kills his family whilst Macduff flees to England.

Meanwhile, Lady Macbeth commits suicide because of her guilt. Macduff joins forces with Malcolm, Duncan's son, and march towards Macbeth's castle. Macduff confronts Macbeth and asks him to surrender, but Macbeth refuses and vows to fight to the end. Macduff kills Macbeth and peace is once more restored to Scotland. Malcolm is crowned King of Scotland.

The AUTHOR – Evelyn Samuel

Evelyn Samuel was born in South Africa, and attained a BA degree in English & Speech & Drama at the University of Durban Westville, and a Higher Education Diploma at the University of South Africa. She now lives in the UK, and has achieved a QTS, Diplomas in writing Stories for Children, Travel Journalism, TEFL. She currently runs a Tuition School and her property business in Wembley, London.

www.ingramcontent.com/pod-product-compliance
Lightning Source LLC
Chambersburg PA
CBHW080907190726
48294CB00008B/2001
9781739998110